The origin of Ireland's Ordnance Survey

For those I've shared happy lunches with by summit trig pillars.

The Origin of Ireland's Ordnance Survey

Finnian O'Cionnaith

FOUR COURTS PRESS

Set in Centaur 11.5pt/13.5pt for
FOUR COURTS PRESS LTD
7 Malpas Street, Dublin 8, Ireland
www.fourcourtspress.ie
and in North America for
FOUR COURTS PRESS
c/o IPG, 814 North Franklin Street, Chicago, IL 60610

A catalogue record for this title is available
from the British Library.

ISBN 978-1-80151-122-3

Printed in England
by CPI Antony Rowe, Chippenham, Wilts.

Contents

Illustrations

FIGURES

PLATES

appear between pages 96 and 97.

Preface

Every map tells a story. This is true for the most basic representation of property to something on the epic scale of the Ordnance Survey of Ireland. Each story involves people in need of information from the land, and who are willing to pay specialists (land surveyors) to gather it for them. The needs of the patron therefore dictate the actions of the surveyor, the content of the map and ultimately guide the story.

I have studied historic land surveying and mapping in Ireland for nearly two decades. During that time I have seen hundreds of manuscript and printed maps, created by generations of surveyors. Despite my best efforts, the full story behind most is rarely discovered. Interpretation and tangential research often help partially fill this gap. However, it is seldom truly sealed. The story behind the formation of the Ordnance Survey of Ireland in 1824, by contrast, is known in remarkable detail, spanning multiple sources. In actuality, there is a near overabundance of information on the survey's establishment, the researcher's job shifting from piecing together fragmentary data to prioritising material amongst volumes of text. Regardless of this change, this story of cartography, imperialism, science and politics has left such a legacy at an island-wide level that it requires telling in similar detail.

The two-century legacy of the Ordnance Survey means different things to each of us. Unusually in the field of historic mapping, it is still actively impacting our lives. As the official mapping branches of the governments of the Republic and Northern Ireland, Tailte Éireann and the OSNI remain critically relevant in the modern world. Each continues to produce information that acts as the cartographic bedrock for both states, though in forms and breadth of interest that would be unimaginable to those who shaped the survey's earliest days. We encounter this output at various stages in our lives, from school, to travel, outdoor activities, voting constituencies or supply of services. Indeed, the survey has expanded far beyond the clinical realms of mapping or mathematics, becoming embedded in literature, art, and arguably cultural identity over the intervening centuries. As a result, the term 'Ordnance Survey' remains synonymous in the minds of most residents of this island with accuracy, officialdom and our shared landscape.

Such a remarkable story had a starting point. Over a few months in 1824, a distinct entity came into being, different from what had proceeded it in either Ireland or Britain. This elemental form in turn was shaped, stretched, and divided by the wider factors of modern Irish history leaving us with the organizations we know today. Yet, the residual character of its initial concept remains. This vestige can be directly attributed to those who argued the survey's specific role in Ireland. Though in essence a cartographic project, this human influence on the survey's inception remains ever-present, and indeed pivotal, when examining its history.

The concepts of period decision makers, the specialists they turned to for advice, public opinion, and of course budget, each had its own role in determining the Ordnance Survey's beginning. These factors are readily seen in the records we are left. In them are the hopes and differences, eloquence and ignorance, moods, attitudes, and knowledge of people who were oblivious to the long-term significance of their words. They form the nucleus of this study and the Ordnance Survey's heritage in Ireland. It is they who tell the story behind the map. Our role is simply to listen and learn.

Abbreviations

BNF   Bibliothèque nationale de France
HC   House of Commons, Westminster
MS   manuscript
NAI   National Archives of Ireland
NLI   National Library of Ireland
OSI   Ordnance Survey Ireland
OSNI   Ordnance Survey of Northern Ireland
RIA   Royal Irish Academy

Acknowledgments

This book came relatively fast on the heels of my last publication and took several rapid steps from its initial concept to its final form. Throughout, it was an immensely enjoyable and interesting journey, aided by several groups and individuals I would like to acknowledge.

I would very much like to thank the Society of Chartered Surveyors Ireland for their generous sponsorship of this book. I am grateful for this aid, along with their ongoing efforts to promote the role of surveyors in Ireland. In particular, I would like to thank James Lonergan, Director of Education and CPD, and the members of the SCSI's Geomatics Professional Group. Additionally, I would like to thank Sarah Sherlock for her ongoing and deeply appreciated support of my research.

This is my fourth publication with Four Courts Press and, as always, I am delighted with the final product. As such I would like to thank my editor Martin Fanning for his insight, clarity (and patience) in bringing the book to life.

I have been fortunate to receive much-appreciated encouragement from both Tailte Éireann and OSNI during my research. Accordingly, I would like to express my thanks to Patrick Kenny of Tailte Éireann, and Suzanne McLaughlin and Ken Stewart of OSNI for their interest. Similarly, I was fortunate to receive similar support from the OS200 research group, especially Professor Keith Lilley of Queen's University Belfast. I am also grateful to have been allowed to present some of my initial findings at the OS200 'Mapping Monuments' conference in Ballykelly, Co. Derry, in November 2023.

As always in such projects, I frequently encounter those whose aid may seem small to those giving it, but whose impact was positively felt in my work. Accordingly, I would like to thank Dr Conchubhar Ó Crualaoich and the team at The Placenames Branch for their generosity in sourcing imagery, and Dr Ruth McManus (Dublin City University) and Dr Fióna Gallagher for their help in unwittingly bringing my cartographic skills up to scratch. Such abilities proved very useful for this endeavour.

Finally, I would like to thank my family, friends and colleagues whose ongoing help made all this possible. And, of course, a very special thank you to Éanna, Réiltín and my wonderful Donna.

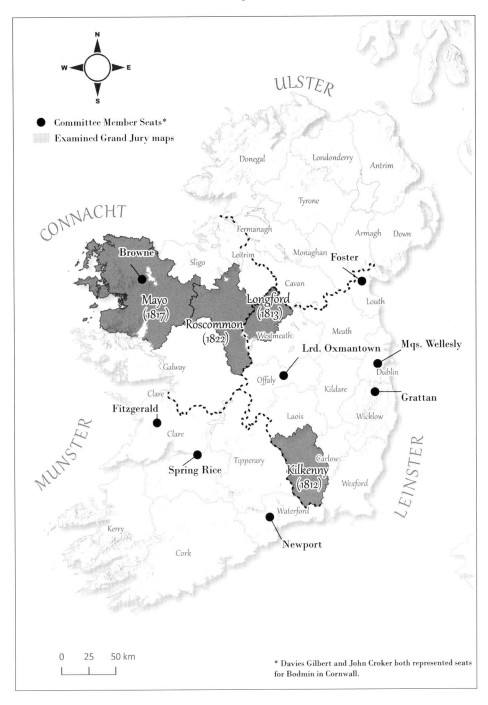

Map 1. Location of parliamentary seats for Spring Rice committee members and county maps examined during their 1824 investigation. By author.

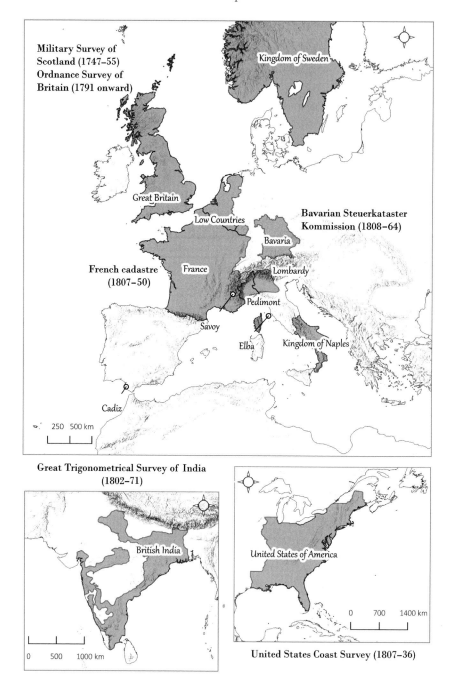

Map 2. Many contemporary surveys from across the world were mentioned by experts during the Spring Rice committee, several of which were of direct relevance to the survey of Ireland. By author.

CHAPTER ONE

Introduction

[A]ll former surveys of Ireland originated in forfeitures, and violent transfers of property; the present [survey] has for its object the relief which can be afforded to the proprietors and occupiers of land from unequal taxation ... Your committee trusts that the survey will be carried on with energy, as well as with skill, and that it will, when completed, be creditable to the nation, and to the scientific acquirements of the present age.

Report from the select committee on the survey and valuation of Ireland,
June 1824, p. 14.

As the official mapping agencies for both the Republic and Northern Ireland, the Ordnance Survey (Tailte Éireann and Ordnance Survey Northern Ireland (OSNI))[1] plays a significant role in life on this island. This point is relevant not only to the modern world but also to historic studies, the Ordnance's cycle of measurement, revision and publication continually capturing an ever-evolving physical, social and cultural environment. Since the foundation of its Irish branch two centuries ago, the Ordnance Survey has comprehensively charted a landscape shaped by enormous changes, creating its own vibrant story in the process. In this manner, both modern organizations have come to embody both authority and legacy within this island's spatial world.

The Tailte Éireann's mapping division and OSNI originate from a single pre-partition organization, the Ordnance Survey of Ireland. Established in June 1824, this body became synonymous with mapping in the public's collective consciousness throughout the nineteenth century and onward. Its earliest output was, however, not initially intended for general usage. Instead, its mission can be traced to a specific issue not normally associated with map-making: tax reform. All subsequent actions by the Ordnance Survey of Ireland can trace their rationale back to this singular point, its initial efforts in

---

1 Ordnance Survey Ireland (OSI) was merged with the Property Registration Authority and Valuation Office in 2023 to form a new organization, Tailte Éireann. Ordnance Survey operations in the Republic of Ireland are based in Mountjoy House, Phoenix Park. Ordnance Survey of Northern Ireland's headquarters are located in Colby House, Stranmillis Court, Belfast.

amending Ireland's inherently flawed land-tax system doing much to shape the organization's enduring legacy. This book explores this connection between mapping and taxation, examining why this organization was needed, the motivations behind those that aided its founding and what external pressures shaped its earliest days.

The events of the spring and summer 1824 can be easily overlooked in the Ordnance Survey's wider history. No maps were produced, nor were any measurements taken. Indeed, compared to the immense volumes of information later produced by the organization, this brief period could be summarized in one short sentence; that a parliamentary select committee recommended extending Ordnance surveying operations to Ireland. This summation, however, fails to highlight the fascinating and often tense discussions that took place in the halls of Westminster about the institution's Irish role. At its heart was an attempt to fix growing differences between two groups within the British government. Each sought to resolve Irish tax problems through mapping, though they could not agree on how this could be achieved. The resulting discussions are a prologue to the better-known aspects of Ordnance's Irish history, taking place before the now-familiar names of Tomas Larcom, William Yolland or John O'Donovan became irrevocably joined to the island's landscape. The events of this short period provided a solid base, centred on reasoned and expert opinion, upon which an influential body would eventually be built.

The Irish survey as we know it was born out of political compromise, being military in essence but civilian in purpose. Initially, the two sides were poor bedfellows, with army officers unfamiliar with key aspects vital to Ireland's administrative needs.[2] The arena in which such divisions were most readily exposed was the *Select committee for the survey and valuation of Ireland* (1824)[3], colloquially known as the 'Spring Rice committee', in honour of its chairman, Thomas Spring Rice MP (b. 1790, d. 1866). Between March and June of that year, this Westminster-based group investigated the most appropriate method of executing a precise, standardized national survey of Ireland, utilizing the best available techniques. After the discussions and debates, this small consortium had the unenviable task of summarizing the complex evidence presented to them and collating it into a series of logical recommendations. These recommendations would become the survey's earliest guide. Despite its brevity, the committee had to pursue a solution sensitive to various needs. In doing so, it set the course for many better-known aspects of the Ordnance Survey's history over the following two centuries (see plate 1).

2 Army control of the OSI continued until the 1980s, when it was transferred to full civilian management.   3 HC 1824 (455), viii, 79.

This book covers the formative days of the Ordnance Survey of Ireland, using the words of those involved as a chronological narrative. As such, it is as much about individuals as it is about cartography and surveying, with the opinions, technical knowledge and political savvy of those in Westminster helping establish the Ordnance's subsequent role.

DISCORD, COMPROMISE, AND MAPPING: THE STARTING POINT
OF THE ORDNANCE SURVEY OF IRELAND

[It was a] peculiar local survey which we required for our peculiar purpose.[4]

To begin, the term 'Ordnance Survey' was not originally a noun as it is today, representing an organization, but rather a verb – an action. It was the act of surveying land, i.e., its physical measurement and conversion into maps, conducted by the Board of Ordnance, a military department, on behalf of the British government. Therefore, from the perspective of early nineteenth-century officials, references were likely to be made to '*an* Ordnance survey' rather than '*the* Ordnance survey'. The latter, modern understanding of this term is used throughout this study.

Since the Tudor era, the Board of Ordnance had controlled Britain's artillery and fortifications, both fields dependent on an understanding of topography.[6] These duties naturally linked the Board to charting the landscape, though this task remained bound to the army's needs.[7] Such military necessities resulted in the Board's understandable preoccupation with 'obstructions to manoeuvrability' in surveys, such as the inclusions of forests, rivers, and marshes, or advantageous features such as roads or hills.[8] The concept of an Ordnance-based survey for the benefit of civilian administration did not emerge in Britain until the late eighteenth century, with Ireland falling within its remit in the early 1820s.

---

4 Evidence of Lord Monteagle, *Report from the select committee on Ordnance Survey* (Ireland) (HOC Paper 664, 1846), p. 26.   6 Peter Barber, 'Mapmaking in England, ca. 1470–1650' in David Woodward (ed.), *The history of cartography*, 6 vols (Chicago, 1989), iii, p. 1601.   7 The Ordnance Survey's use of a crow's foot/broad arrow symbol for benchmarks exemplified this connection; this symbol was commonly used to mark military property or equipment from the sixteenth century onward. The Ordnance Survey became independent with the abolition of the Board of Ordnance in 1855. Cóilín Parsons, *The Ordnance Survey and modern Irish literature* (Oxford, 2016), p. 250.   8 John Andrews, *Maps in those days: cartographic methods before 1850* (Dublin, 2009), p. 230.

The Irish portion was a scheme conducted for the country's benefit but mostly outside its control. Consequently, it reflected Ireland's post-Union status with Britain and the latter's imperialistic approach to its sister kingdom. As a result, the needs of Westminster, i.e., reform of land-based taxes, dictated the methods used for the survey and its approach to charting Ireland. Though explained in further detail below (see p. 39) each county was responsible for collecting a levy, known as a 'cess'. This was used to pay for local infrastructure and associated staff. Individual payments were based on the size and value of property per townland, with over 60,000 of these small and archaic divisions spread across Ireland.[9] Nationally, the collective cess income was estimated at approximately £750,000 per year (£43 million sterling in 2024, or almost €50 million), making it a significant revenue stream. Unfortunately, valuation assessments were static and had become grossly outdated over time. The result was an unacceptably misbalanced system that overly taxed some landholders while others incorrectly paid little or nothing.

Officials had long recognized this problem, with reform efforts steadily gaining traction in Westminster throughout the 1810s and 20s.[10] Not only would the issue of incorrect revenue collection be removed if this issue was addressed, but a major stumbling block on the road to greater political and social stability in Ireland would be achieved. By 1824, such open inequality added to an increasingly unpredictable political situation across Ireland, driving further support toward Daniel O'Connell's (b. 1775, d. 1847) Catholic emancipation movement. Calming tensions in any form would strengthen Ireland's part in both the United Kingdom and the empire and reduce the chance for civil strife. Tax reform was, therefore, of significant interest to members of parliament from both sides of the House of Commons. Unfortunately, there was no quick solution. The information on which the original tax assessments had been based was so old and obscure that no official could accurately trace its source, or even identify when the system had first been set up.[11] The only answer was for a new land valuation of the entire country: in effect, a national cess reset.

Maps would play a key role in this solution, guiding valuers in the field, acting as a referenceable archive and ensuring each assessment conformed to

---

9 Previous attempts had been made to establish local taxation based on the standardization of small administrative territories, namely ploughlands. These came to nothing as 'ploughlands' were found in some counties but not others with no definitive figure supplied of how big they were. 11 James c. 7 [Ire.] (1614)/9 Anne c. 9 [Ire.] (1713).   10 The Tithe Composition (Ireland) Act, 1823, was another reformative attempt contemporary to cess correction.   11 Andrews speculates that it likely emerged in piecemeal fashion during the sixteenth and seventeenth centuries, alongside plantation developments. John Andrews, *Plantation acres* (Omagh, 1985), p. 366.

defined areas as determined through physical measurement. Unfortunately, to the frustration of many, there was no standardized or suitably detailed mapping series with national coverage. Few cartographic resources contained relevant information, with those that did often being highly inaccurate or archaic. Cess reform would therefore have to be preceded by a national survey denoting the physical location and extent of such sub-county entities. The question of who would conduct the survey and how it would be executed understandably left many looking to the Board of Ordnance's expertise.

The proposed survey would differ greatly from what the Board of Ordnance, or Ireland, was accustomed to. The earlier Ordnance Survey of Britain had begun in the 1790s as a general one-inch-to-a-mile map series. It had no specific theme and has been aptly referred to by one geographer as resembling a 'glorified military reconnaissance'.[12] By contrast, the requirement for Ireland was more refined and at a (literal) larger scale, calling for the accurate identification and charting of the perplexing labyrinth of townlands, many only being a few dozen acres in size. This civil necessity understandably caused concern among Ordnance officers. While they would have no problem conducting a topographical survey of the island, few in their ranks had any experience identifying such small administrative areas, or indeed working in Ireland.

The new survey would also significantly vary from previous, often traumatic, surveys for the Irish population. Since the late sixteenth century, the island had frequently undergone extensive mapping projects, usually executed by English surveyors and aimed at the forcible confiscation of land.[13] Suspicions, therefore, remained rife in rural Ireland's collective consciousness of soldiers measuring land, stirring reminiscences of earlier punitive exercises. This added to the recent history of reprisals following the 1798 Rebellion, which was still within living memory for many. The Ordnance Survey, by contrast, would lend itself to more reformative goals. These were, however, restrained within the broader context of British imperialism in Ireland and not immediately apparent to many on the ground.

It is important to note that Ireland had its own surveying and cartographic resources prior to 1824. A capable and extensive domestic land surveying profession had emerged during the seventeenth and eighteenth centuries, staffed by Irishmen. It remained a private practice with its primary commercial interests focused on the needs of landed estates rather than public administration. There were few official surveying posts available in local or national governments and

12 John Andrews, *History in the Ordnance map* (Newtown, Montgomeryshire, 1993), p. 3.   13 *Report from the select committee on the survey and valuation of Ireland* (1824), p. 14.

no organization responsible for the regular production of revised, medium- or large-scale maps.[14] Notwithstanding this scenario, from the 1770s onward, a small group of senior surveyors found patronage from the country's collection of Grand Juries (the forerunners of County Councils). These bodies frequently sought detailed maps of their counties to aid local administration. Each was produced as a stand-alone project, with little standardization and to varying degrees of accuracy. Few contained data relevant to cess reform, and even fewer were considered scientifically correct. Consequently, in early 1824, the Spring Rice committee had the prodigious task of assessing the capabilities of both Ordnance and the Irish surveying community, reviewing existing cartographic sources while keeping those officials with a stake in the matter content or, at minimum, supportive.

Politically invested parties could be divided into two primary camps. Ironically, both were enthusiastic about a new survey, though they differed on how it would be organized. The first was a small but influential group of Anglo-Irish politicians led by Thomas Spring Rice, MP for Limerick. A Liberal Protestant estate owner with a desire for moderate reform, Spring Rice is described in his official Westminster biography as a 'spry, quick-witted, voluble, little man with a gift for hyperbole and the literary sensibilities of a poet'.[15] Within Ireland's popular history, he is also known for first coining the term 'West Britain', denoting his backing of the Union.[16] Though initially supportive of O'Connell, he eventually developed into one of his greatest opponents, becoming known for his dogged determination and persistently long parliamentary speeches. These qualities proved vexing to his Tory opponents, with one official describing Spring Rice as a 'conceited, chattering, provoking elf …'.[17] Despite such dismissive portrayals, he repeatedly proved himself to be a fighter. In one notable instance, shortly before the period covered by this book, Spring Rice demonstrated his valour by facing a fellow MP in a duel. Only their timely apprehension by police prevented the bout, Spring Rice being arrested with a cocked pistol in hand.[18] Such boldness would prove useful in his attempt to shape the survey and valuation of Ireland, especially given the status

14 Finnian O'Cionnaith, *Land surveying in Ireland, 1680–1830* (Dublin, 2022), p. 45.   15 Spring Rice, Thomas (1790–1866), https://www.historyofparliamentonline.org/volume/1820–1832/member/rice-thomas–1790–1866 (accessed 30 Jan. 2023).   16 'Further, it cannot be denied but that North Britain, a name which I prefer as much to Scotland, as I should prefer the name of West Britain to that of Ireland …', Hansard HC Deb., 23 April 1834, vol. 22, cc 1164–284.   17 Spring Rice, Thomas (1790–1866), https://www.historyofparliamentonline.org/volume/1820–1832/member/rice-thomas–1790–1866 (accessed 30 Jan. 2023).   18 *Dublin Journal*, 9 Feb. 1824. Spring Rice's opponent was fellow Limerick MP, Standish O'Grady (b. 1792, d. 1848). The duel took place in Ballsbridge, Dublin, and was accidentally interrupted by police in search of an illegal dog-fighting event. Both MPs were fined £250 pounds for this incident.

of his opponents. He found much support among fellow estate-owning Irish MPs. They were keenly aware of the unjust nature of the land-based tax, its unwelcome impact on rural communities and the potential fuel it provided to the emancipation movement. Though they had little collective knowledge of land measurement, they had long championed the need for reform, concluding that mapping would play a pivotal role (see plate 2).

The second group was composed primarily of two men, the imposing figures of brothers Arthur and Richard Wellesley. By 1824, Arthur (b. 1769, d. 1852), duke of Wellington and victor of Waterloo, was master general of Ordnance and thus a prominent member of Lord Liverpool's Tory cabinet. A noted micromanager accustomed to command, and with a distrust of sharing his intentions, Wellington had come to martial fame in India in the 1790s, his star rising to even greater heights during the Peninsula War (1807–14) against French forces in both Portugal and Spain. A reluctant native of Trim, Co. Meath, his interest in Irish affairs would later dominate a significant portion of his premiership in the years 1829–30 and again in 1834. His older brother Richard, Marquess Wellesley, was lord lieutenant of Ireland (b. 1760, d. 1842) in 1824, based in Dublin Castle. A fellow veteran of the administration of India, he was described as 'self-centred',[19] 'vain and indifferent'.[20] Despite this Wellesley had demonstrated a conciliatory tone toward reform in Ireland since taking up his role and was willing to lend his support to aid the complex political situation in his jurisdiction (see plates 3 and 4).

Wellington and Wellesley were relative latecomers to the story of cess reform compared to the MPs mentioned above. They had, however, significant resources at their immediate disposal. This was most prominent in the form of the Board of Ordnance's surveying department, which fell under Wellington's command. This immediacy was one of the primary causes for the dispute between both groups, ultimately triggering the formation of the Spring Rice committee. In February 1824, Wellesley, prompted by his top aides, urged Wellington to deploy the Ordnance Survey to Ireland to provide accurate mapping for tax amendments. This included the county cess alongside the more controversial issue of land-based tithes, customarily due to the Church of Ireland (see below, p. 42). Wellesley's insistence on using Ordnance personnel was driven by his distrust of the Irish surveying and engineering communities. He firmly stated that the use of Irish civilian expertise in such a project was to be avoided at all costs.[21] Likewise, Wellington would not have his officers and

---

19 Wellesley, Richard (1787–1831), https://www.historyofparliamentonline.org/volume/1820–1832/member/wellesley-richard–1787–1831 (accessed 30 Jan. 2023).   20 George Boyce, *Nineteenth-century Ireland* (Dublin, 2005), p. 44.   21 Wellesley to Wellington, 17 Feb. 1824, *The dispatches of Field Marshal the duke of Wellington*, 8 vols (London, 1835), ii, p. 219.

men fall under civilian control, be they Irish or otherwise, thus limiting the project to a small group of Ordnance staff. Nothing was mentioned about whether a survey of Ireland would differ from that of Britain, with Wellington happy to see a repeat of the survey's British one-inch-to-a-mile output. Within mere days of hearing from Wellesley, Wellington had instructed his department to begin plans for deployment to Ireland.

Spring Rice and his colleagues were understandably alarmed at the speed of this development. Their years of lobbying for tax reform may have proven futile due to Wellington's characteristically prompt actions. Quite justifiably, they feared that the resulting generalized topographic maps would be useless for Ireland's specific problems. The execution of a British-style Ordnance Survey would not help resolve the cess and tithes issues as it would be limited to county boundaries. Only including smaller administrative areas, such as parishes or townlands, which had been missing in the British series, would aid reform. Consequently, these features were of paramount importance to Spring Rice's camp. Unfortunately, the existing Ordnance staff had little familiarity with recording such bounds. Undoubtedly, they could be surveyed if required, but first, suitable people or sources would be needed to locate them on the ground. In light of this development, Wellington vehemently refused to have his highly specialized staff waste their time interviewing local farmers to identify which field lay in which townland or trying to extract the same information from private estate maps. By contrast, such bounds were part of the day-to-day working world of Ireland's civilian surveyors and engineers. These professionals, nontheless, had explicitly been blacklisted by Wellesley. The project, therefore, reached a very early impasse.

With Ireland's immediate cartographic and tax future at stake, Spring Rice formally requested that a parliamentary select committee be established to investigate the matter.[22] As parliament would ultimately have to release funds for the Ordnance's work, Wellington had little choice but to cooperate, temporarily halting his plans. The result was the *Report from the select committee on the survey and valuation of Ireland* (1824), the initial guiding plan for the Ordnance Survey of Ireland.

Both sides were fortunate that they agreed on several key points. Other aspects simply required investigation and clarification. First, there was universal agreement that a new survey and valuation would be immensely beneficial and

22 'The object of that Report was twofold – to consider the best mode of apportioning more equally the local burdens collected in Ireland, and to provide for a general survey of that part of the United Kingdom; and both the evidence taken and the recommendations of the Committee are pointed towards that double object'. Evidence of Lord Monteagle, *Report from the select committee on Ordnance Survey* (Ireland), p. 26.

should be conducted using the best scientific methods available. This task fell to Major Thomas Colby, superintendent of Ordnance's surveying wing. Ireland had no suitable alternative to Colby's experience and resources, though it had a small corps of highly-proficient 'topographic engineers' capable of similar duties.[23] If a national map series were to emerge domestically, it would invariably come from one of this group. Such a scenario was never a true potential as Colby's devotion to scientifically correct mapping distinguished his work both to the committee and Wellington. Regardless, there remained potential scope for some civilian aid. For instance, what exact role the Ordnance would fulfil remained a discussion point throughout the investigation, as did to what level of detail they would be asked to measure. Colby's management of the most technical part of the survey, a triangulation network (in essence a national mathematical scaffold for topographic detail), was evident. Still, there was no guarantee that he had the means to record topographic data in sufficient time. The potential of non-military assistance in the survey, therefore, remained credible throughout the investigation.[24] Equally, the Ordnance Survey was never expected to undertake the near-alien valuation element, again leaving room for civilians.

The acquisition of sub-county civil boundaries was of equal significance during the committee's inquiries. This aspect was referred to as a 'territorial survey', in contrast to the recording of topographic data such as hills or rivers. The committee sought to identify which boundaries were most relevant to their reformative cause, e.g., townlands, parishes, baronies etc., and what sources could aid in their identification. As such, features notably absent in the Ordnance maps of Britain would, in turn, become intrinsic to the Irish survey, though Colby's involvement at this level caused the committee much concern. Much of this unease was due to Wellington, who was determined to keep his approach military in principle. Ever the soldier, he was aptly described by geographer J.H. Andrews as having a 'possessive attitude to topography' regarding the Ordnance's work. The duke, therefore, felt the need to use 'very strong language' when dealing with Spring Rice and the Irish survey,[25] insisting that his staff would not be involved in the bothersome territorial aspect. By contrast, Spring Rice and his colleagues knew that without the inclusion of these divisions, cess reform would remain unresolved.

With no assurance that the Ordnance would manage the entire project, the committee was forced to keep an open mind to alternative routes. One concept to emerge was the execution of several consecutive, independently directed

23 O'Cionnaith, *Land surveying*, p. 191. 24 Andrews, *A paper landscape*, p. 123. 25 Wellington to Sir William Knighton, 6 Nov. 1824: Wellington, *Dispatches*, ii, pp 332–3.

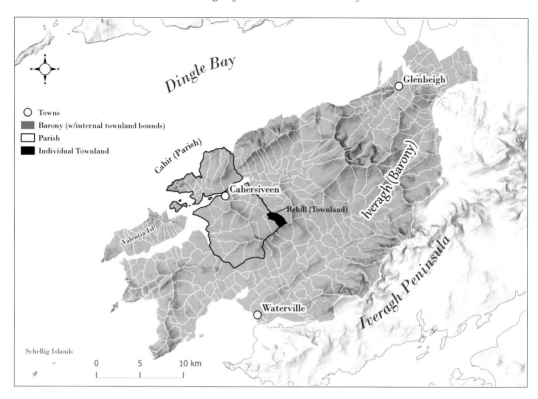

1.1. An example of the labyrinth of townlands in Iveragh, Co. Kerry, just one of Ireland's many baronies. Townlands would be pivotal to any reassessment of land-based taxes such as county cess. By author.

surveys. Each would act as a stepping stone toward the final goal of a valuation based on accurate mapping. Beginning with an Ordnance Survey triangulation network, subsequent elements, such as topographic and territorial information, would be added piecemeal to form an increasingly detailed record. In such circumstances, partial civilian control would be presumed, though questions remained about the standards they would be held to. The committee, therefore, sought to understand if Ireland's civilian and engineering community could accomplish this task if such a scenario developed. While this situation failed to fully materialize, the assessment of Ireland's surveying capabilities remained one of the committee's most significant legacies. Had their investigations gone otherwise, the history of mapping in nineteenth-century Ireland may have been very different from that known today.

Though highly respected, praise of the Ordnance Survey's capabilities was not universal. Several MPs were openly concerned about their methodology and limited staff, stating that the decades it had so far taken to conduct the still-incomplete survey of Britain would not be welcomed by Ireland. The committee, therefore, wanted assurances on the length and estimated cost of the project. The concept of a commercial map series was mainly avoided, the project's cartographic aim remaining initially devoted to valuation.

The select committee was thus left with several key questions related to how a new survey and valuation of Ireland could be conducted. Their task was to find solutions to each of these, basing their findings on evidence given by expert witnesses. This process pitted Spring Rice against Wellington – the latter's off-stage presence felt throughout the inquiry. Meetings began on 22 March 1824 and ended in June. By then the committee had a solution to many of the problems stated above, their journey being one of the most in-depth studies of Irish surveying and mapping ever conducted.

SOURCES

The story covered in this book took place over a concise time frame, accounting for only 129 days. It began in February 1824, with a letter written by Colby to the Board of Ordnance outlining how his organization's work could be extended to Ireland. It ended several months later, in June, with the publication of the Spring Rice report, defining the essence of the soon-to-take-place Ordnance Survey of Ireland. While a thematic analysis would be of use to this study, I felt that a chronological layout shed the best light on the select committee's decision-making processes. This linear approach highlights changing opinions and the depth of evidence over time, while avoiding the pitfall of dedicating large parts of the text to complex thematic reviews of technical minutia.

Much of the information in this book stems directly from the minutes of the Spring Rice committee. The committee acted as a nexus in the history of surveying and mapping in Ireland. It was a rare instance where historical figures examined the strategies and methods of earlier measurement schemes, while simultaneously theorizing how to implement their own system based on period needs and technologies. The committee records thereby provided one of the most in-depth analyses of the use of mapping in Ireland, alongside rare assessments of the country's engineering and surveying communities. Additionally, they offer early appraisals of Colby's plans alongside the varying scenarios that lay before decision makers in 1824. These notes were published with Spring Rice's final report.

Each committee meeting had a similar format, with one or more experts being asked a series of questions relevant to their field of interest. The background of these witnesses varied immensely, ranging from Ordnance officers to civilian engineers, valuers, politicians and even policemen (see below, p. 72). They would respond to the parliamentarians' questions as best they could, with several being called back on multiple occasions to clarify specific points or to expand on earlier evidence. Specialists were often asked their opinion on various scenarios concerning the proposed survey, such as whether townlands or parish boundaries would be most suitable for valuation, or how much the survey would cost per acre. Such exploration allowed the committee to refine their arguments, explore alternatives and come to solid conclusions based on fact. This process also included several dead-end scenarios, which by themselves are of interest due to their exclusion from the final parliamentary report.

Despite their wealth of information, the minutes are often difficult to approach and laborious to read. This is principally due to their complexity and the often-poor structure of questioning. Though the chairman of each meeting was noted, no record was taken of which committee members asked individual questions, thus denying modern readers the opportunity to see what topics concerned specific members. The near continual stream of queries was organized haphazardly, changing subjects at random and emphasizing some technical elements at the expense, or entire ignorance, of others. For instance, one of the most prominent victims of such abandonment was, surprisingly, the project's cartographic component, the committee being happy to follow Colby's lead for map design from an early stage. Also of note was the absence of those onto whom the burden of cess payments fell. Admittedly, the interests of the landed gentry were well represented by Spring Rice himself, who on one occasion swapped his committee seat to provide evidence, however, the voice of the tenant farmer remained unheard throughout.

Irrespective of their faults, the minutes remain of immense historical importance to the study of Irish cartography, engineering, and surveying.[26] This is most evident in the testimony of the many prominent Irish engineers that appeared before the committee. Traditionally, information on these men is limited to formal reports or maps, with their prim and restrained procedural language restrictions. While of obvious use, such formality fails to capture the persona or nuances of this small and influential group. The Spring Rice minutes, by contrast, allow readers greater insight into these individuals at a time when their opinions were of immediate concern to the British government. This includes detailed descriptions, in their own words, of their careers, work

26 One of the most notable contributions to the early history of the Ordnance Survey of Ireland is John Andrews, *A paper landscape* (Dublin, 1975), which, in turn, helped inspire Brian Friel's 1980 play *Translations*.

ON SURVEY AND VALUATION OF IRELAND. 23

Upon what principle do you think the valuation of Ireland ought to proceed?— I conceive that it is essential to the success of such valuation, both with reference to local purposes and to general statistical science, that the principle adopted for the valuation should be uniform in all parts of the country; that the scale of value applied to a northern county should be the same scale of value applied to a southern county, and that we should not have to complain of the anomalies which often exist in other territorial assessments, where a half rate is taken in one part of the country, and a rate upon the rack-rent is taken in another. In order to ensure this uniformity, as well as to prevent abuses arising from local interest or local prejudice, I conceive that there should be a commissioner or commissioners employed by Government, to co-operate with the local valuers in the several counties, baronies and parishes. Such officer or officers should exercise a regulated power of direction and control; and further, in order to insure an uniformity of assessment, I conceive that in taking his valuation, he ought not to refer to the market prices of the day so much as to a fixed scale of value of all the articles of produce. Without such precaution, supposing the valuation to be six years in progress, it is clear that a valuation so made would vary directly with the fluctuating prices of the period of time to which I have alluded; whereas, if for purposes of the valuation, the different prices of wheat, barley, oats, butter and other produce, were assumed as the scale, and the quantity of produce were to be looked to as the mode of reaching the value, by comparing the fixed scale with any subsequent fluctuations of price, the value of the day might always be found. By those means, the valuation would not only apply to the local purposes for which it is directly intended, but it would afford at all times a mode of ascertaining the territorial resources of the country.

T. S. Rice, Esq.

(April 1.)

Veneris, 2° die Aprilis, 1824.

THOMAS SPRING RICE, ESQUIRE,

IN THE CHAIR.

Major Thomas Frederick Colby again called in; and Examined, as follows:

WHEN you were last examined with regard to the time that the proposed Survey would take, did you give your answers under the supposition, that the labours of the ordnance were to continue in Great Britain during the survey in Ireland, or that the whole of the ordnance force was to be transferred into Ireland?—Under the supposition that the survey of Great Britain was to continue.

If the survey of Great Britain was to be suspended, so as to place at your disposition the entire of the engineering force, in what time could your operations be carried into effect?—I do not apprehend that would make any essential difference in the survey of Ireland.

Have the goodness to explain to the Committee why, if the force under your command was to be augmented, the time in which the survey could be effected might not be proportionally diminished?—I estimate the time that would be necessary for training persons for that survey, when the real exigencies of that survey become known.

Do you not think the survey could be executed in a shorter time, if instead of training engineers, you could employ those that were already experienced?—No doubt it could be carried into effect much sooner; but those persons are not existing at present.

If the operations of the ordnance in Great Britain were suspended, placing those persons at your command, would you not have persons experienced for the survey of Ireland?—So small a number, that no essential difference would be made in the time of ultimate completion.

Would it be your intention to undertake the survey of Ireland merely with individuals you intend to train for that purpose?—Certainly not; I should employ some of the persons that are now employed in the survey of Great Britain, and supply their places with others.

What time must elapse before you have persons trained for the Irish survey?— I have estimated, that we might commence the survey of Ireland in the summer of 1825.

Major T. F. Colby.

(April 2.)

C 4

If

1.2. A page from the *Report from the select committee on the survey and valuation of Ireland* (London, 1824), colloquially known as the 'Spring Rice committee' in honour of its chairman. The committee gave most (though not all) parties with an interest in a survey of Ireland a chance to state their opinions (Private collection).

conditions, opinions on specialized subjects, and practical advice, such as how to best interact with Ireland's rural population. Such hugely valuable insight equally applies to senior members of the Ordnance Survey, notably Colby. His true legacy within Irish history is entwined with the Ordnance's ground-breaking six-inch series, first published in 1833. The Spring Rice report would provide him with an outline from which to work. This guidance, coupled with orders from the Board of Ordnance and his own ingenuity, would do much to shape the survey we know today.

At the core of this study is the narrative formed by the Spring Rice committee. This book is a summary of a larger, more expansive record which, in its original form, is difficult to tackle. It provides extensive background and context to topics, themes and concepts discussed in the committee chamber, enhanced with further details from private correspondences, parliamentary debates, and other records. This includes exploring the careers of those involved, examining their personal agendas, and placing them within the context of Ireland's spatial history. Moreover, reminiscences by several key members of Spring Rice's investigation proved helpful. These were often given decades after the committee, outlining opinions not recorded in 1824 or influenced by later events. Understandably, much of this ancillary data is entirely absent from the committee's records, though, when examined with perspective, it adds greatly to the story of the origin of the Ordnance Survey of Ireland. Similarly, research conducted by historians and geographers, notably J.H. Andrews' *A paper landscape* (1975), Col. Charles Close's *The early years of the Ordnance Survey* (1926), and Rachel Hewitt's, *Map of a nation* (2011), alongside others, proved of immense value.[27] As such, this book aims to avoid simply repeating the evidence presented to Spring Rice's committee but instead to use that evidence as the basis to tell a broader story. In the process, it hopes to contribute to the excellent library of modern research available on the history of the Ordnance Survey of Ireland.

---

27 Close, for example, was in direct contact with Colby's children and could draw on private correspondences supplied by them.

CHAPTER TWO

Setting the scene: taxation, townlands, and topography

The task awaiting Colby in spring 1824 was daunting. He had little doubt that he could conduct an Ordnance-style survey of Ireland though his lack of staff was of concern. This caveat aside, he, like Spring Rice, knew that the remit for Ireland meant that it would have its own set of requirements missing from the British survey. Of most significance was the identification and integration of administrative boundaries, this topic becoming one of the main drivers for the eventual Spring Rice committee. Accordingly, their investigations focused on existing cartographic sources, if they could assist in identifying these bounds and what specifics were required for tax reform. Though such topics may seem ancillary in the broader history of the Ordnance Survey, they helped define Colby's earliest work in Ireland and provided the survey with much of its character. Consequently, this chapter reviews the necessity of including townlands in Irish mapping, providing a background to much of the discussions, compromises, and arguments that would follow between Colby, Spring Rice and Wellington.

The history of surveying and mapping in Ireland far predates the arrival of the Ordnance Survey. Starting in the 1570s, it can be split into a series of eras, each relating to varying phases of English expansion. As such, its story documents a multi-century process, deeply entangled with broader forces that shaped early modern Ireland.

The Ordnance Survey of Ireland had various similarities with earlier large-scale surveys conducted on behalf of English, and later British administrations. First, its purpose was to locate and quantify land at the request of the government. Second, it was conducted, at least at its outset, by the military, a common, though not universal, aspect of older surveys. Such similarities, however, cease rather rapidly following these two points, with its methods, purpose and execution being radically different than those that had preceeded it. Given such comparisons, older surveys were frequently examined during

Spring Rice's inquiries to see if they could be used to expedite the Ordnance Survey's work and also, of lesser magnitude, to provide a cartographic context to the project. To accomplish these tasks, the committee turned to the opinions of civil engineers resident in Ireland. Each was accustomed to referencing historical sources and was aware of their various strengths and weaknesses. It was clear to all involved that Colby and the Ordnance Survey was the start of a new chapter in the island's dynamic cartographic journey, marking a clean break from earlier exercises. A review of what preceeded Colby's deployment, therefore, provides a backdrop for the saga of mapping in local governance, helping familiarise readers with earlier surveys while also exploring the social context of large-scale surveys in pre-Ordnance Ireland.

The beginning: surveying and forfeitures, 1570–1700

Though the island had been the subject of multiple and comprehensive surveys from the sixteenth century onward, by 1824 Ireland still lacked an authoritive mapping agency. This was unusual given the often intense interest English authorities took in Irish lands and the frequency they were recorded. In place of such an agency, official cartographic needs were met by either military or civilian surveyors, employed on an ad hoc basis. Before 1700, government-sponsored large- and medium-scale surveys were usually associated with the spoils of war and thus vastly different from the objectives of the Ordnance Survey. The presence of surveyors in the wake of military campaigns was a common feature during this era of conflict and violence. The Desmond rebellions (1569–83) alongside the Nine Years (1593–1603), Cromwellian (1649–53), and Williamite (1689–91) wars were each accompanied by major mapping exercises upon their conclusion.[1] These surveys were designed to facilitate the forfeiture of land from the Gaelic and Hiberno-Norman land-owning nobility and its redistribution to Protestant English settlers and sponsors of the military campaigns. In this manner, the heartland of native Irish political and economic power was both exposed, often for the first time, and subsequently removed. As a result, surveying became part of the violent cycle of rebellion and native defeat that drove the expansion of English authority, Spring Rice duly acknowledging this fact in his final report.[2]

The resulting forfeiture maps were practical documents. They were, for the most part, visually uninspiring, intended to provide qualitative and quantitative

---

1 Peyton Survey of Munster (1584), Bodley Survey (1609), Down Survey (1656–8), Trustees' Survey (1700–3) respectively.   2 '… that all former surveys of Ireland [before the Ordnance Survey] originated in forfeitures and violent transfers of property …' *Report from the select committee*

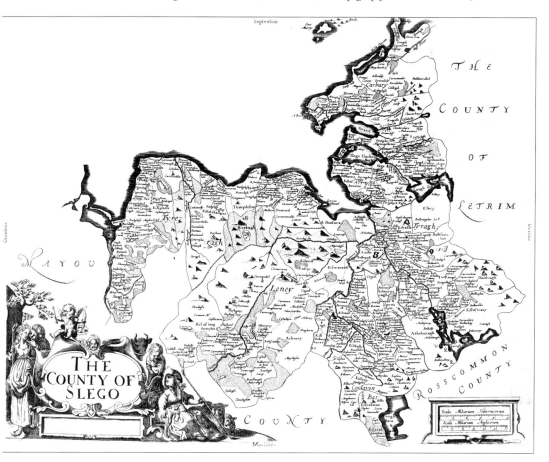

2.1. The cartographic legacy of Sir William Petty's Down Survey in the 1650s was still felt at the time of the Spring Rice committee. Sir William Petty, *The county of Slego* [*sic*] (1685), NLI MS 3137 (courtesy of the National Library of Ireland).

information for the new landowners. Representations of terrain were rarely included (or needed), with acreages, land conditions, resources (such as woodland), and administrative bounds being of greatest significance. Given the intensity of such surveys, Ireland by consequence became a testing ground for the application of mapping in England's growing colonial network. As such, lessons learned on the island were frequently transferred worldwide, with Ireland often being listed alongside Virginia in North America as a lucrative market for aspiring seventeenth-century surveyors.[3] Surveying methods were

on the survey and valuation of Ireland (London, 1824), p. 14.   3 Sir John Davis to Salisbury, 24 Aug. 1609 (Hatfield House, Cecil papers, vol. 127, f. 133).

sophisticated for the era but far below the standards eventually implemented by Colby. Inherent flaws in methodology or the low precision of instruments used consequently decreased Colby's confidence in the usefulness of these historic sources, irrespective of the reverence they were held in by the Irish surveying community.

The Down Survey (1656–8) could be considered the most influential map series to emerge from this forfeiture era. Conducted under the supervision of English philosopher and scientist Sir William Petty (b. 1623, d. 1687), it was created in the wake of Cromwell's brutal Irish campaign. Such was the impact of this near-island-wide project that the resulting baronial and parochial map series set a legal (and cartographic) precedent over the following 150 years in Ireland.[4] In this manner, the Down Survey can be considered a forerunner for state mapping, and a cornerstone of pre-Ordnance Irish land surveying. Like the later Ordnance Survey, it was also conducted by soldiers. Yet, few among their number were men of science or professional surveyors.

Despite its size and prestige, the long-term utility of the Down series was hampered by a lack of revision. It became a snapshot of Ireland in the 1650s and gradually reduced in relevance as time progressed. As a result, it was of limited use to early nineteenth-century administrators. Stagnancy was common in all map series to emerge from the forfeitures. They had been created for a singular purpose, often isolated to a specific area of the country, with none being the subject of periodic updates. This invariably led to the degradation of the information they contained as property bounds and land quality changed. Though useful, the concept of a regularly updated official map archive was understandably unattractive to successive Irish governments due to the financial and time commitments involved, with returns far outweighed by costs. It was also of lower importance to pre-nineteenth-century officials, with existing map sources capable of satisfying the relative basic needs asked of them.

Ireland's lack of an official mapping agency prior to the Ordnance's arrival exasperated this situation. Though there had been a surveyor general of Ireland between the sixteenth and late eighteenth century, this position was more aligned with engineering and architecture. The surveyor general's deputy, however, was often selected from the growing ranks of Ireland's commercial surveyors, though their remit was usually limited to Crown estates.[5] This lack of officialdom within the surveying profession would become painfully apparent during Spring Rice's investigations, with no authoritative voice capable of speaking for the industry as a collective.

---

4 Robert Gibson, *Practical surveying* (Dublin, 1752), p. 207.   5 O'Cionnaith, *Land surveying*, p. 145.

Surveying, mapping, and the eighteenth-century estate landscape

Though developments within government-led mapping were erratic before 1824, progress for surveying's commercial wing was more constant. Not only did technical support of forfeitures prove lucrative for private surveyors, especially toward the end of the seventeenth century, but significant incomes could also be made in inter-seizure periods. Disruption among the landowning classes invariably drew surveyors deeper into estate economics and the legal world of property. For the budding Protestant Ascendancy, surveyors could reveal information on their holdings and highlight how their new Irish estates could be developed. To the displaced, the work of surveyors was one of the few resources available to resist the confiscation of their lands, legally. In this manner, professional surveyors continued to find steady employment. By the 1750s Ireland could rightly claim to have its own well-developed civilian profession, populated by local practitioners, sensitive to regional needs.

As the eighteenth century progressed, civilian surveyors managed to shake off whatever association remained of their link to anglicization. They became relatively neutral in the country's divided social order, servicing the needs of both tenants and landlords alike, regardless of religion.[6] With a central group of between 100 and 200 professionals operating alongside a broader range of amateurs, the vocation spread across the country. It, however, lacked any form of centralized control or licensing, its work focused on practical cadastral surveys rather than the production of commercial prints. Cartographically, most maps remained simple and unadorned, based on long-established forfeiture styles.[7] Medium- and small-scale printed maps were rare and beyond the scope of the typical surveyor's day-to-day work. The inherent financial risks of Ireland's small cartographic market, and lack of government support, did much to dissuade many aspirants.

Regardless, Ireland remained attractive for some print specialists. The arrival of famed city and estate surveyor John Rocque (b. 1709, d. 1762) in 1754 did much to stimulate cartographic tastes among the wealthiest landowners.[8] Drawn by the country's underdeveloped scene for artistically fashionable maps, Rocque's move from London soon attracted patronage from Ireland's top

6 Terence Dooley, *Sources for the history of landed estates in Ireland* (Dublin, 2000), p. 1; Arnold Horner, 'Retrieving the landscapes of eighteenth-century county Kildare: the 1755–60 estate maps of John Rocque', *Archaeology Ireland*, 31:2 (2019), 20.   7 Andrews, *Plantation acres*, p. 152.   8 John Varley, 'John Rocque: engraver, surveyor, cartographer and map seller', *Imago Mundi*, 5 (1948), 83–91; Colm Lennon and John Montague, *John Rocque's Dublin: a guide to the Georgian city* (Dublin, 2010); Anne Hodge, 'A study of the rococo decoration of John Rocque's Irish maps and plans, 1755–1760' (BA, NCAD, 1994); Finnian O'Cionnaith, *Mapping, measurement and metropolis: how land surveyors shaped eighteenth-century Dublin* (Dublin, 2012), p. 156.

aristocrats. He straddled the worlds of estate mapping and commercial prints, incorporating the latest creative trends into his works (mostly emanating from France). In the process, he cornered a lucrative and extremely wealthy client base. This mixed output became a trait of subsequent generations of his French School style, though none came close to matching the renown of their master.[9] A similar Scots School of surveyors also emerged in the following decades. These Scottish immigrants preferred topography and engineering, thereby filling another gap in the local trade.[10] Both the French and Scottish groups would forge significant legacies in early nineteenth-century Ireland, with many of their most prominent members aiding the Spring Rice committee.

Problems of the early nineteenth century

Irrespective of such developments, by 1824, most commercial surveying remained fixed in the realm of property and estate mapping. Practitioners still employed traditional measurement methods with complex procedures, such as triangulation networks, becoming synonymous with a small elite.[11] Overall, provincial and national mapping, alongside surveying education, lagged far behind many European countries, thus limiting its usage for good governance.

There were several inherent factors to explain this deficiency. First, as it was an island under one government, Ireland lacked an international border. The need to accurately determine where the country ended therefore did not exist. As a result, the need to create high-accuracy, medium-scale mapping, at least from a security perspective, was reduced. Second, the local surveying profession remained focused on estate economics. Such emphasis accompanied the overwhelming dominance of agriculture in the Irish economy, the influence of the Industrial Revolution being muted compared to Britain.[12] For surveyors, more money could be made in measuring farms than factories. Third, the lack of serious interest from the Irish government in land measurement cannot be overlooked, the surveying profession lacking the vital economic impetus brought by parliamentary funding to seriously invest in new methodology or equipment.

Though a large portion of the profession's cartographic output remained fixed on property mapping at large scales,[13] some surveyors maintained a more expansive view when it came to mapping. County mapping had been relatively common among their forfeiture-era predecessors, guided by immediate 'big-picture' demands of the military and subsequent mass distribution of lands.

9 Evidence of William Bald, *Report from the select committee on the survey and valuation of Ireland* (1824), p. 73. 10 O'Cionnaith, *Land surveying*, p. 192.   11 Ibid., p. 210.   12 O'Cionnaith, *Mapping, measurement and metropolis*, p. 211.   13 40 perches to an inch was commonly used in Irish property mapping.

By the eighteenth century, the demand for county-level maps had dipped notably, though there remained a small but growing interest from local government, such as Grand Juries, or from philanthropic organizations such as the Dublin Society.[14] In turn, county maps became a prolific sub-genre of land surveying.

Few surveyors became involved in such work due to its technical complexity and financial risk, ensuring it remained an area of specialization for the elite native or attuned foreign surveyor. Early local leaders in the post-forfeiture industry included Gabriel Stokes (b. 1682, d. 1768.) and Walter Harris (b. 1686, d. 1761), who produced maps of counties Dublin and Down, respectively, in the 1740s and 50s. Each had been employed by the Physio-Historical Society, which sought new county mapping from local 'men of ability' to accompany their studies of Ireland's history, geography and economy.[15] Other mid-century leaders included the McCrea family of surveyors, who maintained a multi-generational presence in Ulster county mapping for fifty years.[16] Such success was countered by the many proposed county surveys that failed to materialize.[17] Unfortunately, the collective efforts of Irish county surveyors were later dismissed *en masse* by Colby during his Spring Rice interviews. This had little to do with any direct experience of such sources but rather stemmed from his suspicion of any non-Ordnance data and his wish to avoid mixing the two.[18] Others, by contrast, fared better during the Spring Rice review. Notable was William Duncan, whose 1821 map of Co. Dublin was executed with rigorous triangulation methods, as was the work of William Edgeworth and Richard Griffith in Roscommon. The latter two would both be interviewed by Spring Rice's committee, providing valuable insight to Colby and the gathered MPs.

County mapping also proved attractive to an equally select group of non-Irish-born surveyors. Included in this cohort was the aforementioned John Rocque, whose methods proved adept at county, city and estate levels. Massachusetts native Henry Pelham (b. 1749, d. 1806) and Scots partners George Taylor (d. 1741) and Andrew Skinner (fl. 1760–82) equally found the medium-/small-scale mapping gap in Ireland lucrative. Both Irish and foreign groups showed a preference for comparable map scales, with two inches to a mile being popular between 1750 and 1820 (see table 1 below), closely followed by one inch to a mile. The latter scale proved equally prevalent in the mass-

---

14 Wilkins, *Alexander Nimmo*, p. 128.   15 O'Cionnaith, *Land surveying*, p. 158.   16 Andrews, *Plantation acres*, p. 351.   17 Ibid., p. 344.   18 Portlock, *Memoir*, p. 111. Colby's caution also applied to other British military surveyors, such as Gen. Charles Vallancey's (b. 1731, d. 1812) incomplete topographic survey of Ireland in the 1770s. John Andrews, 'Charles Vallancey and the map of Ireland', *Geographical Journal*, 132:1 (1966), 48.

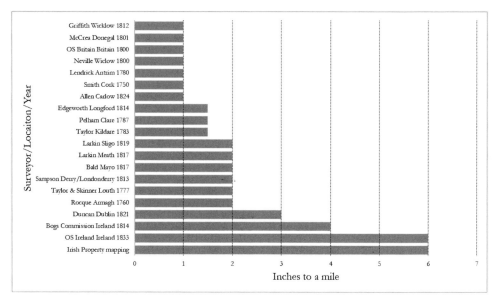

Table 1. Various map scales used in prominent Grand Jury and county maps in Ireland, 1750–1833. The Ordnance Survey's proposed scale of six inches to a mile would be far more detailed than such maps and remarkably close to the scale of forty perches to an inch traditionally used in Irish property mapping.

resurveying of English counties during the same period, though this preference can be partially traced to patronage requirements laid out by the London-based Society in Arts.[19]

The topic of traditional county map scales is worthy of note, given Colby's critical decision to survey Ireland at six inches to a mile. His adherence to a national six-inch series was remarkable in light of the above-mentioned norms, and that the Ordnance survey of Britain remained fixed as a one-inch series. Surprisingly, the topic of scale was rarely mentioned throughout Spring Rice's 1824 investigations, with the assembled committee happy to follow Colby's lead with little argument or detailed scrutiny. He did, nonetheless, have some historical and practical justification for this choice, decisively settling the matter with the assembled parliamentarians early in their proceedings (see below, p. 37).

Though Colby retained caution around pre-Ordnance medium- and small-scale surveys, they could not be judged as a singular entity. A case in point was the excellent work of the Bogs Commission (1809–14) to whom the committee paid special attention. The Bogs Commission surveys were the first significant (near) national survey in post-Union Ireland. Driven by the needs of the

19 J.B. Harely, 'The re-mapping of England, 1750–1800', *Imago Mundi*, 14 (1965), 60.

Napoleonic wars, this organization was tasked with charting Ireland's peatland for its conversion to agricultural use. This complex scheme was based on medium-scale topographic surveys, using triangulation control, and covered about a third of the island. Accomplished by the best civilian staff available, the Bogs Commission was arguably the pinnacle of pre-Ordnance mapping in Ireland and did much to encourage a new professional elite. Indeed, many of the Commission's chief engineers would later give evidence before the Spring Rice committee, with one, Richard Griffith, eventually holding a prominent role alongside Colby.

Despite the sophistication and quality of the Bogs Commission, such projects remained a minor part of the surveying communities' efforts. Even the Bogs Commission surveys fell short of potential national mapping, each of its surveys conducted as an isolated, independent entity. This disjointed approach later became a critical point levelled against the Commission by Spring Rice's committee. Ireland in 1824, therefore, had an extensive history of land measurement, with an experienced local workforce of surveyors, ranging from literate part-time practitioners to well-regarded professional civil engineers. It had, however, few examples of high-accuracy, uniform mapping integrated with regional or national governance.

Ordnance Survey in Britain

By contrast, efforts in Britain had a notable advantage in the form of the Ordnance Survey. Founded in 1791, the Ordnance Survey of Britain owed much to the influence of General William Roy (b. 1726, d. 1790). Roy was a strong proponent of a large-scale national survey, having played a prominent role in the survey of Scotland following the Jacobite rising (1745). In the 1780s, he coordinated the British portion of the great triangulation between the Royal Observatory in Greenwich and its equivalent in Paris.[20] As a result, he encouraged the use of scientific-grade surveying at the highest levels of the British government, successfully petitioning for the acquisition of sophisticated equipment. This investment soon paid off, with the then master of ordnance, the third duke of Richmond, ordering a series of isolated six-inch (1:10,560) surveys of strategic locations along the English Channel coast. Driven by the growing security concerns emanating from revolutionary France, these individual surveys were soon linked up and eventually extended across southern England.

20 Hewitt, *Map of a nation*, p. 89.

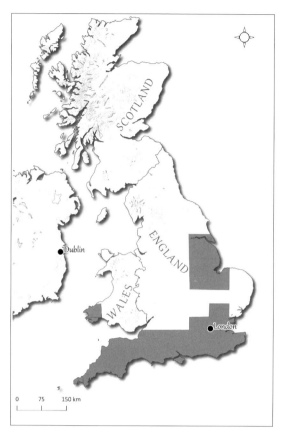

2.2. Approximate limit of published Ordnance mapping
in Britain by early 1824. By author.

This significantly wider scope would soon take a different form under the
command of Roy's successor, Captain William Mudge (b. 1762, d. 1820).[21] Most
notably, the scale of the survey would be reduced from six to two inches to a
mile (1:31,680). It was eventually published as a one-inch-to-a-mile map series,
beginning with a map of Kent in 1795 (see plate 5).[22] The first maps produced
during the Ordnance Survey of Britain's early years reflected the army's needs.
Initially, maps concentrated on areas most vulnerable to invasion from France,
namely the south coast, the approach to the river Thames, and Pembrokeshire
in Wales. The inclusion of Pembrokeshire was in reference to the last landing
of French troops in Britain in 1797; the powers-that-be determined not to let
their old enemy have the same advantage twice.

21 Mudge initially ran the Ordnance Survey alongside Major Edward Williams (d. 1798).
22 Tim Owen and Elaine Pilbeam, *Ordnance Survey: map makers to Britain since 1791* (Ordnance
Survey, 1992), p. 12; Charles Close, *The early years of the Ordnance Survey* (New York, 1969), p. 44.

Colby would later do much to revitalize these initial Ordnance maps when he obtained command in 1820. His insistence on revising, correcting and redistributing these early maps did much to amend mistakes and update noticeable changes. With his near-obsessive attention to detail, he ensured that standards rose drastically in the years immediately preceding the Spring Rice committee, with even Wellington commenting that his promotion to succeed Mudge had more to do with his aptitude than his seniority.[23] By the time the Spring Rice committee sat in 1824, Ordnance maps were being released of Lincolnshire. Though out of sequence for the organization's slow northward movement through Britain, Mudge had decided to prioritize the Lincolnshire survey at the behest of local landowners who offered to purchase 500 printed copies.[24] This decision would significantly test Ordnance resources and later have unforeseen consequences for Colby's approach to the survey of Ireland (see below, p. 62).

Despite some localized lapses in quality, the Ordnance Survey of Britain remained far superior in scope, accuracy and uniformity than anything produced to date in Ireland. Its military essence ensured that retention of specialized staff remained high, creating a small, elite body with a strong sense of purpose and *esprit de corps*. Besides needing additional resources, Colby and his team would have little difficulty transferring their skillset to Ireland for a general topographical survey. Issues surrounding land-based taxation, however, remained well outside their know-how and soon became a stumbling block for their plans.

LAND-BASED TAXATION: THE HEART OF THE ORDNANCE SURVEY OF IRELAND

While [Ireland] has run with complaints of party violence, of oppression from the rich, and of injustice from the Magistrate, very little has been said of another mischief, more extensive in its operation than any of the former, and less open to remedy from its fixed and prescriptive nature – we mean the partial and unequal manner in which the local taxes ... [that] have pressed upon the people of Ireland, owing to the imperfect measurement and valuation of the soil.

Freeman's Journal, 29 Sept. 1824.

Land-based taxes lay at the core of the Ordnance Survey of Ireland. They were the driving force behind the survey's methods and the critical factor

23 Close, *The early years of the Ordnance Survey*, p. 83.   24 *The Economist*, 'How intrepid Victorian surveyors mapped the length and breadth of Britain', 6 Apr. 2023.

distinguishing it from its British equivalent. They were also the justification
Spring Rice needed to form his committee and the root cause of his dispute
with Wellington. Yet their topicality was far from unique from a European
perspective, with the broader picture of tax reform through mapping being of
note when assessing the Spring Rice committee's activities.

Throughout the seventeenth and eighteenth centuries there had been a
general drift toward the combination of accurate medium-/large-scale national
mapping with tax re-assessments across Europe.[25] As in Ireland, the success of
systematic mapping programmes depended on various social and administrative
needs of the ruling classes, and how receptive they were to the penetrating view
of surveys. The common theme for such projects was increasing tax revenue
through reform rather than expansion. Several central European states felt this
need most prominently in the aftermath of the Thirty Years War (1618–48).
The mass loss of life among agrarian taxpayers during the conflict and the
ongoing costs of maintaining standing armies in its aftermath proved prime
motivators to invest in mapping for improved revenue.[26] Such stimuli remained
valid well into the eighteenth century, with pre-industrial economies remaining
heavily reliant on agricultural land for tax income. The Netherlands, for
example, commissioned detailed and widespread surveys to fund the expense
of dike maintenance early in the century. Cleves and Hanover in Germany
followed suit, undertaking equivalent examinations of land-based taxation
through mapping, notably tithes. Unfortunately, success in these early ventures
was far from certain.[27] The Cleves venture, for example, was abandoned in the
1730s due to its expense, with even the king of Poland, Stanisław August,
remarking that a planned national survey was in trouble as 'it seemed that the
earth itself rose up in opposition so as not to be measured'.[28]

Indeed, one of the chief inhibitors to these reformatory projects was, as in
1824, what investment politicians, nobles and monarchs were willing to make.
Imbalances in period political and ruling systems were a notable stumbling
block to success. Across the Continent, not all citizens were equal before their
local law system or in the eyes of their regional tax collectors. In France, for
example, reformative tax surveys were actively blocked by the nobility, where,
unlike Ireland or Britain, they held near tax-exempt status. As a result of this
social class wishing to keep the extent of their privileges hidden from the
masses, collective influence was placed on autocratic French kings to limit
funding for tax-based land surveys. This obstruction would remain until the

---

25 Maria Luisa Sturani, 'Topographical surveying in the Enlightenment' in *The history of cartography*,
iv (Chicago, 1989), p. 1417.   26 Roger Kain, 'Taxation and cartography' in *The history of cartography*,
iv (Chicago, 1989), p. 1348.   27 Ibid., p. 1350.   28 Ibid., p. 1351; quoted in Lucyna Szaniawska,
'Topographical surveying in Poland' in *The history of cartography*, iv (Chicago, 1989), p. 1469.

1789 Revolution, when the nobility's prestige, along with many of their heads, was forcibly removed.[29]

The *censimento* in Austrian-ruled northern Italy (Lombardy, Venetia and Tirol), by contrast, proved a better model of what could be achieved in Ireland. Completed in 1759, this large-scale (1:2000) map series helped rebalance the burden of tax payments from the poor to the nobility. It was later adopted in Spain alongside the neighbouring Italian regions of Piedmont and Savoy, the latter two mentioned during the Spring Rice committee's investigations.[30] The *censimento* was also relevant to the case of the Ordnance Survey of Ireland as it involved one European state charting lands in another that it controlled.[31] While this particular point was overlooked during the Spring Rice investigation, the execution of similar mapping projects across Europe remained of active interest. As shall be seen however, such interest remained limited to policy or general cartographic design rather than detailed examination of their execution, with Colby's plans for Ireland exceeding most regarding scale, accuracy and scientific expertise. Regardless, taxation remained a common factor shared across the Continent.

The taxes at the centre of Ireland's new survey took two principal forms, cess and tithes. Each represented a separate charge for all landholders and financed different services. Cess was the primary concern of the Spring Rice committee. It was a form of community tax collected by each county and used to pay for local administrative costs and infrastructure, such as roads or salaries of officials. In theory, it was based proportionally on the size and productivity of land within a county, with each landowner and tenant paying their respective share. Unfortunately, by the 1820s, valuations had become grossly outdated, with acreage estimates being equally questionable. The result was a 'mass of clumsy partiality and injustice',[32] with payments often utterly incorrect due to the poor base information.[33]

Cess was calculated on a townland basis. Townlands are Ireland's most minor administrative subdivision, with many predating the Norman invasion. Numbering around 60,000, they form the foundation level of all geographic areas on the island, with the respective larger units of parishes, baronies, and counties based on what townlands they contain.[34] Though by 1824 there was no official record of each townland's size, location, or quality of land the townlands' names and boundaries were generally well-known to locals at ground level.[35] If

29 Kain, 'Taxation and cartography', p. 1352.   30 Ibid., p. 1351.   31 Elizabeth Baigent, 'Topographic mapping and the state' in *The history of cartography*, iv (Chicago, 1989), p. 1404. 32 *Freeman's Journal*, 29 Sept. 1824.   33 Wilkins, *Alexander Nimmo*, p. 130.   34 Andrews, *Paper landscape*, p. 14. There were a total of 61,098 townlands according to the Irish Placenames Database of Ireland, https://www.logainm.ie/en/ (accessed 22 Feb. 2023).   35 Nationally, the

a revised, accurate and official record was used as the basis of valuation, it would do much to rectify this imbalanced and flawed system of cess.

While cess reform was the initial target of the Spring Rice committee, and the subsequent Ordnance Survey, tithes were the more topical and divisive issue of the day. Regardless of its many errors, cess was mostly implemented independent of social conditions. Tithes, by contrast, had a distinctly sectarian edge. All landholders paid this tax (equating to one-tenth of agricultural produce) directly to the Church of Ireland, regardless of religion.[36] As the Church of Ireland remained the official state church and a minority religion, tithes were deeply resented by non-Anglicans such as Catholics and Presbyterians alike. Neither group could benefit from the services they paid for, with the Anglican clergy growing exceedingly wealthy as a result.

There was also a significant socio-economic imbalance in tithes, which increased their unpopularity. By the early nineteenth century, pasture farming had become the predominant realm of wealthier landowners, while tillage remained that of the poor. Before the Tithe Composition Bill (1823), the former had been chiefly exempted from this levy, thus increasing the burden on lower-income households.[37] As a result, tithes became a flashpoint in the complex, often violent world of post-Union rural Ireland. Despite the unpopularity of this second levy, the Spring Rice committee focused its efforts on cess reform. It was, however, intended that the maps and valuations from cess amendments could equally be adopted to correct tithe rates. This initial strategy avoided the problem of immediate conflict with the Church of Ireland, though did little to reduce opposition to tithes, which eventually erupted into widespread civil disobedience in the 1830s. Anglo-Irish MPs were understandably eager to reduce the potential of another Irish revolt. Many remembered the widespread violence that accompanied the 1798 Rebellion and saw tax reform as a means of calming tensions. Any attempt at restructuring would be welcome.[38]

The journey of cess reform

Discussions on cess amendments far pre-dated the Spring Rice committee. The topic had been brought before the Irish parliament as far back as 1711 but little

average townland covers 325 acres (1.32km sq): G. Brendan Adams, 'Prolegomena to the study of Irish place-names', *Nomina*, 2 (1978), 49–50; cited in Terence Dolan, 'townland', *A dictionary of Hiberno-English: the Irish use of English*, 2nd ed. (Dublin, 2006). Spring Rice knew of one townland near his estate in Limerick that was just three acres in size, with another nearby which measured nearly six thousand: Evidence of Lord Monteagle, *Report from the select committee on Ordnance Survey (Scotland)* (1851), p. 23. **36** Boyce, *Nineteenth-century Ireland*, p. 68. **37** *Freeman's Journal*, 29 Sept. 1824. Stephen McCormac, 'The tithe war; reports by Church of Ireland clergymen to Dublin

had been achieved. Admittedly there had been a half-hearted request following the Act of Union for each Grand Jury to survey and value their respective territories, though only two had yet to make any actual headway on the issue (Armagh and Kilkenny).[39] In 1815, a Westminster investigation took aim at Grand Jury inactivity on the issue of making '[cess] assessment more equal...'.[40] This investigation noted their ineptness in curbing '... the extensive corruption which pervaded the ... system', including deceit among cess collectors. Unfortunately, by this stage, the entire system of Irish Grand Juries was falling increasingly under Westminster's spotlight due to its inefficiency and would soon be marginalized.

Shortly after the 1815 investigation, another parliamentary group concluded that a new land valuation system for taxation would be advisable.[41] They suggested that new assessments be conducted at a sub-barony level (i.e., per parish or townland), independent of the local Grand Jury authority. Furthermore, this second investigation recommended that each barony, parish, and townland should also be surveyed and mapped to aid the valuation process. Unfortunately, these recommendations failed to gain traction in parliament.

Yet another attempt was made in 1819 by Arthur Chichester, MP for Belfast (b. 1783, d. 1869), who submitted a similar bill to parliament. Again, this proposal included both a survey and valuation element and, like previous attempts, fell by the wayside.[42] Chichester's efforts were, however, not in vain. Though his bill was unsuccessful, he had reached an agreement, in principle, with the Board of Ordnance to conduct a supportive triangulation survey in Ireland. An essential first step in the organization's Irish venture was thereby taken.[43] Also of note for the 1819 investigation was the involvement of several future members of Spring Rice's committee, including Sir John Newport (b. 1756, d. 1843) and John Wilson Croker (b. 1780, d. 1857), the latter publicly linking the potential expansion of the Ordnance Survey's remit with the needs of the Admiralty (see below, p. 90).[44]

Two years later, another champion of local Irish taxation was found in Spring Rice. His reformative political aspirations, and position as an Irish estate owner, gave him a solid understanding of the ongoing tax issues. In 1821 he submitted two separate reports to parliament analysing cess systems in Dublin

Castle', *History Ireland*, 4:13 (2005). **38** William Smyth, 'Sir Richard Griffith's three surveys of Ireland, 1826–1864' (PhD, NUIM, 2008), p. 29. **39** Andrews, *Paper landscape*, p. 14. **40** *Report from the select committee on Grand Jury presentments of Ireland*, HC, 1815 (283). **41** *Two reports from the select committee on Grand Jury presentments of Ireland*, HC, 1816 (374, 435). **42** *Report from the select committee on Grand Jury presentments of Ireland*, HC, 1819 (378); Hansard, vol. 40, 26 May 1819, cc 805. **43** This debate also brought about a cost assessment of the project, estimated at £300,000 by Leslie Foster (12 million acres at 6*d.* per acre to survey). This would be the eventual cost submission made to parliament by Colby in 1824. Ibid. **44** Andrews, *Paper landscape*, p. 17.

and his native Limerick. Each was scathing of the inefficiency and corruption of Grand Juries, highlighting a skewed system riddled with loopholes easily exploited by the wealthy, to the detriment of the poor.[45] A concurrent report by Newport further supported the reform movement, concluding that the existing land valuation system should be steered toward a more impartial and proportionate model. Importantly, Newport hoped that the improvement of valuations would be accompanied by a general survey of Ireland, as it was,

> ... most essential to this very important object, that the system hereafter to be adopted should be uniform in every part of Ireland, founded on an accurate survey of the whole acreable contents of the country; on a subsequent division of the land into profitable and unprofitable, and on a subdivision of the profitable lands, to make them hereafter proportional by [sic] contributory to payment of these assessments.[46]

Newport recommended that any new survey should be conducted outside the control of Grand Juries 'by the employment of proper officers under the direction of government – and at the public charge'.[47] This invariably led to the door of the Board of Ordnance.

WHAT WOULD A NEW SURVEY INVOLVE?

The Spring Rice committee members did not begin their review with a set plan, or an exact understanding of the technicalities that would be required. They did nonetheless have an approximate idea of what was needed, loosely based on a combination of the existing work of the Ordnance Survey of Britain and data required for reform in Ireland. The Irish project would consist of four separate entities, some of which Colby and his team were accustomed to, while others were entirely unfamiliar:

- a *triangulation network* using trigonometrical techniques, covering the entire island. This mathematical model would be like that already measured in Britain.
- a detailed *topographic survey* from which maps were to be produced. This would include information on Ireland's physical landscape such as roads, buildings, rivers, etc.

45 Smyth, 'Sir Richard Griffith's three surveys of Ireland', p. 32; *First report from the select committee on Grand Jury presentments* (1822), p. 4. 46 *First report from the select committee on Grand Jury presentments*, p. 1. 47 Ibid.

- a *territorial/boundary survey* of small administrative areas (e.g. townlands). Their borders would first need to be identified on the ground and then transcribed onto mapping. From this, their respective areas could be determined in acres, roods and perches.
- once the above was completed, a *valuation* could then take place using the new maps and acreages as a guide. Valuations were based on soil quality and acreage per townland and would become the basis of reformed cess charges.[48]

The committee started its work without a clear picture of each element's technicalities, or the sequence in which they should be executed. Many of the witnesses called had differing opinions on these two aspects of the investigation, with Spring Rice and his colleagues facing the unenviable task of determining which made the most sense based on the scope of the project and the time involved.

The terminology used by the committee was the root of some confusion with the general public of the period. This was most obvious regarding the frequently mentioned 'trigonometric survey'. The committee and witnesses mostly aligned in their comprehension of this term, agreeing that it only referred to the triangulation portion of the project. Period commentary and newspaper reports however often grouped the triangulation and topographic elements into one, becoming a 'trigonometrically' executed survey. Additionally, mention of topography in the committee minutes was reserved for measuring physical features such as hills or rivers. This, in turn, differed from the less restrictive duties of the Ordnance Survey's eventual 'Topographic Department', whose interests focused on an expansive range of subjects with greater cultural and historical significance.[49] Regardless, such tasks lay many years in the future.

The Board of Ordnance was virtually guaranteed control of the triangulation network from the start of the investigation, having the greatest experience in this field. Most witnesses supported this point, including many Irish engineers called to provide evidence. However, a frequent line of questioning was to what depth Colby and his team would be asked to participate. It was clear to all that the proposed survey of Ireland and the

---

48 Maps were not necessarily essential for valuation using area calculation, though they were highly practical. Thomas Burgh (b. 1670, d. 1730), surveyor general of Ireland between 1700 and 1730, published a well-received treatise on how to calculate areas based on coordinates rather than cartographic data. Thomas Burgh, *A method to determine the areas of right-lined figures* (Dublin, 1724).   49 Evidence of William Bald, 13 May, p. 58, Evidence of Mr Hyett, 19 May, p. 99, Evidence of Richard Griffith, 7 May, p. 45, Evidence of Alexander Nimmo, 17 May, p. 79, *Report from the select committee on the survey and valuation of Ireland* (London, 1824); Andrews, *Paper landscape*; p. 147; Andrews, *Maps in those days*, p. 224; *Dublin Journal*, 26 Apr. 1824.

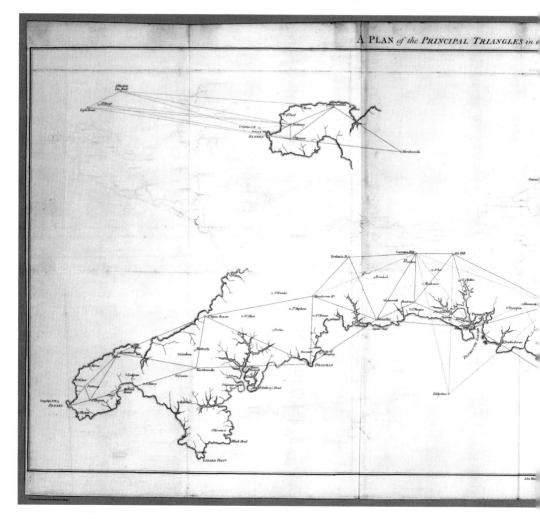

2.3. The primary triangulation of Dorset, Devon and Cornwall in south-west England, surveyed by the Board of Ordnance in the 1790s. William Mudge, *A plan of the principal triangles in the trigonometrical survey, 1795–1796* (London, 1797) (David Rumsey Map Collection, David Rumsey Map Centre, Stanford Libraries).

existing Ordnance Survey of Britain were two very different entities. While Colby was agreeable to conducting the triangulation and topographic portions, he expressed concerns about the territorial section and rejected the valuation. Management of the territorial issue would remain problematic throughout the committee meetings. The survey's remaining components threw up their own range of questions and queries, though there was often an abundance of options suggested by expert witnesses to soothe any fears.

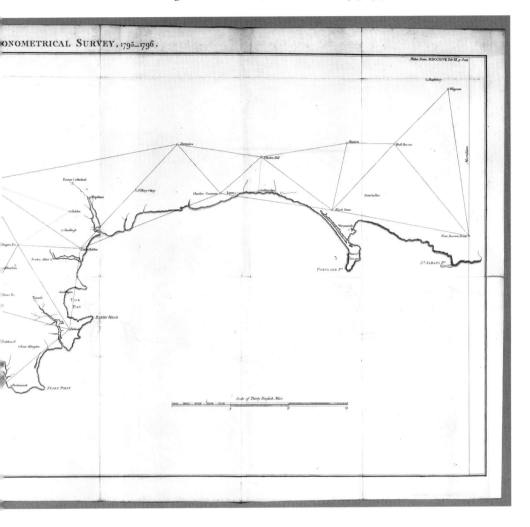

ONOMETRICAL SURVEY, 1795–1796.

Triangulation network

The triangulation network created by the Ordnance Survey is what defined the scheme in terms of scientific precision. Before the advent of GPS, such networks were the best available method for accurately measuring vast areas, justifying the extra effort and time needed for their execution.[50] As the name suggests, this network consisted of a series of angular observations in the form of large triangles covering the landscape. The meeting point of each triangle corresponded to prominent objects visible from other (though not all) points

50 A national triangulation network of Ireland had been suggested by William King, archbishop of Dublin, as early as 1709. King was an active member of Ireland's scientific community and maintained close connections with the country's top surveyors. O'Cionnaith, *Land surveying*, p. 52.

in the network. In the case of the eventual Ordnance Survey of Ireland, these objects came in the form of uniform pillars located on the tops of mountains, 'trig pillars', now familiar sights on summits around the island.

Triangulation was a well-established methodology by the 1820s. It had become synonymous throughout the eighteenth century with some of the most scientifically accurate mapping projects ever attempted in Europe and had played a significant part in the 'second scientific revolution' in period cartography.[51] Distances were no longer based on a direct measure between two points but instead would incorporate concepts designed to improve precision, no matter how minute. Increasingly sophisticated devices were deployed to record lengths and angles, new calculations were developed, optics were improved for telescopic sights, and naturally occurring facets, such as the earth's curvature or the expansion and contraction of metals, were now acknowledged and compensated for. Notable examples referenced by the Spring Rice committee included the *carte de France* (1750–1815), the Anglo-French survey (1784–90), the principal triangulation of Great Britain, the great trigonometrical survey of India (1802–71), and, more locally (though less renowned), the work of the Bogs Commission.

Within the context of early nineteenth-century Britain and Ireland, the topic of triangulation was irrevocably connected to the Board of Ordnance. It was one of the few organizations with experience conducting triangulation control for extensive surveys, thus having a near (though not absolute) monopoly on experienced staff and high-grade equipment. While no one directly challenged Colby's authority over this portion of the Irish survey, the committee occasionally felt obliged to ask resident Irish engineers about their interest in managing this aspect. All reverted to Colby's expertise.

A triangulation network begins with the measurement of a hyper-accurate baseline. For national surveys, this line is usually several kilometres long. The baseline for the Ordnance Survey of Britain in 1791, for example, measured across Hounslow heath near London, was over eight kilometres in length but was accurate to just one part per million (an error tolerance of 25mm over 8.3km). This was a remarkable achievement given the manual nature of such work, reliant on metal chains and labour-intensive calculations, testament to the quality of the Ordnance's proficiency in geographic science. By comparison, the purely 'mathematical' standards practised in private commercial surveying meant that errors propagated with distance, thus making them unsuitable for a national survey. The simple issue of several stretched links in a surveyor's

---

51 The first scientific revolution was driven by the research of Sir Isaac Newton and Nicolaus Copernicus during the sixteenth and seventeenth centuries. Hewitt, *Map of a nation*, p. 125.

chain could result in significant distance errors when multiplied out over several kilometres. Equally, issues with substandard angular instruments were difficult to detect unless compared to a reference triangulation network. Disputes frequently found their way into period newspapers when two rival surveyors' measurements disagreed, causing harm to the collective profession.[52]

Such accuracy was required for the Ordnance baseline as this became the reference for all subsequent measurements in the triangulation network, and thus the entire survey. Once measured, angular observations could be taken from the baseline to nearby trig pillars. Slowly, these angular measurements expanded one triangle at a time, creating a lattice whose nexus points were precisely known. This network, not visible in the final mapping, acted as a mathematical scaffold from which geographic detail could then be accurately added. Any errors within the triangulation element could be dissipated across the entire network, thus lessening their impact on overall topographic detail.[53] The baseline for the eventual Ordnance Survey of Ireland would be taken along the east side of Lough Foyle, Co. Derry, taking nearly two years to calculate.[54]

Angles between triangulation points within the network were measured using an instrument called a theodolite. This instrument consists of a horizontal circle divided into degrees, minutes and seconds, combined with a similarly divided perpendicular vertical circle attached to a telescopic sight. The vertical and horizontal angle to a distant point could therefore be obtained, thus positioning it within three-dimensional space compared to the instrument. Given the accuracy required, the design and condition of individual instruments therefore directly impacted the quality of measurements within a network. The availability of such higher-spec theodolites consequently became a subject during Spring Rice's investigations, providing an important record of the rarity, and value, of such devices (see plate 6).

While focus would have been placed on a primary triangulation, a secondary and even tertiary triangulation networks were required for very large survey areas. These lower networks were created inside each of the primary triangles, becoming a network within a network. Their purpose was to provide local reference points for field surveyors to record topographic detail (e.g., roads, property boundaries, etc.). The density of this hierarchical model would prove to be an important point for the committee witnesses as the greater the

52 O'Cionnaith, *Land surveying*, p. 69.   53 Or as aptly described by Andrews, 'When the map of Ireland is picked up and shaken, it is only the mathematician who hears the rattle', Andrews, *Paper landscape*, p. 23.   54 Colby would also use chain measurements to check the accuracy of his trigonometrical observations, in essence physically measuring one side per triangle. This allowed for easier checks to be performed and gave additional support to detail measurements within

density, the more time would be spent on calculation, with its associated costs. (See Appendix A for further details of triangulation networks.)

Detail/topographic survey

The topographic portion of the survey would constitute the physical element of the Ordnance's mapping. This thus formed the majority of information on the finished map. It involved surveyors gathering measurements in the field using surveyors' chains and lower specification theodolites than those used in the triangulation.[55] In turn, this information would be placed in context by positioning it relative to the reference triangulation points. In this manner, all recorded physical detail in the country would have the same spatial accuracy, regardless of how far it was from the initial baseline.

In theory, Ireland's new survey did not need this topographic element. Earlier map series, such as the Down Survey, had mostly avoided accurate depictions of terrain. Instead, this part of the project would help tie civil divisions, such as townlands and parishes, with the island's physical landscape, giving the resulting maps greater cross-vocational appeal.

The level of detail required for the survey was occasionally mentioned during the Spring Rice committee's meetings, though not as prominently as might be expected. It was assumed that surveyors would gather physical data (rivers, towns, mountains), though who these surveyors would be remained a more topical issue than what information would actually be collected. The topographical element would become the Ordnance's most recognizable component to the general map user and remain crucial to cess revaluation (figures 2.4a–d).

Territorial survey

The territorial section of the survey drew great interest from witnesses and committee members. This data would quantify and name the areas valuers would eventually assess, overlaying the topographic mapping, and thus be pivotal to cess calculation. The main problem faced by the committee was identifying which sub-county division to use and how to locate their boundaries in the field. Several witnesses urged that civil parishes should be examined as

each triangle. Andrews, *Paper landscape*, p. 26.   **55** Though less accurate, the theodolites used were more portable than those of triangulation portion, but still significantly better than the outdated circumferentor (surveyor's compass) that remained stubbornly in service across rural Ireland in the 1820s. O'Cionnaith, *Mapping, measurement and metropolis*, pp 61–7.

the local diocese often had records of their bounds. Others argued that the smaller townland divisions should be studied, as these had been the traditional basis of cess collection. Unfortunately, no complete list, let alone a map, of Ireland's thousands of townlands existed, turning the territorial portion into a formidable task.

Irish-based engineers interviewed by Spring Rice had greater confidence in this matter than their British equivalents. Many had worked across the island and felt that townland boundaries were well known to rural communities. They believed that by calling on the assistance of farmers or local authorities, such information could be correctly determined through questioning. This may have been a less scientific approach than the Ordnance Survey was used to, but it was effective. Regardless, there was no alternative available. Townlands were entirely alien to Colby and the existing Ordnance Survey corps, the organization understandably preferring to focus on more specialized and technical tasks such as the triangulation. This was echoed in the testimony of civilian engineers, who agreed that the experience of the Ordnance teams was so rare that it would be a waste of resources to have them conduct such interviews. Wellington also disapproved of his specialist surveyors undertaking such a mundane task. Eventually, the boundary element would fall under the management of engineer Richard Griffith, though this only occurred after the committee had concluded, and this decision was not part of their recommendations.

A conspicuous facet of documenting townlands involved standardizing their names.[56] Many townland names were unrecorded or known only in their original Gaelic version, notably in the country's west. This process was complicated due to the vast number of 'mangled' anglicized variants across the island, provided as alternatives by centuries of English administrators.[57] To cut through such confusion, Colby invested significant resources to identify each townland's most commonly used title. This strategy included hiring prominent Gaelic scholars, such as John O'Donovan (b. 1806, d. 1861), to trace their original linguistic roots. As such, it improved on earlier efforts implemented by Mudge in Wales, where, like Ireland, 'the language barrier was like the Himalayas'.[58] Welsh translations had met with much criticism and Colby was determined to avoid similar mistakes in Ireland. Part of this desire may have originated from the time he spent living in Wales as a youth, hoping for accuracy and consistency in Ireland though aware of the overarching need for accessibility to English

56 Proinsias Ó Drisceoil, 'Civilizing Ireland, Ordnance Survey 1824–42, ethnography, cartography, translation', *History Ireland*, review, 15 (2007). https://www.historyireland.com/civilizing-ireland-ordnance-survey–1824–42-ethnography-cartography-translation/ (last accessed 22 Feb. 2023).   57 Andrews, *Paper landscape*, p. 121.   58 Hewitt, *Map of a nation*, p. 192.

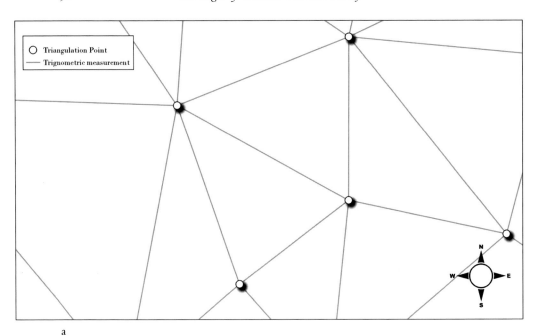

a

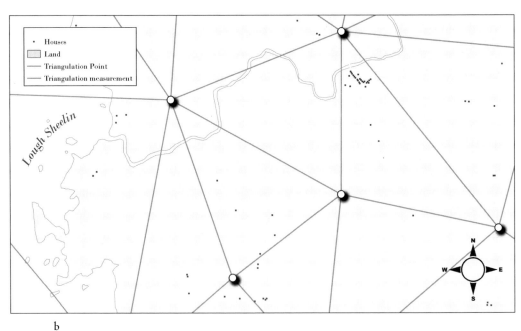

b

2.4a–d. The four components of the Ordnance Survey of Ireland. Beginning with a
triangulation network (**a**), followed by a topographical survey (**b**), the inclusion of
townland boundaries (**c**) and finally their quantification (in acres, roods and perches),
and valuation (**d**). By author.

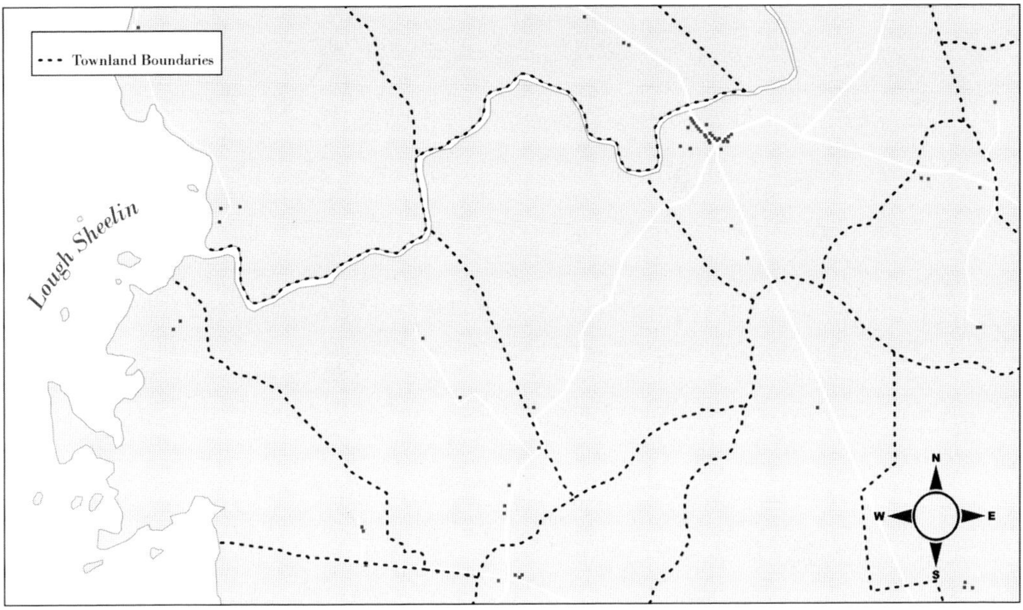
Townland Boundaries
Lough Sheelin
N
W
E
S

c

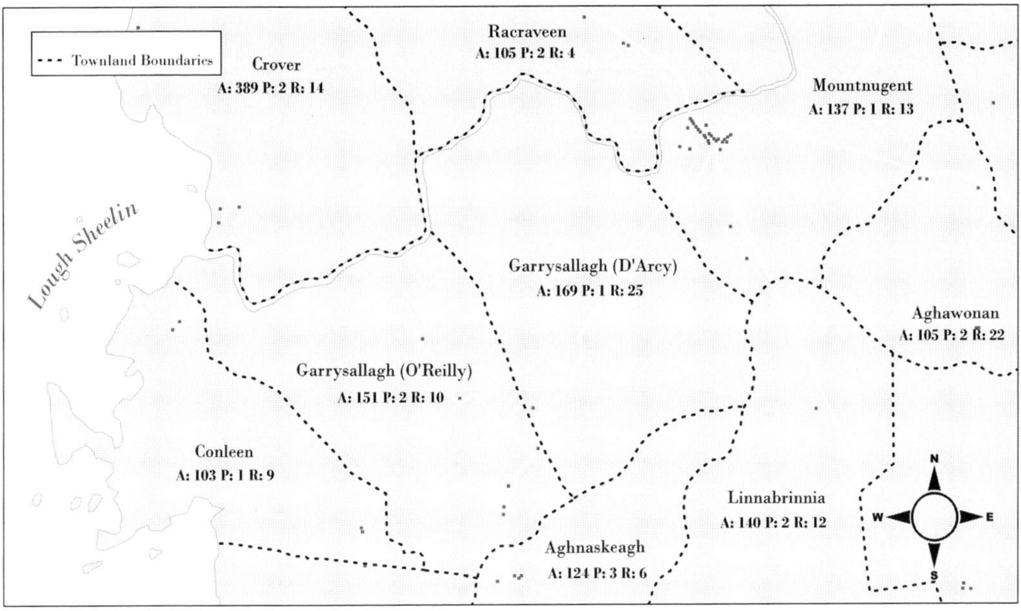
Townland Boundaries
Lough Sheelin
Racraveen
A: 105 P: 2 R: 4
Crover
A: 389 P: 2 R: 14
Mountnugent
A: 137 P: 1 R: 13
Garrysallagh (D'Arcy)
A: 169 P: 1 R: 25
Aghawonan
A: 105 P: 2 R: 22
Garrysallagh (O'Reilly)
A: 151 P: 2 R: 10
Conleen
A: 103 P: 1 R: 9
Linnabrinnia
A: 140 P: 2 R: 12
Aghnaskeagh
A: 124 P: 3 R: 6
N
W
E
S

d

readers.[59] Andrews describes this sensitivity regarding Irish placenames as well-intentioned deference to local culture, backed by extensive academic research by Ordnance staff. In this manner, it was a 'rational, scholarly and practical' approach, thoughtfully deployed by the standards of the era.[60] Admittedly, the Ordnance's rigorous investigations could never be perfect, with one Colby biographer openly admitting that many local names had been adjusted to be 'more suitable to the English tongue'.[61]

The prominence of this orthographic element in modern culture can be traced to Brian Friel's (b. 1929, d. 2015) influential play *Translations*, written in 1980. Set in the fictional Irish-speaking village of Ballybeg, Co. Donegal, the play recounts the arrival of the Ordnance Survey and the ensuing clash of cultures between locals and army officers. Covering the complex aspects of politics, post-colonialism and cultural identity, the play's primary themes were given added emphasis due to the era in which it was written, at the height of the Troubles. The process of identifying townland names provides the play's title, with Ordnance characters producing anglicized alternatives to appear on mapping. While a superbly written piece of literature, the play is however a work of fiction, exaggerating the renaming process for dramatic effect.[62] The actual work of the Ordnance Survey was more complicated than the 'purely imperialist endeavour that Friel described'.[63] For example, most Ordnance staff in the year in which the play was set were, in fact, civilians, contrasting with the predominantly military composition seen on stage. Such factual liberties were noted by several academics upon the play's release, remarking that it provided

---

59 Nicholas Wolf, *State, religion, community, and the linguistic landscape in Ireland, 1770–1870* (Wisconsin, 2014), p. 65. 60 Andrews, *Paper landscape*, p. 122. This episode of the Ordnance Survey of Ireland was noted in Colby's biography: 'In the Ordnance Survey the importance of a correct determination of names was felt and fully appreciated, and "Name Books" were established by Major Colby, in which the officers entered the names, according to the best information they could acquire; but the enquiry did not rest here, but became the subject of the most careful antiquarian research. Lieut.-Colonel Larcom [Thomas Larcom (b. 1801, d. 1879)], who took so active a part in this and other branches of the survey, observes in respect to names, that, "as for the orthography of the names engraved on the maps of the Ordnance Survey, the different spellings and alias names of every townland were collected from all accessible documents, some (where the names were ancient) of very great antiquity; and finally, local inquiry and examination were made by an Irish scholar on the spot, to render the name ultimately adopted as nearly as possible consistent with the ancient orthography …"', Joseph Portlock, *Memoir of the life of Major-General Colby* (London, 1869), p. 198. 61 Portlock, *Major-General Colby*, p. 198; *Irish Times*, 'More than a map: the Ordnance Survey's huge but hidden cultural impact', 1 Sept. 2016; *Irish Times*, 'Distorting the past, true to the present', 31 July 1996. 62 John Andrews, '"More suitable to the English tongue": the cartography of Celtic placenames', *Ulster Local Studies*, 14:2 (1992), 7–21; John Andrews, 'Irish place-names and the Ordnance Survey', *Cartographica*, 31:3 (1994), 60–1; C. Nash, 'Irish placenames: post-colonial locations', *Transactions of the Institute of British Geographers*, new series, 24:4 (1999), 457–80. 63 Hewitt, *Map of a nation*, p. 281.

a medium to cover the broader story of 'anglicization of Irish place-names in its totality, over hundreds of years, rather than the specific events under Ordnance control'.[64] In this regard, *Translations* should not be taken as an accurate historical record of the Ordnance Survey's work, but rather a sublime and rightly celebrated commentary on the long-standing cultural differences between England and Ireland. The orthographic portion of the Ordnance's duties was left entirely untouched during the 1824 investigations (and thus outside the remit of this book), the Spring Rice committee content to leave such technicalities to others at a later date.

Outside this naming parameter, the charting of townlands did, however, touch upon the significantly broader relationship between mapping and English rule in Ireland. The territorial aspect of the Ordnance Survey was the final step in the centuries-long journey of documenting Ireland's civil divisions. This had begun with the coarse charting of post-medieval fiefdoms, such as those of the Desmonds' and O'Neills' by Tudor surveyors.[65] Analysis of administrative depth widened with the expansion of English rule, notably with Petty's baronial and parish surveys on behalf of Cromwell. This process reached its most base level with the Ordnance's townlands. While the scope of each phase differed, cumulatively, the vestiges of Gaelic Ireland were slowly exposed to English administrators. Colby's work marked the end of this journey. There was simply nowhere to go below townlands. In this manner, the survey's strongest link with imperialism was manifested through its territorial element.

Valuation

Unusually for a project with the specific aim of determining land values, the committee gave the valuation portion little attention. In the introduction to their findings, they, almost repentantly, addressed this gap, stating:

> Your committee are not as yet in possession of sufficient evidence to enable them to form a detailed plan, or to do more than to suggest, some leading general principles: they, however, regret this the less, because the survey must necessarily take precedence, the basis of the valuation being obviously the proposed maps of the counties, baronies and parishes, divided into their respective townlands.[66]

Undoubtedly, attempts to alleviate pressures from Wellington pushed the committee's valuation element to a lower rung. Yet, as stated above, valuers

64 John Andrews, Kevin Barry, Brian Friel, '*Translations* and *A paper landscape*: between fiction and history', *The Crane Bag*, 7:2 (1983), 118–24.   65 O'Cionnaith, *Land surveying*, p. 36.   66 *Report from the select committee on the survey and valuation of Ireland*, p. 9.

simply could not do their work without accurate maps to guide them. As the survey and territorial portions of the project would take many years to complete, the valuation element could afford to wait. Regardless, several valuation experts were called during the committee's meetings, though these remained a notable minority. What little valuation evidence that was provided appears to have convinced the committee that this section was less technically complex than creating the maps the valuers would work from, thus being of lesser concern.

Cess valuation would eventually take place in the 1830s, again under Griffith. Griffith was an exceptionally talented individual frequently interviewed by Spring Rice. He had an ongoing interest in valuation, having worked in this field initially in Scotland in 1806. Between 1825 and 1844 he was employed as the head of the Ordnance Survey's boundary department, establishing townland locations. In 1827, he was also appointed to the pivotal role of commissioner of valuation.[67] Beginning this work three years later, Griffith guided the valuation of all rateable property in Ireland for nearly the next forty years, 'Griffith's Valuation' becoming a pivotal part of nineteenth-century Ireland land management. This work lay far in the future. It first needed a cartographic bedrock on which to build.

---

67 Evidence of Richard Griffith, *Report from the select committee on Ordnance Survey* (Scotland), p. 136. Griffith was the sole commissioner for the general valuation of Ireland, stating 'I was at the head of one of the departments myself; the general boundary department was under my direction. I determined the whole of the [townland] boundaries which were afterwards surveyed by the Ordnance surveyors.'

CHAPTER THREE

Westminster, February 1824

Major Colby entered upon the task [of surveying Ireland] with all the skill and energy he so pre-eminently possessed. This was really the great work of his life, for which all his previous labours were only the fitting preparation, and for this he may be said, to have created the means of execution, whilst devising the mode of proceeding.[1]

The Ordnance Survey's true involvement in Ireland began on 13 February 1824 with a communique by Colby to the secretary of the Board of Ordnance.[2] This memo, now unfortunately lost, outlined his concept of the proposed survey and what resources he could call upon. This evaluation was stimulated by a series of earlier, off-the-record conversations that had taken place between Colby's superior, the duke of Wellington, and Henry Goulburn (b. 1784, d. 1856), chief secretary of Ireland, concerning land-based taxation. Colby's opinion would help shape their initial expectations for the survey and, simultaneously, create concerns from those more familiar with Irish tax reform.

The prompt for Colby's appraisal was in large part thanks to Goulburn. While rarely featuring in Spring Rice's later investigation, Goulburn's activities proved instrumental in the earliest portion of the Ordnance's Irish mission. The son of a wealthy Jamaican plantation owner, he had entered parliament in 1808. Appointed chief secretary of Ireland in 1821, the initial years of his tenure were dominated by the Composition for Tithes (Ireland) Act (1823), providing him with a solid foundation in Irish taxation and the wider emancipation movement, which he opposed.

Ireland's executive government was officially led by the lord lieutenant, based at Dublin Castle. However, this role became more symbolic than administrative following the Act of Union. Instead, much of the country's day-to-day running fell to the lord lieutenant's subordinate, the chief secretary.[3] Goulburn, therefore,

---

1 Thomas Colby, Obituary, *Annual Report, Institution of Civil Engineers*, 1852–3, p. 4.   2 Andrews, *Paper landscape*, p. 20: referred to in Colby's report of 15 Feb. 1827 to the clerk of ordnance Sir Henry Hardinge regarding the progress of the Irish survey.   3 The position of chief secretary of Ireland was also previously held by Wellington for the period 1807–9.

held significant influence over political life and policy on the island. Travelling extensively between Dublin and London, he acted as a liaison to the British cabinet on Irish issues and represented the Irish administration before the House of Commons. As such, Goulburn bore responsibility for official appointments and policies, compared to the lord lieutenant's figurehead role. His favour was therefore widely sought by those seeking positions in the civil service.

Later mentioned in passing by the duke,[4] Goulburn had met privately with Wellington in London regarding Irish taxes. For his part, Wellington had grown increasingly concerned about unrest in Ireland over the preceding months, frequently voicing his worries of another Irish rebellion or civil war to acquaintances. His contacts in Ireland echoed these fears, with one informing him that 'this country is in a far worse state of disaffection than immediately before the Rebellion of 1798'.[5] The chief secretary's warnings over tax were thus well-timed. One of Goulburn's main objectives was to reduce tensions through reformative acts instead of dealing with more radical demands, such as emancipation. Tax reform was an ideal candidate, given its range and impact. The chief secretary informed Wellington that though this strategic move would be of benefit, there were no available cartographic resources to guide valuers. Accordingly, he sought assistance in the form of a national Board of Ordnance survey, which would subsequently act as the basis for any reassessment.[6] The duke assured Goulburn that such support from his department would be forthcoming, turning to his resident expert, Colby, for advice.

Major Thomas Frederick Colby (b. 1784, d. 1852) of the Royal Engineers was a driven, talented and fastidious administrator when it came to land measurement. An archetypical early nineteenth-century 'man of science', he dedicated his career to making the most correct and accurate mapping possible for his nation.[7] Aptly dubbed by Andrews as 'the dominant character' in the Irish Ordnance Survey's early history, Colby's energy, vision and determination gave the organization much of its distinctive character.[8] He was described by his peers as physically short, with a notable facial scar and possessing 'a singularly nervous and elastic frame'.[9] Naturally drawn to others with strong scientific interests, Colby could sometimes appear highly eccentric.[10] Irrespective of his obvious intellect, Colby also showed immense physical hardiness in the

---

4 Wellington's letter to Wellesley, 23 Feb. 1824, *Dispatches*, ii, p. 221.   5 Lord Clancarty to Wellington, 16 July 2814, *Dispatches*, ii, p. 291.   6 Wellington to Lord Wellesley, 23 Feb. 1824, *Dispatches*, ii, p. 220.   7 In 1820 Colby became a fellow of the Royal Society and a member of the Board of Longitude. By the end of his career, he had achieved the rank of major general. Thomas Colby, Obituary, *Annual Report, Institution of Civil Engineers, 1852–3.*   8 Charles Close, *The early years of the Ordnance Survey* (New York, 1969), p. 53.   9 Portlock, *Memoir*, p. 6.   10 Ibid., p. 8.

3.1. Henry Goulburn, chief secretary for Ireland. His lobbying in Westminster helped gain Wellington's cooperation for a new survey of Ireland. Francis Holl, *The Rt. Hon. Henry Goulburn* (*c.*1850).

execution of his work. This willingness to lead from the front had gained him the respect of his subordinates, while his intellect did the same for his superiors.[11] Such endurance would soon become one of his most admirable

11 Colby personally inspected many mountains used in the subsequent primary triangulation, spending a significant amount of time on exposed peaks, a trait appreciated by his men.

characteristics while working in Ireland. One observer noted a typical example of his stamina on a journey to northern Scotland;

> We were joined at Huntley [Aberdeenshire] by Captain Colby, he having travelled through from London on the mail coach … This was Captain Colby's usual mode of travelling, neither rain nor snow, nor any degree of severity in the weather, would induce him to take an inside seat, or to tie a shawl round his throat; but, muffled in a thick box-coat, and with his servant, Frazer, an old artilleryman, by his side, he would pursue his journey for days and night together, with but little refreshment … commonly only meat and bread, with tea or a glass of beer.[12]

Though robust, Colby was equally courteous and generous. He frequently allowed his officers to publish their own accounts of their work in Ireland while being 'quite indifferent as to [his own] personal fame'.[13] Despite this leniency, he likewise maintained ruthless standards when it came to the quality of work emanating from his department. Any concerns around the precision of measurements, no matter how small, were checked and investigated back to their source. One observer noted that Colby 'never blinked [ignored] an alleged fault, but in a manly straightforward manner proceeded to probe and rectify it'.[14] He could also be a pedantic, hot-headed, and demanding opponent to anyone who impeded his work, displaying a propensity for hands-on micro-management. In this regard he had much in common with Wellington, the two men being very much in step when it came to a potential survey of Ireland (see plate 7).

Born in 1784 near Rochester, Kent, Colby was commissioned as a second lieutenant in the Royal Engineers aged sixteen.[15] Excelling in his duties, he was chosen to join the Ordnance Survey in 1802 at the direct request of its commander, William Mudge.[16] Mudge had been with the Ordnance's survey operations since 1791, having previously served with the Royal Artillery during the American War of Independence (1775–83). Following the war, he devoted himself to the study of mathematics and was recommended for the primary triangulation of Britain on the strength of this skill. Within a few years, he had taken responsibility for much of the everyday work of the survey, keeping a lookout for young officers, such as Colby, who could boost his staff's capabilities.[17] Colby also had the added benefit of having supporters at high

---

Portlock, *Memoir*, p. 129.   **12** Portlock, *Memoir*, p. 133.   **13** *Biography, or third division of 'the English encyclopaedia'*, ed. Charles Knight, 22 vols (London, 1867), ii, p. 214.   **14** Portlock, *Memoir*, p. 133.   **15** Hewitt, *Map of a nation*, p. 177.   **16** Letter from chief engineer's office to Maj. Mudge, 12 Jan. 1802, quoted in Close, *The early years of the Ordnance Survey*, p. 53.   **17** Owen and Pilbeam, *Ordnance*

levels within the army. While obviously qualified for the role, and welcomed by Mudge, the influence of Colby's maternal uncle, General James Hadden, then surveyor-general of Ordnance, in his transfer was also likely.[18]

The young subaltern's blossoming career, and life, were almost cut short in 1803. Aged only nineteen, Colby was involved in a tragic accident during his duties. While working in Cornwall, he placed an overloaded pistol on the ground triggering the gun to detonate. The explosion caused extensive damage to his left hand, which 'was taken off [by amputation] just above the wrist the same evening'.[19] The severity of this injury was also exacerbated by a skull fracture caused by shrapnel from the pistol. Lucky to survive, Colby would escape this secondary wound 'without the smallest injury to his intellects', though he would carry a prominent scar on his head for the rest of his life. The fracture also caused him significant pain, which was exasperated by the long periods of concentration required by his work, potentially contributing to some of his more eccentric qualities later in life.[20]

Returning to duty, the young lieutenant resumed his work with great dedication regardless of his injuries. His time was split between supervising fieldwork across England and Wales and computing measurements in the Ordnance office in the Tower of London. Mudge continued to show immense faith in Colby's talents, entrusting him with command of much of the Survey's day-to-day operations in Britain.

The involvement of the Ordnance Survey in Ireland was not entirely alien to Colby. As early as 1819, Mudge had been approached about creating a new map series for Ireland. Mudge had agreed to the work in principle, though did not conduct any major investigation on the topic.[21] No guarantees were offered either. The following year, upon Mudge's death, Colby was promoted to superintendent of the Ordnance Survey by Wellington. He devoted his immediate efforts to correcting existing maps of southern England rather than continuing the incomplete British survey northward.[22] He would serve as director of the survey for another twenty-six years though it was in Ireland that Colby would establish his true legacy.

survey, p. 15.   **18** Close, *The early years of the Ordnance Survey*, p. 85.   **19** Mudge to General More, 16 Dec. 1803, quoted in Close, *The early years of the Ordnance Survey*, p. 85.   **20** Andrews, *Paper landscape*, p. 188; Colby was noted as having a preference for running over walking and 'His personal deportment was not perhaps dignified, but there was about him an air of will and determination which secured for him the obedience and respect of his subordinates', Portlock, *Memoir*, p. 6.   **21** Andrews, *Paper landscape*, p. 13.   **22** Owen and Pilbeam, *Ordnance survey*, p. 25; Hewitt, *Map of a nation*, p. 235; Mudge died on 17 April 1820, though Wellington did not appoint Colby his successor until July. While Colby was the forerunner throughout, the delay invariably caused him significant concern. He appealed directly to the duke in June to allow him to succeed

Given his later testimony before Spring Rice's committee, the contents of Colby's 13 February letter mentioned at the start of this chapter can be assumed. The Major had little experience of Ireland, its cartographic records, or surveying resources. This would, however, be of little impediment to his assessment. He undoubtedly recommended that such a survey be based on a hierarchical triangulation network, such as that implemented in Britain. Invariably this would have included assurances that his team was the highest British authority in this field. Conversely, he would have warned that existing Ordnance resources were limited and could not cover a new project of this size while completing work in Britain. The needs of Ireland, therefore, gave Colby a golden opportunity for any commanding office – a legitimate reason to request further funding and men.

To bolster such a request, he likely advised against employing civilian surveyors.[23] This was based on the hard-earned experience gained during the British survey. As mentioned above, the sequence of the Ordnance Survey of Britain had been sensitive to military concerns, focusing on areas vulnerable to invasion from Europe. One outlier to this work was the prioritization of Lincolnshire, in the east midlands. This unusual amendment was based on an appeal by local estate owners who, in 1811, promised to purchase 500 maps of the county, thus promoting its measurement. Colby's predecessor, Mudge, had unfortunately been unable to acquire enough military surveyors to fulfil this task due to constraints caused by the Napoleonic War. As a result, he had been granted permission by the Board of Ordnance to hire a small number of civilian surveyors to supplement his team there. These men were paid based on the area of land they surveyed daily with the intention of promoting a reasonable work rate. This clause soon backfired. While the civilians were supposed to operate to strict Ordnance guidelines, it was quickly found that they were happy to sacrifice accuracy for speed. As a result, they surveyed large areas of land with less attention to detail, thus increasing their income. Some even employed unvetted assistants to hasten their work. By 1816 Mudge had recognized that neither he, nor Colby, had sufficient time to root out such malpractice, resulting in 'slovenly' results.[24]

Colby and his officers were still busy revising Ordnance maps produced by these contracted civilians at the time of his letter to Wellington. This shoddy

Mudge, noting that he refused to have his prominent scientific acquaintances campaign on his behalf. Wellington, however, personally interviewed several of these acquaintances on his own initiative and was satisfied with their response. Close, *The early years of the Ordnance Survey*, p. 83. 23 Colby to Goulburn, 12 Nov. 1824 (NAI CSO/RP/1824/1950). 24 Hewitt, *Map of a nation*, p. 237. Mudge's son, Lieutenant Richard Mudge (b. 1790, d. 1854), was appointed full-time civilian liaison officer from 1816 and would find additional duties under Colby. Owen and work had obviously offended Colby's professional pride and he remained suspicious of any civilian involvement in Ordnance duties. This caution was therefore passed to the proposed survey of Ireland, with Colby determined to avoid Mudge's unfortunate mistake. While such an attitude may have seemed dismissive of the Irish surveying profession, with whom he had little previous contact, it was simply in Colby's character to reject data gathered outside of his direct control. This caution was regardless of the nationality of the surveyors in question. As such, there is 'no need to credit him with more than the average Englishman's prejudice against the Irish' regarding civilian involvement.[25]

Colby's expertise, determination and directness, coupled with the growing political interest in the survey, ensured his letter received Wellington's immediate attention. In response, the duke acted with surprising promptness, more akin to a campaign decision rather than an administrative one. Within a week he ordered Colby to select a group of twenty cadets from Woolwich military academy for training and eventual deployment to Ireland.[26] These cadets would allow Colby to keep a portion of his existing staff in Britain and simultaneously support the development of a new Ordnance corps in Ireland, bolstered by a few experienced supervisors. What the exact duties of the Ordnance officers in Ireland would be, or the limits of their involvement, had yet to be agreed upon by Colby or Wellington. Either way, Colby's immediate future lay west of the Irish Sea.

The Woolwich recruitment drive would form a significant part of Colby's initial evidence to the Spring Rice committee. Indeed, his February letter turned into the catalyst for the committee's formation. The speed of Wellington's response had caused obvious concern among those MPs with a longer and more personal connection with the reform of Ireland's taxes. With Colby's expertise now in play, those parliamentarians who had championed cess restructuring began to see their project take a more tangential course. A direct repeat of the military-focused Ordnance Survey of Britain would be of little use in their quest to re-value Ireland's landscape, with Colby having no experience in either Irish concerns, valuation, or charting areas as small as

Pilbeam, *Ordnance survey*, p. 18. **25** Andrews, *Paper landscape*, p. 21. In the 1840s Colby would express his shock at poverty levels in Ireland, laying blame squarely on policymakers and governmental mismanagement. In a letter to his subordinate Thomas Larcom (b. 1801, d. 1879), Colby noted that the Irish were '… a people both willing and able to labour, and posing sufficient intellectual power to be readily trained to form the successive grades of a happy and wealthy society. Yet all these gifts of nature were paralysed by an ignorant system of government, and the people were reduced to the verge of starvation'. Colby to Larcom, 26 Dec. 1842, Larcom papers, NLI, MS 7553, quoted in Gillian Doherty, *The Irish Ordnance Survey: history, culture and memory* (Dublin, 2004), p. 42. **26** The Royal Military Academy, Woolwich, London, was home to the survey school of Military Engineering until 1833, when the course was transferred to Chatham, Kent. Owen and Pilbeam, *Ordnance survey*, p. 17.

townlands or parishes. Likewise, Wellington would also have been happy with a uniform map of Ireland in a similar format to that of Britain, reserving Colby to his long-established roles regardless of the change of scope for Ireland.[27] As a result, both Spring Rice and Newport would bring the topic before the House of Commons within a month of Colby's letter, attempting to guide what was rapidly becoming a generalized military mapping enterprise back to the realm of taxation.

WELLINGTON RECEIVES A LETTER FROM DUBLIN, 17 FEBRUARY 1824

Only a few days after Colby had written his assessment, Wellington received another related letter. This communique had arrived from Dublin and was written by his older brother, Marquis Richard Wellesley, lord lieutenant of Ireland.[28] It too concerned a new survey of Ireland, with Wellesley also calling upon Wellington's assistance.

Referring to Wellington as 'My dear Arthur', Wellesley began by highlighting the importance of a new general survey to avoid the 'numberless abuses now existing in the local and municipal taxation in the provinces of Ireland'. He felt that all concerned parties in Britain and Ireland agreed that such an endeavour was needed and that he had expressed the same to the prime minister, Lord Liverpool. Continuing, Wellesley mentioned he had discussed 'this plan' with Goulburn but had yet to approach Lord Liverpool directly for resources. Instead, he preferred to confide in his brother, who, as master of ordnance, could provide direct aid. Unaware of developments in London between Goulburn, Wellington, and Colby, Wellesley felt that the time was right for such an enterprise.

Wellesley shared Colby's concerns about the use of civilians. This criticism, however, had a more discriminatory edge than Colby's practical worries, urging

---

27 Evidence of Lord Monteagle, *Report from the select committee on Ordnance Survey* (Ireland), p. 26. 'The circumstances which led to the appointment of that Committee were as follows; It was in the contemplation of the Government of the day, prior to the appointment of that committee to proceed with the Ordnance Survey of Ireland; but, as I believe, there had been no intention, at that time, to do more than to follow up the Ordnance operations of Great Britain, and to obtain the materials of an Ordnance map of Ireland. Being perfectly aware, that however important such a measure was in itself, yet that, even if attained with the utmost success and accuracy, it still would not tend in the slightest degree to the accomplishment of any of the objects in which Ireland was interested in relation to local finance, namely, the apportionment of our grand jury taxes, the apportionment of tithe, or any other territorial object of that description, I represented both to the Government and to Parliament the necessity of taking a more enlarged view of the case.' 28 See Appendix B for full transcript.

Wellington to keep Irish engineers and surveyors away from the proposed survey as:

> Neither science, nor skill, nor diligence, nor discipline, nor integrity, sufficient for such a [survey] can be found in Ireland.[29]

By contrast, Wellesley felt that Wellington's Ordnance department was ideal for the task:

> I am therefore satisfied that the only source from which the means of executing the survey can be derived is the Ordnance; and that you are the only authority capable of infusing the spirit which such an operation would require into the agency which must be employed.[30]

The lord lieutenant used the example of several errors in Irish coastal charts to highlight the supposed incompetence of local engineers. Such an argument likely originated from Wellesley's connection to John Wilson Croker, the first secretary of the Admiralty. Croker had long favoured the Ordnance Survey's involvement in Ireland and had previously asked for their aid in the creation of improved navigation mapping. Trigonometrically based hydrographic charts of the combined coasts of Britain and Ireland would drastically reduce dangers to shipping. When addressing parliament on this issue in 1819, Croker noted the 'disgrace' the Admiralty felt about the quality of Irish and Western Scottish charts, which, in his opinion, were the most defective in all of Europe.[31] This request had met with mixed results due to Mudge's limited resources. The subsequent grounding of the sloop HMS *Pandora* on an unmarked sandbank near Wexford stimulated further pressure from Croker. He had also been a member of Newport's 1822 land valuation committee (see above, p. 44) which had recommended that 'proper officers' conduct a new survey of Ireland. This again drew the Ordnance Survey into an inevitable association with Irish affairs.[32] Therefore, if Wellington and Wellesley could get the Board of Ordnance to complete a scientific-grade survey, including Ireland's coasts, then the Admiralty support could be forthcoming. With no apparent Irish champion, Colby's expertise was becoming increasingly valuable across multiple fronts.

---

29 Wellesley to Wellington, 17 Feb. 1824, *Dispatches*, ii, p. 219.   30 Ibid.   31 Hansard HC Deb., 26 May 1819, vol. 40, cc 805–6. William Vesey Fitzgerald, MP for Clare, followed Croker's parliamentary statement by expressing concern about such a request given the complexity of the subject. He suggested that no decision be made unless the members be 'made [better] acquainted with its machinery'.   32 Andrews, *Paper landscape*, p. 18; *First report from the select committee on Grand Jury presentments*, p. 4.

The letter between the duke and marquess was the most official to date concerning the use of Ordnance expertise in Ireland. While previous parliamentary committees recommended the involvement of the Board of Ordnance,[33] Wellesley's letter was a direct request for their assistance. Ever a man of action, Wellington would soon have a clear response ready for his brother.

WELLINGTON RESPONDS, 23 FEBRUARY 1824

In a short reply to Wellesley's letter, Wellington voiced his full support of using Ordnance resources to aid the situation in Ireland.[34] The duke informed his brother that Goulburn had been actively pursuing the topic in London and that the two had met several times. These conversations had helped Wellington formulate a better understanding of how such a survey could be used, but he now had the added advantage of having Colby's 13 February assessment at hand. As such, Wellington was able to caution Wellesley that while he supported the scheme, and that aid would be forthcoming, it would be delayed 'owing to the want of persons properly trained'. No survey would begin in 1824, but it would 'commence next year with such force as will enable us to complete the survey of the whole of Ireland in five or six years [1830/1]'.[35] Such warnings were apparently necessary as 'we should only mislead you if we were to promise to do more.'

The Board of Ordnance was now committed to involvement in a new survey of Ireland. There was, however, an obvious gap between their previous British output and what would be required for Ireland. It is possible that Wellington believed that others, more familiar with Irish needs, would eventually use generic Ordnance mapping as a foundation for tax reform. As a result, Colby's initial instructions held no specific references to civil boundaries or valuation. Throughout February, Wellington and Colby had begun to take steps to ensure sufficient Ordnance resources would be available for this project. These earliest actions marked the beginning of Colby's Irish venture, though much still remained to be determined.

---

33 *Report from the select committee on Grand Jury presentments of Ireland*, Hansard HC Deb., 26 May 1819 vol. 40, cc 805.   34 See Appendix B for transcript.   35 Wellington to Wellesley, 23 Feb. 1824, *Dispatches*, ii, p. 220. This assessment must have been based on Colby's advice and may have only related to the triangulation portion of the survey, rather than the detail or territorial elements.

SIR JOHN NEWPORT ADDRESSES PARLIAMENT,
27 FEBRUARY 1824

The speed of Wellington's actions over the previous fortnight had caused genuine concern among some members of parliament. One was Newport, MP for Waterford and a long-time champion of Irish tax reform. During a House of Commons discussion on the Ordnance budget for Britain's colonies, he rose to speak about the proposed survey of Ireland, both topics being Wellington's responsibility. Newport had recommended a new general survey of Ireland for many years but was now worried about Colby's involvement. Expressly, he explained that a new survey of Ireland could not take as long as the still incomplete survey of Britain, which by then had been underway for over thirty years. Hoping to create a map series adequate for equalizing Irish taxes, he believed that the complexity of a national triangulation network, as the Board of Ordnance proposed, was excessive and that perhaps local surveying expertise could be deployed to reduce the time frame. Additionally, he emphasized that a repetition of the one-inch-to-a-mile map produced for Britain would be of little use as the Irish equivalent would still require data suitable for valuation.[36] If the same scale were used for Ireland, the resulting maps would poorly suit the vital boundary information.

Goulburn responded on behalf of the government, stating that the cabinet was satisfied that such complex measurements were necessary. After all, Colby was the top expert in Britain on the matter, and investment in a scientifically accurate map would be more appropriate than a swift, but coarse alternative. In addition, he assured the house that Wellington had 'made arrangements for carrying through the survey with a rapidity far exceeding that with which the work had proceeded in England', hence the recruitment of cadets.[37] In reply, Newport stated that he had first raised this topic as far back as 1813, but that 'not one step had yet been made' before Wellington's unexpected action over the previous days.

Finding a middle ground, fellow MP Davies Gilbert (b. 1767, d. 1839)[38] interjected. A Cornish-based engineer with a flair for scientific research, Gilbert believed that the proposed survey would be of little use to the topic of Irish tax reform. Given the resources Wellington had committed to Ireland, however,

36 This final point was echoed over twenty years later when Spring Rice recollected parliament's concerns about the Ordnance Survey's deployment to Ireland: 'Could the counties of Ireland be furnished with a map as perfect in its execution and as accurate in its details as the Ordnance Survey of Great Britain, it would [still] not answer for the purposes of the grand jury taxation unless a minute subdivision … were superadded.' Evidence of Lord Monteagle, *Report from the select committee on Ordnance Survey* (Ireland), p. 26.   37 Hansard HC Deb., 27 February 1824, vol. 10, cc 525–51.   38 Member of parliament for Bodmin (1806–32).

Gilbert felt that a triangulation of Ireland would take only one year and that cartographic detail 'would be afterward filled in by degrees' (it is not known if this pun was intended). Though a prolific researcher and author, the origins of Gilbert's over-optimistic time frame remain a mystery. Feeling the need to support Wellington and Colby's work before parliament, Gilbert rightly assured his fellow members that the Ordnance Survey of Britain had 'raised the country in the eyes of the scientific world' and could do the same in Ireland. This assessment was sustained by Col. Frederick Trench (b. 1775, d. 1859),[39] MP for Cambridge, who, following Gilbert's statement, asserted that such scientific methods would be far better than the slipshod 'loose parochial surveys' supported by Newport.

Newport's concerns were justifiable. Despite the obvious qualities of the British survey, it remained glaringly incomplete. Growing tensions in Ireland meant that tax reform could not wait until the 1850s for suitable information. While his suggestion for a rapid survey had been deflected, the 27 February House of Commons discussion helped establish three issues that would later dominate much of the Spring Rice committee's proceedings: 1) how long would a survey of Ireland take?; 2) could local administrative needs be melded into the Ordnance's already proven methods?; and 3) could Ireland's existing engineering and surveying community be used to supplement existing Ordnance resources? This list of concerns would be expanded further over the following month as Colby's involvement in Ireland grew more complicated than he, or Wellington, had initially envisaged.

39 Member of parliament for Cambridge (1819–32).

CHAPTER FOUR

The Spring Rice committee,
March and April 1824

With Colby's recruitment drive underway, those MPs with a long commitment to cess reform began to worry. The likelihood of a new survey of Ireland taking on a different character than they had intended was becoming more probable with each passing day. While the competence of Colby and his team was not at issue, at least regarding accuracy, concerns about their suitability remained. The length of time an Ordnance-based survey would take, the body's lack of mapping experience in Ireland, and their ability to obtain civil data all hung above Wellington's scheme. The parliamentarians who had so far tried to steer cess reform understandably demanded clarification and assurances that their needs would be met.

On 10 March 1824, Spring Rise rose to speak in the House of Commons. His aim was to try and manoeuvre Wellington's plan back on course based on two primary points. First, he wished to reinforce that a new survey and valuation of Ireland were badly required. Second, given the complexities of the task, it would be wise to appoint a select committee to explore the subject in greater detail, thus avoiding an unsuitable duplicate of the British survey. The new survey would take place regardless of any select committee's outcome, parliament having already made initial funds available for its execution.[1] The committee's purpose, therefore, was to refine the factors that would differentiate the Irish and British surveys, ascertain available resources, and determine if the project was to be conducted entirely by the Board of Ordnance or with the aid of others.[2]

George Dawson (b. 1790, d. 1856), MP for Derry, followed Spring Rice's speech, expressing his full support. He represented a county that had 'suffered

---

1 *Freeman's Journal*, 12 Mar. 1824.   2 Speaking in 1851, Spring Rice (then Lord Monteagle of Brandon) retained his concerns that a duplication of the British survey would have missed its true purpose, stating '[A repetition of the British Survey] would be ineffectual for the purposes of adjusting our local taxation … [he thus called for] a committee to consider in what manner and subject to what modification the Ordnance survey should be carried on; the Government readily acquiesced in that proposal'; Evidence of Lord Monteagle, *Report from the select committee*

more from the present [cess] system than any other in Ireland' and was keen to
see such reform. Unsurprisingly for a military officer, Col. Trench in response
once again urged that the Board of Ordnance be directed to manage the survey,
as they were proven 'men of science', echoing Wellesley's concerns about
Ireland's engineers. Not to let the military dictate a scheme he had been
supporting for years (particularly in public), Sir John Newport rebutted the
colonel's suggestion. Newport again outlined to the House that he had genuine
concerns about the Board of Ordnance's involvement as it would 'take too
much time, and when completed would not be sufficient for the required
purpose'. Camps were therefore emerging. Each agreed that a survey was
necessary but differed on Colby's level of involvement. Goulburn took a
conciliatory approach when responding on behalf of the government. He
argued that the topic of who controlled the project would 'be most
advantageously discussed' by Spring Rice's proposed group, thus taking the
intricacies out of the government's hands. The resolution for a select committee
to study the survey and valuation of Ireland was thus passed.[3]

The brief exchange between Trench and Newport would become the guide
for Spring Rice's committee over the following months. There was obvious
weight behind the argument that the Board of Ordnance would be the best
choice to manage the project. However, given the small size of Colby's
command, it was unknown if they could satisfy all requirements within a
suitable time frame, including the vital civil divisions. Two days later, these same
concerns were raised by Arthur Hills, marquis of Downshire (b. 1788, d. 1845),
in the House of Lords. He also emphasized the need to include sub-county-
level administrative information in any new valuation survey, thereby adding
additional political urgency to the need for an investigatory committee.[4]

Reflecting in 1851, Spring Rice (then Lord Monteagle) still felt that a
British-style Ordnance map of Ireland would have been 'ineffectual' without
further investigation. Summarizing, he believed that had the survey gone ahead
without sensitivities to Irish issues, then 'the gross injustice and the grievous
[public] discontent' in Ireland would have continued.[5] Within just a few weeks
of his Commons proposal, his new committee would begin hearing expert
testimony on surveying, valuation, and the eccentricities of Irish land
administration. Each deposition would help determine the extent of the
Ordnance's role and identify who could fill in the gaps that they could not, or
would not, execute.

The parliamentary select committee for the survey and valuation of Ireland
(1824) consisted of ten members, including Lord Lieutenant Wellesley. Most

on Ordnance Survey (Scotland), p. 23.   3 Hansard HC Deb., 10 March 1824, vol. 10, cc 870–1.
4 Hansard HC Deb., 23 March 1824, vol. 10, cc 936; *Freeman's Journal*, 16 Mar. 1824.   5 Evidence

represented Irish constituencies and came from both sides of the House. Based in Westminster, this small group would delve deep into the history and technicalities of land measurement in Ireland in a way rarely seen before. The committee members were:

- Thomas Spring Rice (chair), [Whig] MP for Limerick City.
- John Leslie Foster, [Tory] MP for Co. Louth.
- Davies Gilbert, [Tory] MP for Bodmin.
- William Vesey Fitzgerald, [Tory] MP for Co. Clare.
- Dominick Browne, [Whig] MP for Co. Mayo.
- William Parsons, Lord Oxmantown, [Tory] MP for King's County.
- James Grattan, [Liberal] MP for Wicklow.
- Marquees Richard Wellesley, Lord Lieutenant of Ireland.
- Sir John Newport, [Whig] MP for Waterford City.
- John Wilson Croker, [Tory] MP for Bodmin.

The presence of so many Irish MPs was self-explanatory, given the relevance of the survey and valuation to their seats. Some, such as Spring Rice and Newport, had been involved with proposed tax reform for years, further reinforcing their presence. The inclusion of two members from non-Irish constituencies, namely Davies Gilbert and John Wilson Croker, was, however, noticeable. Both represented Bodmin in Dorset, and had little political connection to Ireland. Nevertheless, their presence was a deliberate move to strengthen the committee's support and credibility. Croker, alongside his parliamentary position, was first secretary of the Royal Navy, and, as mentioned above, had been seeking to update charts of the Irish coast. The new survey of Ireland could potentially fulfil this need, thus bringing the project within the Admiralty's interests. Gilbert (born Davies Giddy), by contrast, was a gifted academic, mathematician, and future president of the Royal Society. He would act as the committee's scientific lead and be able to assess the technicalities of evidence presented to them. Fortunately, Gilbert and Croker would also provide their own evidence to the committee, further outlining their specialist areas.

On the same day that Spring Rice and Newport called for the committee's formation, William Gregory, undersecretary for Ireland based in Dublin Castle, received a letter from an Ordnance officer. He was informed that Wellington had 'consented to undertake the Survey of Ireland' and that Colby would oversee the exercise.[6] Consequently, while Spring Rice and Newport began to

of Lord Monteagle, *Report from the select committee on Ordnance Survey* (Scotland), p. 23.   6 Maj. Gen. Brooke Young to William Gregory, 10 Mar. 1824 (CSO/RP/1824/1121).

assemble their committee in London, preparations were already starting across the Irish Sea for Colby's arrival.

The strength of the committee's ultimate findings greatly depended on the quality of the experts they interviewed. In total, nineteen witnesses were summoned between the committee's commencement in March 1824 and the publication of its report in June of the same year. They came from various backgrounds and social standings, offering insight and opinions on many aspects of the proposed survey. Some proved more capable and informative than others, though the final ensemble collectively covered most fields and specialist topics. Their testimonies helped the committee understand what 'additions to [the Ordnance Survey of Britain] were absolutely necessary, with a view to the local taxation of Ireland and the equalization of our burthens [there] …'.[8] In this regard, the committee's selection of examinees was mostly successful, but some with a more active stake in cess reform were excluded, as discussed further below.

Committee meetings took the form of an interview, with the MPs asking a series of questions to individual experts. Several could be interviewed in a single session, though most meetings usually involved just one or two testimonies. Only a few key experts were called back repeatedly to add to or clarify previous statements. Evidence from each session was recorded in a book of minutes. Based on actual testimony, this created a valuable first-hand account of the opinions and attitudes of some of the prime influencers in the Irish survey's foundation. Such insight was most relevant to Ordnance officers, such as Colby, and a collection of Ireland's senior civil engineers invited to Westminster for the occasion. As a collective, the engineers could be considered the elite of land surveying in early nineteenth-century Ireland. Their testimonies clarified the pivotal need for high-quality, uniform mapping, with members of the military and politicians also adding their respective interests. Notably, the minutes also provide some of the first, detailed commentaries of Thomas Colby on Ireland, as well as the Ordnance Survey's original viewpoint and concerns about working there.

Despite the various strengths of the Spring Rice minutes, they can be a laborious maze to work through. The committee had an unfortunate tendency to fixate on detail, frequently lurching from one technicality to another without

7 Thomas White, *The Ordnance Survey of the United Kingdom* (London, 1886), p. 63.   8 Evidence of Lord Monteagle, *Report from the select committee on Ordnance Survey* (Scotland), p. 22.

Drawn by Jn.º Shury & Son
Printed by Day & Haghe lithrs

4.1. The Houses of Parliament, Westminster, as they would have appeared in 1824. The building was damaged by fire in 1834 and subsequently replaced with the current gothic structure. John Shury, *Palace of Westminster* (London, *c*.1830).

a clear agenda. Not all witnesses underwent the same structure of questioning, with topics often varying within a short time. As noted by Andrews, the meetings often took 'on a quality of a nightmare' due to their poor structure, though this lessened toward their later sessions.[9] While detailed, the committee records were also an official account, likely missing off-hand comments or elements of conversation between committee members and witnesses that might provide a further understanding of personalities, or even touches of humour.

A distinctive trait among those called to testify during the committee's first weeks was their availability, each present in London in March and April. This was advantageous in many ways, with high-profile (and on-hand) witnesses such as Colby and Spring Rice laying a foundation concerning cess and the existing survey of Britain. Testimonies from Irish-based experts were more common from May onward; by then these individuals had been provided sufficient time to travel to Westminster from various parts of Ireland. This latter group was

9 Andrews, *Paper landscape*, p. 25.

mostly comprised of civilian engineers who, according to Andrews, had been 'a hitherto neglected source'.[10]

Many of the Irish engineers had forged their careers with the Bogs Commission a decade earlier. As a result, they were acquainted with the practicalities of charting remote areas of the Irish landscape in high detail. Ironically, despite Wellesley's concerns about this group in his February letter to Wellington, many were, in fact, Scottish and were considered some of the top land measurement experts on the island. As Andrews notes, the evidence given by the Irish-based engineers was 'heard at length and generally with respect' by the committee, their knowledge of Ireland's landscape and people, coupled with their experience, being of obvious value. Such deference was impressive given the criticism they had received from Wellesley. Yet, if the issue over civil boundaries had not been as necessary, it remains possible that the survey may have been executed entirely without their advice.

Though considered capable, even by loftier British standards, the engineers were few in number. At an industrial level, they lacked a recognized figurehead or official body to represent their interests or to speak with a collective voice in Westminster. They had no bond with each other apart from professional and personal camaraderie. Consequently, their testimonies were given as an assortment of individuals, and though, while respectful to their professional brethren, they occasionally differed on details.

Their British equivalent, by contrast, presented a more unified voice. Most British witnesses of this class were members of the existing Ordnance Survey. They were considered Britain's foremost authorities on triangulation, which would shortly become a core element of the Irish survey. Despite this, few had professional experience in Ireland or in measuring sub-county civil boundaries. Regardless, they presented themselves as experienced, proficient and knowledgeable, the primary difference between the civilian and Ordnance camps being the obvious procedural clarity of the latter.

Chief among the Ordnance witnesses was Colby. He was the first and last to testify before the committee, often setting the agenda regarding the survey's triangulation and topographic element. The committee would usually accept his opinions as fact, offering little argument in return. One such instance was his insistence that valuation maps be set at six inches to a mile.[11] Another was his insistence that historic cartographic sources be kept separate from any data generated by his team, a point accepted without significant dispute by the parliamentarians.[12] His knowledge, however, was not exhaustive, especially

---

10 Andrews, *Paper landscape*, p. 22.   11 Evidence of Thomas Colby, *Select committee for the survey and valuation of Ireland* (1824), p. 14.   12 Colby would later repeatedly have his staff consult the Down

concerning civil boundaries in the unfamiliar Irish countryside. The evidence of others would soon help him refine his concept of the new Ordnance survey.

Despite the quality of evidence provided by witnesses, the committee was prepared to avoid some glaringly obvious technical matters. Little was asked concerning the expected accuracy of the triangulation network or precision of instruments to be used. Even the final design of maps was glossed over, striking the modern reader with some alarm. Somewhat timidly, the committee was again happy to follow Colby's lead regarding many of these elements. Fortunately, he capably covered most of these in his later instructions to Ordnance officers.[13]

Both officers and engineers were open about their weaknesses as much as they were their strengths. Many Ordnance witnesses were uncomfortable with the concept of identifying civil boundaries, a task significantly removed from their usual duties. Equally, some engineers specifically asked not to be involved with the primary, or even secondary, triangulation networks, conceding to the Ordnance's experience. Separately, both groups sought to set their professional boundaries courteously to each other. It should be noted, however, that none of those interviewed had ever conducted a national large-scale survey from the beginning. This included Colby, who had inherited an already functioning organization from Mudge. Thus, Ireland became his arena to improve the British survey system by avoiding some of the costly mistakes made by others in the past.

The remaining witnesses mainly consisted of politicians, a few technical experts, or non-Ordnance military members. Surprisingly only one valuer was called to testify throughout the entire investigative process, making his appearance on the committee's final day. Equally, only one commercial land surveyor was interviewed. The surveyor, a Dr Patrick Kelly, is a virtual unknown in the history of Irish surveying and mapping outside the committee minutes. As far as is known, his experience in Ireland was limited to a single estate survey and valuation, with his testimony being of limited use. The committee therefore ignored the remainder of Ireland's diverse and highly seasoned surveying trade, preferring to hear evidence from the smaller and more prominent group of civil engineers. Irrespective of their deep involvement and extensive experience with determining property boundaries, land surveyors were effectively dismissed as 'practical' rather than 'scientific' surveyors by Spring Rice and his colleagues.[14]

Survey though did not incorporate its spatial data into Ordnance mapping. Colby to Goulburn, 12 Nov. 1824 (NAI, CSO/RP/1824/1950).   **13** Close, *The early years of the Ordnance Survey*, p. 119. **14** O'Cionnaith, *Land surveying*, p. 206.

Their absence was not unique. No representatives of the Irish civil service were called to testify, let alone representatives of the local scientific or legal fields. No delegate from Ireland's grand juries was invited, irrespective of their central role in the cess issue. At best, the latter's absence can be seen as a deliberate snub stemming from a frustrating lack of administrative reform.[15] At worse it was discrimination, London circumventing Dublin's remaining influence to decide how Irish taxes would be assessed. Likewise, the case of landowners was also restricted, primarily to Spring Rice's evidence, the MP owning an extensive estate in Munster. Concerns of tenant farmers were entirely without representation, and no female voices were heard.

Though absent, the attitudes of Ireland's 'peasantry' remained a concern for the committee. Despite the reformative spirit of the endeavour, fears of resistance troubled the committee members.[16] The Irish engineers were questioned at length about any opposition or violence they had previously met in the field. Indeed, many had been at the receiving end of sabotage, suspicion or occasional confrontations. Generally, these acts were usually driven by ignorance, boredom or local grievances, rather than organized political civil disobedience. In response, most engineers found that politeness and openness concerning their work alleviated fears, with initial mistrust from locals frequently replaced by curiosity. Direct conflict was more likely when a landowner objected to the presence of surveying teams on their property, a fact that still affects the day-to-day work of surveyors (globally).

Regardless, Spring Rice and his colleagues remained keenly aware of the tensions surrounding cess and tithes. They also had concerns that armed military officers involved in the new survey could stoke tensions.[17] Memories of the violence of 1798 remained vivid in many rural communities, being yet another point that differentiated the Irish from the British survey. The proposed survey, however, was not to be a repeat of the Down Survey and would see no seizure of lands. Regardless, at least one period commentator felt that the project was 'consistent with imperialism', indicative that some sections of society objected to further British intrusion into regional concerns.[18] Localized hostility was encountered over the coming years, though the most common form of resistance to the Ordnance Survey remained non-cooperation. Throughout, Colby was insistent on police, rather than military protection, and only when needed.[19]

Wellington was the one prominent member of the British establishment whose non-attendance at committee meetings was highly noticeable. Andrews

---

15 *Committee on Grand Jury presentments* (1815).   16 Gillian Smith, 'An eye on the survey', *History Ireland*, 9:2 (2001).   17 By the 1840s the majority of the Ordnance Survey's 2,000 staff were civilian, Andrews, *Paper landscape*, p. 91.   18 Smith, 'An eye on the survey'.   19 Ibid.

speculates that the field marshal may have been too Olympian to provide evidence on the menial subject of topographic mapping and property tax. Regardless, his presence was occasionally felt behind the scenes.[20] Wellington's faith in Colby's technical knowledge also may have justified this absence, being, like the committee, happy to defer to the major's judgment. Nonetheless, as master of ordnance, Wellington remained Colby's commander, and the key target Spring Rice needed to convince to adjust the survey to more civil needs. This eventually culminated in an in-person confrontation between Spring Rice and Wellington on the eve of the committee's report in June. Therefore, a full understanding of Wellington's private opinion concerning the survey of Ireland must, unfortunately, remain unknown.

COLBY'S PLAN, 22 MARCH 1824[21]

Major Thomas Colby, superintendent of the Ordnance Survey of Britain

The select committee for the survey and valuation of Ireland sat for the first time a little under two weeks after it was first proposed. No roll call of committee members, ancillary staff, or clerks was kept for this, or any subsequent committee meetings, though it can be assumed that all members were present for this inaugural gathering. First to present evidence was Major Thomas Colby, who had by this stage been employed for over two decades in the Ordnance Survey of Britain. Over the coming weeks, he would repeatedly prove himself as one of the committee's most able and formidable witnesses, presenting an air of authoritative confidence. His various testimonies would do much to shape their final conclusions though it should be noted that Colby was never the mouthpiece of Wellington, with the duke looking to his subordinate's expertise rather than directing him.[22] During his evidence, he demonstrated restrained independent command and an openness towards concepts not previously applied to the survey of Britain. Above all, he justifiably sought to be seen as a geographic scientist and military officer capable of handling whatever mission was laid before him.

Colby had laid out his thoughts on the proposed survey of Ireland in his 13 February letter to Wellington. Still, it was the parliamentarians gathered before him that required the most guidance. As noted above, Newport and Spring Rice were reluctant to see an extension of the existing British one-inch series in Ireland, as it would have been unsuitable for displaying small civil

20 Andrews, *Paper landscape*, p. 27.   21 *Report from the select committee on the survey and valuation of Ireland*, pp 13–16.   22 Wellington to Sir William Knighton, 6 Nov. 1824: Wellington, *Despatches*, ii, 332–3. Portlock, *Memoir*, p. 257.

boundaries. Nevertheless, all generally understood that the Ordnance Survey would be heavily involved with the project, even if limited to the triangulation element only. While his level of commitment had yet to be established or agreed upon by this early stage, Colby would soon become intrinsically and irrevocably linked with the measurement and mapping of Ireland.

The committee's initial goal was to understand what was involved in a national survey and how experiences in Britain could be applied to Ireland. They commenced by asking their star witness about the status of the survey of Britain. Colby replied that the triangulation portion had been completed apart from the western isles of Scotland and some parts of eastern England. The 'filling up' process (i.e., adding geographic detail between triangles) was approximately two-thirds complete for England and Wales, with maps produced for a few choice areas.

Colby presented the committee with a sample six-inch map of Kent to demonstrate the Ordnance's cartographic output.[23] He felt that the same scale would be most suitable for Ireland though noted that the British survey had initially begun at six inches to a mile (1:10,560), but that had been quickly superseded by a one-inch variant (1:63,360).[24] None of the committee objected to using this scale in Ireland, deferring to Colby's expertise. This choice of scale would become one of the defining aspects of Colby's work in Ireland. Such was its ambitious approach that one late nineteenth-century commentator noted that 'the idea of a cadastral survey of an entire country like Ireland, on so large a scale as six inches to a mile, was quite a novel one'[25] (see plate 8).

Colby and Spring Rice recollected this demonstration when speaking before another committee examining the Ordnance Survey of Ireland in 1846. Colby remembered his initial orders were to prepare maps at a six-inch scale for valuation only, rather than publication. However, a general one-inch scale map of Ireland was to be created for sale, as in Britain. The eventual publication of the six-inch series only came about by chance when, several years later, a cost analysis found it was cheaper to have maps engraved than repeatedly copied for valuers.[26] Likewise, in the same 1846 meeting, Spring Rice also concurred with 'the gallant officer [Colby]', stating that by this early point in the investigation, no consideration had been given to a published six-inch series.[27]

23 This six-inch map of Kent was the first issued by the Ordnance Survey in 1795, Close, *The early years of the Ordnance Survey*, p. 44.   24 During an 1851 parliamentary review of the Ordnance Survey of Scotland, the six-inch scale employed in Ireland was considered 'generally useful' for Irish needs. It was however discouraged in Scotland as at this scale the largely uncultivated and extensive Scottish highlands would result in a large number of 'mere blank sheets with a few figures dotted over them here and there …' *Select committee on Ordnance Survey* (Scotland), p. viii. 25 Thomas White, *The Ordnance Survey of the United Kingdom* (London, 1886), p. 63.   26 Evidence of Thomas Colby, *Report from the select committee on Ordnance Survey*, p. 15.   27 'I believe that previous

Andrews notes that the six-inch scale (as used in Kent) was not customarily applied in England before the Ordnance Survey. In this regard, it 'might plausibly be claimed as a tradition of the Survey itself.'[28] In a strange coincidence, it was, however, remarkably close to the preferred Irish property map scale of forty perches to an inch (1:10,080). Though this alignment was purely unintentional, the correlation, if noted, would have appealed to the mostly Anglo-Irish committee for strictly practical reasons. Within its first hour, therefore, the critical issue of a scale for the Irish survey had been settled, at least in Colby's head. When asked about his opinion of scale in a subsequent interview, he abruptly reminded the members of what had been discussed during this initial meeting.[29] The choice of a six-inch scale was a considerable achievement for the first day of the committee, its true long-term significance passing undetected by those present.

It was clear to Colby that a larger scale for Ireland was required due to the need to record sub-county divisions. When asked what administrative divisions the Ordnance had previously recorded in Britain, he responded that they had been limited to county boundaries. The only exception had been Lincolnshire maps, which included local 'hundreds' subdivisions.[30] Such variation remained rare. In Britain, county boundaries had been determined independently by Ordnance surveyors in the field and without local assistance. Colby foresaw that measurement to even parish level in Ireland would incur far 'greater difficulty' but could be aided with an act of legislature, to 'compel the inhabitants [of parishes] to put some additional marks' on the ground. Once marked, Colby's men could record them.

Questions then turned to triangulation. Colby estimated he would need twenty-five additional staff in the first year and a further twenty-five in year two. Overall, he did not believe it would take much longer to create a triangulation network in Ireland than Britain and that Wellington had already asked him to train twenty cadets. These men were undergoing a six-week course on surveying near Cardiff, and would then depart for Ireland.[31] Colby also

to that Committee, his Grace the Duke of Wellington, who was then Master-general of the Ordnance, had taken steps to proceed with the Ordnance Survey of that part of that country; and I think it appears in the evidence of a gallant officer, a friend of mine, who was examined, Major Colby, that there were 20 young Ordnance officers at the time actually in training for the purposes of carrying on that survey; but, as I have already stated, I do not believe that it was in contemplation to give a six-inch detailed survey, or to show the territorial divisions of Ireland in a manner that was essential to the local taxation of Ireland.' Evidence of Lord Monteagle, *Report from the select committee on Ordnance Survey* (Ireland), p. 26.   **28** Andrews, *Paper landscape*, p. 23.   **29** *Report from the select committee on the survey and valuation of Ireland*, p. 23.   **30** Parish boundaries had been included in mapping commercial English county surveys since the eighteenth century but were not a traditional part of military mapping. J.B. Harely, 'The re-mapping of England, 1750–1800', *Imago Mundi*, 14 (1965), 57.   **31** *Freeman's Journal*, 29 Mar. 1824; *Belfast Newsletter*, 30 Mar. 1824.

assured the committee that he had access to Mr Troughton's[32] highly accurate two-foot theodolite to aid with primary triangulation measurement. When questioned further about funding, the Major responded that his Ordnance officers were paid daily, while their subordinate surveyors received payment per square mile measured.[33]

Ever the astute project manager, Colby comforted the committee that he was also watching similar European developments. The highly detailed Bavarian national survey ('Steuerkataster Kommission', 1808–64) was particularly interesting to him as private landowners funded it in return for lithographic prints of their estates.[34] Conversely, he admitted that he had not examined the Bogs Commission series for comparison, despite their modernity. At this point, he felt the need to inform the members that his organization had no interest in land valuation, only its measurement (and ideally its triangulation only). He also remained entirely unfamiliar with identifying sub-county civil boundaries, such as townlands. Even so, the project's broader scope remained crucial to him, as it allowed him to be the first to bring both Ireland and Britain under the same cartographic system. Once the Irish survey was complete, both islands would have a comparative one-inch reference map made to similar standards. As such, he felt that any measurements should be taken in an English system rather than the Irish, thus establishing a shared standard between both islands.

The committee thus received a solid and rational introduction to the processes and essential finances of surveying and valuing Ireland – one that they would significantly build upon over the following weeks. Colby had demonstrated that some areas of the Irish project were already firmly set in his mind, such as scale. Other topics, however, remained outside of his comfort zone. This would be just one of many appearances Colby would make before Spring Rice prior to any conclusions about the project's future being reached.

SETTING CARTOGRAPHIC AND PROFESSIONAL BOUNDS,
29 MARCH 1824[35]

Lt Col. Richard Keane, Waterford militia

A week after Colby's inaugural appearances, the select committee sat to hear their next witness, Lt Col. Richard Keane (b. 1780, d. 1855). Holding his commission in the Waterford militia, Keane came from a prominent military

---

32 Edward Troughton (b. 1753, d. 1835) was a noted British manufacturer of high-precision mathematical and astronomical instruments.   33 Re: Colby's initial Irish budget.   34 The Ordnance Survey would begin commercial sales of their maps sheets the following year from 163 Regent Street, London. *The Gazette*, 5 Jan. 1825.   35 *Report from the select committee on the survey and*

family, being the eldest son of Sir John Keane, 1st baronet of Belmont. Educated at Trinity College Cambridge, the colonel was well informed on cartography, trigonometric observation and Ireland in general. These reasons alone, plus his availability in London, led to his appearance before Spring Rice.

Keane had a notable habit of providing long-winded, though informative, answers throughout his testimony. This markedly contrasted with Colby's shorter and matter-of-fact responses given a week before. Keane's first significant contribution was to explain to the committee the hierarchal difference between primary, secondary, and tertiary triangulation networks, which he did ably. He felt that the French method of organizing their great *cadastre* survey (1790–1850)[36] was worthy of study. This had fallen under the management of the Ministry of Finance, with a supervising civil engineer assigned per *arrondissement,* similar in format to the Bogs Commission. The cadastre's scale of 4cm to 100m was large enough to include individual gardens, which exceeded what the committee envisaged. However, the French method of grouping land types into five separate sub-categories for valuation, e.g., five classes of arable land etc., was noted with much interest.

Turning closer to home, Keane informed the MPs that he had been 'in every part Ireland' and,

> I look upon it, that Ireland is the easiest country in the world to survey because you have so many rivers and eminences which mark the country; perhaps you have not so many churches as there are in England, but you have as many [reference] points [for triangulation surveys].

He believed it would take at least four years to complete the primary triangulation of the island and that one hundred engineers should be sufficient to fill in detail over ten years (working at 100 acres per day for a 200-day work year, due to weather). In his opinion, townland boundaries would be too complex to measure accurately, suggesting that subdivisions be limited at parishes. Additionally, he noted that some parts of Cork and Waterford did not use 'townlands' but rather another archaic subdivision known as a 'ploughland', further muddying the water.[37]

Keane finished his evidence optimistically, stating that the local populace would welcome the revaluation of the country given the imbalances in the current tax system. In this manner, he was one of the few witnesses to voice

valuation of Ireland, pp 17–19.   36 Like the Ordnance Survey of Ireland, the French cadastre was a post-revolutionary topographic survey for land-based taxation conducted between 1807–50, Hugh Clout, 'The "cadastre" as a source for French rural studies', *Agricultural History*, 43:2 (1969), 215.   37 Andrews, *Paper landscape*, p. 15.

the concerns of small landholders who bore the burden of cess inefficiencies. While he would play no significant part in the eventual survey of Ireland, Keane retained an active interest in the project throughout 1824. In May that year, only two months after his appearance before Spring Rice, he sent a letter from Dunkirk, France, to Goulburn. In it, he asked to be appointed as a valuer for the upcoming survey and wished to produce a corresponding lithographic atlas of Ireland. The chief secretary informed him that it was simply impossible to 'enter into an engagement concerning any future proceedings' regarding the survey, especially as Spring Rice had yet to conclude his investigations.[38]

Around the time of Keane's interview, Goulburn also began to receive separate letters of inquiry from some of Ireland's top commercial land surveyors. These included former Bogs Commission engineers John Longfield (b. *c.*1775, d. 1833)[39] and William Edgeworth as well as Arthur Neville (d. *c.*1856), son of the official surveyor to Dublin corporation, A.R. Neville (d. 1828). Each asked for the same thing: to become involved with the topographic portion of the Ordnances work.[40] Word of Colby's deployment had obviously disseminated among the country's surveying community by this stage, thus stimulating their applications.

The surveyors appear to have incorrectly assumed the project would take a similar approach as the Bogs Commission, with prominent surveyors and engineers being assigned large swathes of the country with a team at their command.[41] This earlier scheme provided steady employment and a notable career boost for the commission's 'topographic engineers' corps. Unfortunately for them, the Ordnance Survey would be a very different organization. As per Wellington and Wellesley's instructions, each applicant was informed that the work would be conducted by military staff only. There would be no room for civilian surveyors in Colby's plan. Others of similar professional rank would strongly object to the exclusion of Irish surveyors from the scheme, though it would take several weeks for their complaints to reach the press.

---

38 Keane to Goulburn, 30 May 1824 (NAI CSO/RP/1824/1429). Keane would later succeed his father to become 2nd baronet in 1829, receive a knighthood, and stand as MP for Waterford; Henry Stooks Smith, *The register of parliamentary contested elections*, 2nd ed. (London, 1842), p. 155. 39 John Longfield was an estate surveyor who was a leading early-nineteenth-century member of Rocque's French School. Educated at the Dublin Society's drawing school, Longfield became an apprentice to surveyor John Brownrigg (b. *c.*1746, d. 1838). By 1805 he had set up his own firm in his master's former workshop on Grafton Street, Dublin, becoming a Bogs Commission engineer in 1809. A large collection of his manuscript estate maps is currently held by the National Library of Ireland. 40 Longfield to Goulburn, 10 Mar. 1824 (NAI CSO/RP/1824/1443); Edgeworth to Goulburn, 25 Mar. 1824 (NAI CSO/RP/1824/2226); Neville to Goulburn, 29 Mar. 1824 (NAI CSO/RP/1824/540). 41 O'Cionnaith, *Land surveying*, p. 188.

Goulburn's response was not the end of these men's involvement with the Board of Ordnance. Edgeworth, for example, would soon find himself on his way to London to present before Spring Rice. The young engineer had already completed detailed maps of Roscommon and Longford, thus making his knowledge base of interest to the parliamentarians. Additionally, he was well acquainted with similar national mapping projects in Europe and had been in contact with Colby during the survey of Britain.[42] Longfield's involvement would be more limited, being called upon in November 1824 to assist Ordnance staff using the Down Survey as a reference source.[43] Neither would ever work for Colby in the field.

TAXES AND TOWNLANDS, 1 APRIL 1824[44]

April's committee activity was restricted to the month's first week. Though short, three meetings were conducted during this brief period, followed by a one-month hiatus. This break (ending 7 May) allowed Irish-based witnesses the time to travel to London. While no committee sessions took place during that period, behind-the-scenes activity continued as Wellington further reinforced his stance regarding his men. In the meantime, the committee would hear additional testimony regarding background topics and concerns surrounding the survey's execution.

Thomas Spring Rice, MP for Limerick

In an unusual move, Thomas Spring Rice, chairman of the select committee, decided to present before his colleagues. Outside his obvious political interest in cess reform, Spring Rice was also an estate owner, possessing lands across Munster, focused on Foynes, Co. Limerick. While most of Ireland's rural population remained without representation during the investigation, Spring Rice was at least able to provide some insight on land and taxation from the perspective of the gentry.

He began by explaining how the existing county cess system worked on a baronial basis, with each expected to supply an expected amount of tax. This income was then summarized at a county level. Spring Rice believed that the existing assessments did not agree '… either with the Down Survey or with any other survey or authority which I know to be in existence.' To prove his point, he highlighted issues with the barony of Upper Connolloe in Limerick. This

---

42 See Appendix D.   43 Colby to Goulburn, 12 Nov. 1824 (NAI CSO/RP/1824/1950).
44 *Report from the select committee on the survey and valuation of Ireland*, pp 20–2.

region paid tax for fifty-three thousand acres of farming land but contained almost twice that, resulting in significantly less cess income than should be expected.

The unscrupulous behaviour of some local tax collectors exaggerated such macro-issues. Spring Rice found many collectors were 'wholly irresponsible' in their duties. According to him, each of these officers was responsible for collecting a set amount of tax, which was then handed over to the local high constable. Any payments above their quota could be quietly pocketed, a point resented by the local populace. Collectors were also free to 'charge the taxes upon such portion of land as he shall think fit', with some lands avoiding cess payment, leading to further bitterness. Spring Rice warned his colleagues that '… in many instances I have known breaches of the peace, and a general disposition to resist the law, as consequences of this system of collecting the county taxes.'

The only solution he could envisage was a new, accurate survey and valuation, by which each townland would be measured and assessed from a single standardized source. If the tax due from the smallest official civil division was known, i.e. townlands, then calculating baronial and county level cess would be made much easier, thus reforming the entire cess system from its administrative base. He noted that given their small size, many townlands coincided with the boundaries of estates. This correlation could be traced to the system of forfeitures over the sixteenth and seventeen centuries, with townlands affording appropriately minor divisions for mass seizure and redistribution. Their limits would therefore coincide with better-documented property bounds, thus making townland identification easier in the field. Spring Rice also believed that public opinion would support such a project if it respected such 'old-established boundaries' rather than create new administrative areas.

Concluding his statement, the MP asserted that the valuation of lands should be controlled by a commission and based on 'a fixed scale of value of all the articles of produce' (e.g., wheat, barley, oats, etc.),

> By those means, the valuation would not only apply to the local purposes for which it is directly intended, but it would afford at all times a mode of ascertaining the territorial resources of the county.

The timing of Spring Rice's testimony is unusual within the committee's agenda. Such evidence would have been of greater use on its opening day, followed by Colby's assessment of the project. Most committee members were well versed on cess issues in Ireland given their Irish constituencies and the topic's repeated discussion in parliament. Spring Rice's statement thus added little to their collective knowledge. He potentially wanted an explanation of the issue to be included in the committee minutes, thereby justifying his concise evidence. Regardless, such testimony highlighted the occasional haphazard planning that went into the committee's agenda. Case in point, Spring Rice's comments, while very interesting, could have been summarized and presented to the committee as a memo. Nonetheless, no committee member could now claim not to understand the problems and inefficiencies county cess collections were having across rural Ireland.

COLBY AND CIVILIANS, 2 APRIL 1824[45]

Maj. Thomas Colby, superintendent of the Ordnance Survey of Britain

Colby returned for his second appearance before the committee. He was the sole witness for the day and was present to discuss the specifics of equipping the new survey with suitably trained staff. All of Colby's answers were based on the assumption that his department would only be responsible for the triangulation and topographic portion of the new survey. As per Wellington's instructions, no consideration had been made for the territorial element.

The Major's initial staffing estimates, provided on 22 March, had been made under the assumption that the survey of Britain would continue in tandem with the proposed triangulation of Ireland. Most of his Irish corps would be comprised of the cadets currently being trained, supplemented with some veteran staff to bolster their numbers. A skeleton staff would be left in Britain, under the command of Royal Engineer Richard Mudge (b. 1790, d. 1854), William Mudge's son, to continue work there.[46]

Colby remained confident he could begin measurement work in Ireland as early as the summer of 1825 if requested. This would involve a personal reconnaissance of suitable locations, which he indeed undertook during the second half of 1824.[47] Initial staff and budget estimates were based on a team of twenty-five to thirty engineers, each of whom would be placed in charge of up to six surveyors, giving an eventual total of around 200 personnel. Engineers would be paid £200 a year but would be expected to cover their own food and lodgings. At that time, he had ten officers working in Britain, with ten surveyors under their command. It was his preference to keep these officers at their

45 *Report from the select committee on the survey and valuation of Ireland*, pp 23–9.   **46** Tim Own and Elaine Pilbeam, *Ordnance Survey: map makers to Britain since 1791* (Ordnance Survey, 1992), p. 36. **47** *Freeman's Journal*, 4 Nov. 1824.

existing duties though he was willing to transfer seven or eight to Ireland, at least on a temporary basis.

Surprisingly, Colby seems to have had limited exposure or understanding of existing surveying and engineering resources in Ireland. As noted in his 22 March evidence, he had never seen any of the Bogs Commission map series produced in the period 1809–14, despite their relative sophistication, scale and extent. This attitude falls well within his pedantic nature, dismissing anything to have preceded Ordnance measurements as unacceptable, regardless of their modernity. He also remained reluctant to employ Irish engineers as he felt they may demand a higher salary, and 'it would make every person employed at a lower rate of pay dissatisfied'. This concern was doubtlessly a result of the issues he and Mudge had experienced when dealing with civilian engineers in Lincolnshire. Placing military staff under the authority of senior civilian engineers was, undoubtedly, another potential source of dispute, not to mention an issue of professional military pride for Colby. Junior Irish surveyors, however, were a different matter, Colby stating that:

> We should certainly look to every source for surveyors, and if those could be found in Ireland whose integrity could be depended upon, we should be happy to employ them at the same rate as we employed other surveyors.

Despite this apparently open stance, Colby's preference was to avoid employing any civilian surveyors unless speed was a prime requirement. This evasion was not due to any apparent anti-Irish sentiment but rather his previous negative experience with civilians in Britain. Colby found they had been often in 'want of sufficient skill, and want of sufficient integrity', with an unfortunate tendency to abandon their duties if more profitable roles arose elsewhere. He was quick to highlight that most of these civilians had been hired before his tenure as superintendent and, therefore, he had not been able to interview them all personally. Nonetheless, he was sure that it would take him at least four months to retrain any civilian surveyors to meet his specific requirements, should, in fact, they be needed.

So far, Colby had been open and helpful with the committee's queries. Yet some of his less-flattering traits presented themselves during this session. After outlining his stance on employing civilians, the Major was asked directly if he would propose the same map scale for Ireland as used in Britain. This topic had already been discussed during his previous appearance and may have been asked a second time in error. The committee minutes do not record who asked this specific question, but Colby's irritation was immediately apparent. His response was brisk, firmly stating that 'it has been proposed in this committee, to execute the survey of Ireland on a scale of six inches to an English mile'. This swiftly (and permanently) cemented this point in the committee's collective consciousness. Colby's abruptness not only demonstrated his propensity to be short with others but also emphasized the importance that scale would play in his planning. That six inches had been set during the committee's first meeting was apparently fixed in his mind as an explicit parameter for his planning process. Though the topic seems to have been more open-ended for his interviewers, Colby's response settled the matter.

The discussion then moved swiftly to existing cartographic resources in Ireland. As one of Britain's leading scientific geographers, Colby only trusted spatial information if it had been measured directly by him, or by those in whom he had confidence. Accordingly, as in Britain, he was comfortable disregarding any existing cartographic source in Ireland as none 'would afford us any assistance'. This standpoint had become something of a personal philosophy for Colby, which he passed onto his men, once stating 'never mind the testimony of anyone; trust to your instrument.'[48] To support this argument, he referred to a recent seventeen-part, two-inch to a-mile map of Mayo created by William Bald (b. 1789, d. 1857) between 1809 and 1817.[49] Colby felt his staff could produce maps 'superior in execution and accuracy', displaying an Ordnance map of Llangollen in Wales as a comparison. Supremely confident, he assured the committee that the author of the Llangollen map (a Mr Boscawen) was now training his Woolwich recruits for the Irish project and that any future maps of Ireland would be even more accurate.

Suitably impressed, the committee wished to understand how such maps would be created, mentioning the emerging field of lithographic printing. Colby responded that he would create any maps of Ireland through this process and that he had seen some impressive lithographic maps of Cadiz produced by French cartographers. He also warned that lithography was less developed in Britain than in France though it was obvious to all that the production of finalized maps would not be an immediate concern.

To conclude Colby's interview, the committee enquired about the cost per acre for a six-inch series of Ireland. Such estimates were near impossible at this stage however as the committee had not set what administrate boundaries would be required for the proposed survey. The inclusion of smaller administrative areas, such as parishes or townlands, would invariably increase

---

48 Portlock, *Memoir*, p. 111.   49 Bald's map met with much acclaim, with Spring Rice later stating 'We had no good trigonometrical survey of any one county in Ireland before the Ordnance Survey, excepting of the county of Mayo, of which there was a really good map by Bald, well engraved in Paris'. Evidence of Lord Monteagle, *Select committee on Ordnance Survey* (Scotland) (1851), p. 28.

costs. As such, Colby avoided placing a definitive price on the project, for now at least.

Colby's second day of evidence was important for the investigation for several reasons. The committee had heard the concerns of the head of the Ordnance Survey regarding civilian surveyors and his insistance on only using staff trained under his high standards if possible. The exact role of the Ordnance teams remained open for discussion, as did the inclusion of civilians, the latter being dependent on the time given for the survey. The topic of scale was also further reinforced with Colby's brusque reminder to the committee that he considered the matter resolved, likely noted by all present.

THE BOGS COMMISSION'S LEGACY, 5 APRIL 1824[50]

John L. Foster, MP for Louth

John Leslie Foster (b. *c*.1781, d. 1842), MP for Louth and select committee member, appeared before his colleagues. A prominent Irish barrister and well-travelled gentleman, Foster's central relevance to the project came from his previous position as a board member of the Bogs Commission. Formed during the Napoleonic wars, this government body had been responsible for surveying large parts of Ireland's lowland bogs, marking the beginning of a new chapter between post-Union government and land measurement. The commission had employed surveyors and engineers *en masse* to investigate the draining and converting bogs to farmland, all based on new, accurate mapping. Once converted or 'improved' in the commission's vernacular, this land would help alleviate pressure on wartime supply lines. Though Waterloo ensured that the commission could not complete its remit, the organization had accurately charted a significant portion of the country, using the best available staff and equipment. Therefore, Foster's experience was directly relevant to a new, island-wide survey.

He informed the committee that he had been involved with the Bogs Commission for four years, though 'attention of the commissioners was not very often required'. With a team of engineers taking a leading day-to-day role, the organization had charted over one million English acres across the island 'with perfect accuracy' at a scale of four inches to a mile. When asked, he could not estimate the cost of the survey per acre as the project's expense had been increased by technical elements, such as taking borings and soil samples.

Expanding on this initial outline, he described how the Bogs Commission had assumed a hierarchical stance regarding its field staff, placing a team of subordinate surveyors under the supervision of each engineer. Usually, individual engineers were assigned a specific district in which to work, establishing their own network of triangulation points from which their topographic detail would be based. The commission, unfortunately, failed to instruct their engineers to link up their respective networks, thus missing a chance to create a near-nationwide set of survey control points. Regardless, had such a shortcoming been avoided, it was still likely to have been rejected by Colby as unsuitable due to its non-Ordnance origin. This omission aside, Foster rightly felt that the Commission had played a significant part in improving Ireland's measurement resources by encouraging the employment of many young talented engineers and surveyors:

> I consider that the elements of accurate surveying were almost unknown in Ireland before the bog survey … we have in Ireland at least twenty individuals not inferior to any twenty that could be selected in England …

As of 1824, most of these former bogs engineers were still operating in Ireland. Several veterans, such as Alexander Nimmo (b. 1783, d. 1832), were heavily involved in improving public infrastructure at the time of Foster's testimony. Another, William Bald, had recently completed a Grand Jury map of Co. Mayo (referred to by Colby on April 2) and had begun to make a similar example for Co. Clare. Their colleague, Richard Griffith, had become one of the foremost experts on Irish geology. Foster felt that Griffith's services would be 'most desirable' for any geological aspects of the new survey. Nimmo, Bald, and Griffith would each make several appearances before the select committee over the coming weeks (see plate 9).

Though the proposed survey differed greatly from the Bogs Commission work, Foster remained acutely aware of the ongoing cess problem. He noted that tax records had not kept up with local improvements, allowing some landowners to underpay their due. He also concurred with Spring Rice's evidence[51] that measuring the island at a townland level would be far better for tax calculation as parish level would be too coarse. Conversely, he warned that measuring each field might be impractical given their complexity and the frequency at which their boundaries were altered.

The committee remained curious about older cartographic sources. They proceeded to question Foster about the suitability of these archives for their purposes, notably the Down Survey. He warned that townland data in the Down series could not be fully trusted due to changes in boundaries made since

51 Given to the committee on 1 April.

the 1650s. He also felt that that survey, though not made through trigonometric techniques, '… was laid down by the chain, and with wonderful accuracy, considering the period at which it was executed.' Such praise was indicative of the lingering cultural impact the Down Survey had on the Irish authorities. Foster also observed that nearly two centuries had passed since 'the period at which it was executed', with the science of land measurement evolving greatly in that time, thus diminishing its acceptable accuracy. He noted that the Down series was held in Dublin Castle, where tracings were still frequently made of it for use in property disputes.[52]

When questioned about other historic surveys, Foster stated that he was aware of both the Strafford survey of Connacht (1630s) and the Trustees' survey (1700) but had seen neither. He was also familiar with modern county surveys, though noted that only seven or eight had been conducted using triangulation methods. Case in point were several county maps produced by surveyor William Larkin. While 'extremely beautiful', Larkin's maps were unfortunately insufficient 'for the purposes for which they were executed' due to a lack of trigonometric control. None of the recent county maps seen by Foster had included townlands.

In conclusion, Foster clearly stated that any future survey and valuation scheme should be conducted as two separate entities: a survey, and valuation. He also urged that the involvement of local authorities in valuation (i.e., barony or parochial officers) should be avoided, another clear sign of the distrust Grand Juries were held in. His status as a former Bogs Commissioner carried significant weight with the committee, and he provided clear and relevant information for the task at hand. The committee was particularly impressed by his knowledge of trigonometric surveying, an unusual skill set for someone of his social standing, though over the coming days, they would see he was not alone in this regard.

NAVAL AMBITIONS, 7 APRIL 1824[53]

John W. Croker, first secretary to the Admiralty and MP for Bodmin

As befitting its initial exploratory phase, the committee's attention turned to areas outside the realm of taxes where a new survey could be beneficial. This included a potential link between the project and the Royal Navy. The

---

52 Finnian O'Cionnaith, 'Piracy, property and politics: Charles Vallancey and the Down Survey of Ireland', *Irish Architectural and Decorative Studies*, 14 (2011), 96; Robert Gibson, *Practical surveying* (Dublin 1752), p. 285; O'Cionnaith, *Land surveying*, p. 136.   53 *Report from the select committee on the survey and valuation of Ireland*, pp 34–42.

4.2. John Wilson Croker, first secretary of the Admiralty, understood the importance a new survey of Ireland could play in the safety of naval and merchant shipping. Henry Meyer, *Rt Hon. John Wilson Croker* (London, 1822) (courtesy of the National Library of Ireland).

individual responsible for this deviation in evidence was committee member John Wilson Croker, who was next to testify.

Born in Galway and a close associate of Wellington, Croker first entered parliament as a representative of Downpatrick in 1808. From 1809 onward he held the prestigious position of first secretary to the Admiralty, being the Navy's representative in parliament, much as Goulburn was Ireland's parliamentary delegate. Croker's opinion was of significance to the committee given the Royal Navy's long experience in creating coastal charts. Spring Rice was also interested in exploring the potential of cooperation between the armed services in this matter.

Like Foster in the previous meeting, Croker began with a demonstration of his familiarity with Ireland's cartographic heritage. He too had personally examined the Down Survey and found it in 'a very perilous state', showing signs of both fire damage along with general wear and tear from users taking tracings.[54] In an act of post-Napoleonic diplomacy, he had hoped to get a dubiously obtained French copy of the Down Survey held in Paris,[55] and anticipated that the French might be willing to trade it for something comparable. This Parisian version was one of the most complete editions of William Petty's masterpiece and had been seized by a French privateer while being shipped to England. A similar exercise had been attempted by General Charles Vallancey (b. 1721, d. 1812) in the 1780s, with Croker's efforts proving equally fruitless. This French copy of the Down Survey can still be found in the Bibliothèque Nationale, Paris.

Something of a cartophile, Croker's interest in mapping was primarily based on his general interests rather than professional practicalities:

> I have seen a great many [county maps], and as I had a pretty extensive knowledge of all parts of Ireland, I have amused myself occasionally, with comparing the maps with the places I have visited, but I have never made any very accurate observations upon the subject, nor indeed thought of this part of the subject with any precision until this morning.

Croker also believed, with some justification, that existing Grand Jury maps, and the Bogs Commission series, were 'less scientific' than those created by the Ordnance department.

His concern with maritime charts had greater relevance to his role as first secretary to the Admiralty. Overall, Croker felt that existing charts of the Irish coast were poor (especially concerning longitude) and represented a direct threat to the safety of Royal Navy vessels. In comparison, charts of the English coast were, according to him, much better, and any future charts of Ireland would be quicker and easier to execute if supplied with Ordnance data. Croker had argued these points in parliament as early as 1819. He had been one of the first parliamentarians to call for the Board of Ordnance to conduct a scientifically-correct survey of Ireland and had expressed his concerns about Irish charts to Goulburn and Wellesley. Recent Admiralty surveys conducted by HMS *Shamrock* had found charts by engineer Alexander Nimmo, on behalf of the Fisheries Commission, to be defective.[56] This information was

---

54 A significant portion of the Down Survey's baronial and parish maps were damaged and destroyed in the 1711 fire at the Treasury Office, Dublin. O'Cionnaith, *Land surveying*, p. 137. 55 O'Cionnaith, 'Piracy, property and politics', 96. 56 Andrews, *Paper landscape*, p. 18.

undoubtedly passed onto Wellesley, reinforcing the lord lieutenant's concerns about Irish engineers. Attempts by the Admiralty to connect with the Board of Ordnance on this matter dated back to 1822. Each had met with failure as the Board did not have the resources for concurrent maritime and general surveys. Maritime surveys were also more expensive than their land-based equivalents as they involved keeping a ship and crew at sea, thus making the proposal less attractive to army engineers.[57]

Returning to terrestrial matters, Croker believed that one scientific grade map of the country would make existing Bogs Commission and Grand Jury surveys obsolete, as a 'general trigonometric system, could with advantage be spread over the whole face of Ireland …'. He also had comments concerning the makeup of Colby's team in the field, noting:

> … there must be, in any case, two or three classes of surveyors; in the first, you must have engineers and instruments of established character; the time of Major Colby and his assistants is infinitely more precious to the public than that of mere local surveyors [for detail or boundary surveys].

Irrespective of such unsolicited advice, Croker was willing to admit where his practical knowledge ended. The first secretary explained he did not have 'very much experience' when asked about the valuation element. He had however seen the rapid rate of agricultural improvement in Ireland and felt that any valuation would be of use 'but for a limited time' without being appropriately fixed.

In conclusion, Croker's position was based on how the new survey could benefit the Royal Navy. The accurate plotting of the Irish coast through a general survey would be advantageous, as future maritime charts could make use of this data, thus saving the Navy time and money. Though he had little to add regarding how such a project could be implemented on the ground, it was clear, from his testimony, that the new survey could play a far wider role than simply calculating cess.

The next committee meeting would not take place until 7 May. Following this one-month break, evidence began to be heard from some of Ireland's top engineers, the committee's pool of London-based experts having been depleted. If an Irish champion could be found for the survey, it would be from among this elite group. In the meantime, the duke of Wellington was active in

Throughout May 1824 Nimmo would frequently give evidence to the Spring Rice committee and prove himself to be an expert in his field. He was also joined by fellow engineer William Edgeworth, who had been in contact with the Admiralty about new surveys of the Irish coast as early as 1815. **57** Murdoc Mackenzie, *A treatise of maritime surveying* (London, 1774), preface.

expressing his private opinions about the use of military surveyors to committee members. His behind-the-scenes influence would do much to dictate the line of questioning the committee would take for the remainder of their investigations.

7 April–7 May break

The committee paused its investigation following its first six meetings, which ended with the 7 April interview of Croker. So far they had heard evidence from a diverse, though small range of officials, technicians, and politicians. There were notable successes during this short time. They had received a solid explanation of the county cess issue (to complement their prior individual knowledge) and understood the importance of a new survey and valuation. They also now recognized the significance of townlands in the Irish landscape and the key role such territories played in the hierarchy of civil divisions. Even so, the issue of which administrative level (barony, parish or townland) to base the new survey remained outstanding. Perhaps of greatest significance was the evidence provided by Colby, who had helped set the scale of the survey, expressed the need for suitably trained staff, and highlighted the clear differences in objectives between the Irish and the British surveys. Colby had also stated his concern about existing Irish cartographic sources to support the project due to their unsuitability or antiquity, a point echoed by Croker and Foster.

Despite all the above, many questions remained. Technical aspects of the project stayed mostly unexplored, though would feature more frequently following the April/May break. Experts in these fields would be questioned on the practical realities of conducting fieldwork in Ireland. Topics would range from the dependability of local surveyors to valuations, the availability of precise instruments, and the expected reactions of the local populace. Upcoming testimonies would also look abroad, seeking inspiration from France, Bavaria or Italy, stressing the importance of scientific grade mapping in developed European economies. Examinations, however, would always be drawn back to the key problem of identifying administrative civil boundaries and who would do this task. The topic of valuation had yet to be seriously tackled and would remain as such for some time to come.

By this stage, Colby's involvement was taken as a given, especially with the commencement of cadet training. To what extent his participation outside of the triangulation and topographic aspects would take remained undecided. Croker, for example, highlighted the value of Colby's time and specialism regarding triangulation compared to that of 'plebian' surveyors, thus recommending civilian surveyors for mundane tasks.[58] Colby, however, had clearly expressed his concerns surrounding a non-Ordnance workforce, though had left the committee the option of their involvement should time be imperative. Others objected to the displacement of Irish expertise in favour of English replacements. In mid-April, the *Belfast Newsletter* protested the 'exclusion of the native surveyor' from the Spring Rice committee meetings and pointed out that local knowledge would be necessary to denote 'the mears and boundaries' so necessary to tax reform:

> We cannot conceive any just cause why men of acknowledged ability and honour [Irish surveyors] should be thus neglected in the land of their nativity, and be suffered to remain idle, if not mortified spectators of the operations of other men, in no respect superior, in point of professional information or experience, to themselves … It is beyond all question, that native merit should be warmly patronized by every statesman who is anxious to promote the welfare of his county.[59]

Other commentators had their own concerns about the Ordnance's involvement. An article in the *Dublin Journal* on 26 April noted that the length of the survey could be far more than the six years estimated by Colby. If so, it would make all associated data from the last census (1821) obsolete. The same article also expressed concern that the whole project rested on the work of a few cadets with just a few weeks of surveying education:

> Before the trigonometrical staff can proceed from one end of Ireland to the other, a whole generation will pass away, so that the names and occupations of the inhabitants will be changed, and what is really valuable in the late census will be lost … The [Spring Rice] committee will do their duty, and we trust they will deem something more necessary for Ireland than a mere trigonometrical survey.[60]

---

58 This term was coined by novelist Maria Edgeworth in an 1810 letter to friends. In it, she lamented that the family company for dinner one evening was 'reduced to the society of three plebian surveyors', in contrast to the greater engineering profile of her brother. Maria was a friend of Spring Rice, the two being in regular contact throughout the 1820s (NLI, Monteagle papers, MS 13,346/2). Maria's brother William would later testify before the Spring Rice committee, 9 Mar. 1810; Maria Edgeworth to Charlotte and Mary Sneyd (NLI, Edgeworth papers, MS 10,166/7 Pos. 9031 (740)).   59 *Belfast Newsletter*, 13 Apr. 1824. This article heavily refers to the work of William Armstrong (b. *c*.1781, d. *c*.1861) who had recently produced a map of Co. Armagh. It is likely he was the article's author, objecting to the involvement of Ordnance engineers in Ireland – a point never mentioned by any of the Irish surveying witnesses called to testify before Spring Rice.   60 *Dublin Journal*, 26 Apr. 1824.

Somewhat ominously, this piece also mentioned that the proposed six years could be further delayed if the Ordnance suffered 'casualties'. Whether such attrition would be caused by men leaving the corps or by some other, more nefarious means, was not clarified.

Andrews theorized that it was during this one-month adjournment that committee members were approached by parties interested in the survey. As mentioned in the committee's final report (see Appendix C), the admiralty, for one, had felt it necessary to follow up on Croker's testimony with a letter to the committee on 22 April. Of more significance, however, were memos from Wellington commenting on the increasingly prominent issue of townland boundaries.[61] As the master general of Ordnance, Wellington still had obvious concerns about his officers wasting their time performing such mundane duties, or, worse, falling under the supervision of civilians. This stance was emphasized due to the obvious lack of an Irish alternative to Colby to champion the topographic and boundary element, leaving Colby as the frontrunner whether he (or Wellington) wanted it or not.

Wellington considered it a misuse of resources to have his scientific staff tramp around the countryside trying to identify non-marked townland or parish boundaries. Instead, he would prefer them to dedicate themselves to the triangulation and topographic surveys only, as in Britain. In a letter to an acquaintance, Wellington mentioned using 'very strong language' in getting his point across to committee members, threatening to withdraw support if he did not get his way.[62] In the same letter, the duke also 'positively refused to employ any surveyor in Ireland upon this service', echoing Wellesley's comments in February. As a result, Wellington, through intimidation or otherwise, would not allow the Ordnance Survey to take full responsibility for the entire project. Spring Rice later confirmed this interference, stating that 'the illustrious person [Wellington] … felt rather indisposed to undertake [the measurement of civil boundaries]'. By contrast, Spring Rice thought the territorial element remained of secondary importance in the eyes of the Board of Ordnance, 'though by me and by the Committee [it was] considered the primary one.'[63]

Wellington's stubbornness undoubtedly perplexed both Spring Rice and Colby during April, as they sought a practical resolution. Both remained aware of the need to record topographic detail and civil boundaries for tax reform. They were also conscious that some form of local assistance would be needed

61 Andrews, *Paper landscape*, p. 27.   62 Wellington to Sir William Knighton, 6 Nov. 1824: Wellington, *Despatches*, ii, pp 332–3.   63 Evidence of Lord Monteagle, *Report from the select committee on Ordnance Survey* (Ireland), p. 26.

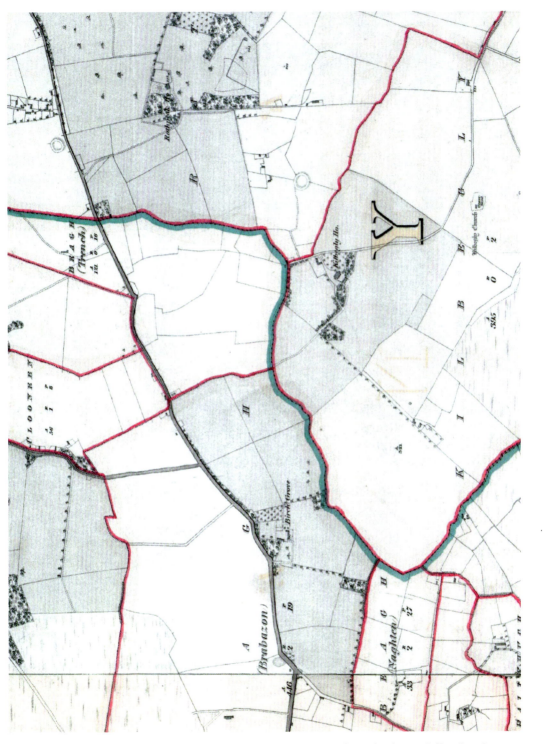

Plate 1. A first edition six-inch (1:10,056) Ordnance Survey map of townlands near Ballinasloe, Co. Galway. The information contained in such maps, along with its national coverage, came to define the Ordnance's work in nineteenth-century Ireland (© Tailte Éireann copyright permit no. MP 000124).

Plate 2. Thomas Spring Rice, MP for Limerick. Sprightly and tenacious with a keen knowledge of economics, Spring Rice had a clear administrative objective for a new national survey of Ireland. John Linnell, *The Right Honourable Thomas Spring Rice* (London, 1836) (courtesy of the National Library of Ireland).

Plate 3. Arthur Wellesley, duke of Wellington and master general of Ordnance. His opinions proved vital to the path a new survey of Ireland would take. Sir Thomas Lawrence, *Arthur Wellesley, 1st duke of Wellington* (London, 1820) (© National Portrait Gallery, London).

Plate 4. Richard Wellesley, lord lieutenant of Ireland. His push for land-based tax reform helped encourage Wellington's decisions about an Irish survey in early 1824. John Le Conte, *Richard Colley Wellesley, Marquess Wellesley* (London, n.d.) (courtesy of the National Library of Ireland).

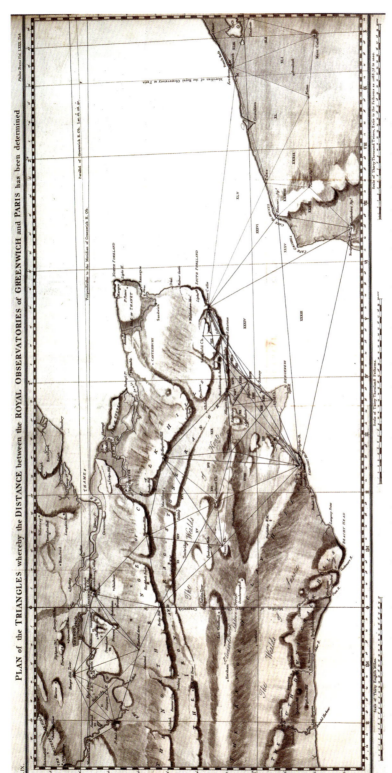

Plate 5. The great triangulation between the Royal Observatories of Greenwich and Paris (1784–90) was a landmark in late eighteenth-century surveying. William Roy, *Plan of the triangles whereby the distance between the Royal Observatories of Greenwich and Paris has been determined* (London, 1790) (David Rumsey Map Collection, David Rumsey Map Centre, Stanford Libraries).

Plate 6. William Roy encouraged investment in high-quality surveying equipment, such as this theodolite built by renown instrument maker Jesse Ramsden. William Roy, *General view of the instrument* (London, 1790) (David Rumsey Map Collection, David Rumsey Map Centre, Stanford Libraries).

27. 6. 37

Plate 7. Major Thomas Colby, superintendent of the Ordnance Survey. His insight and intentions for the Irish survey would guide both Wellington and Spring Rice. William Brockedon, *Thomas Frederick Colby*, chalk, 1837 (© National Portrait Gallery, London).

Plate 8. William Mudge, Colby's predecessor, supervised the production of this 1801 multi-part map of Kent, England. It was subsequently used as an example of what could be achieved in Ireland. Ordnance Survey of Great Britain, *An entirely new & accurate survey of the county of Kent* (London, 1809) (David Rumsey Map Collection, David Rumsey Map Centre, Stanford Libraries).

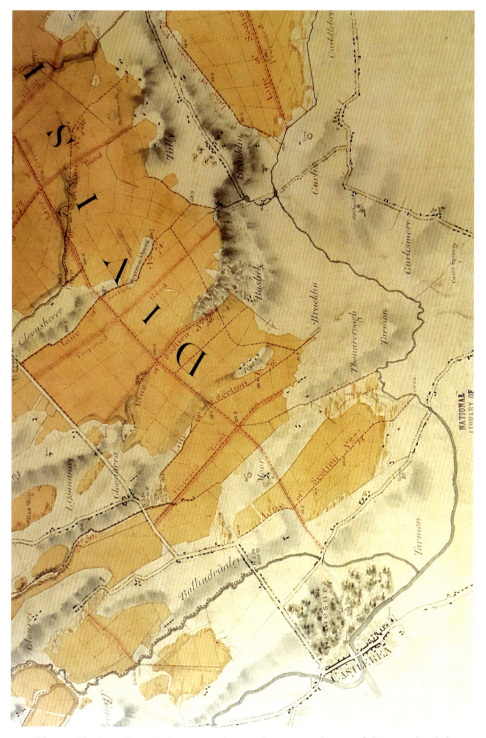

Plate 9. The Bogs Commission surveys (1809–14) represented some of the most detailed, medium-scale mapping made in Ireland before the Ordnance Survey. John Longfield, *A survey of the Lough Gara district, in the county of Roscommon* (1811), NLI MS 16D16 (courtesy of the National Library of Ireland).

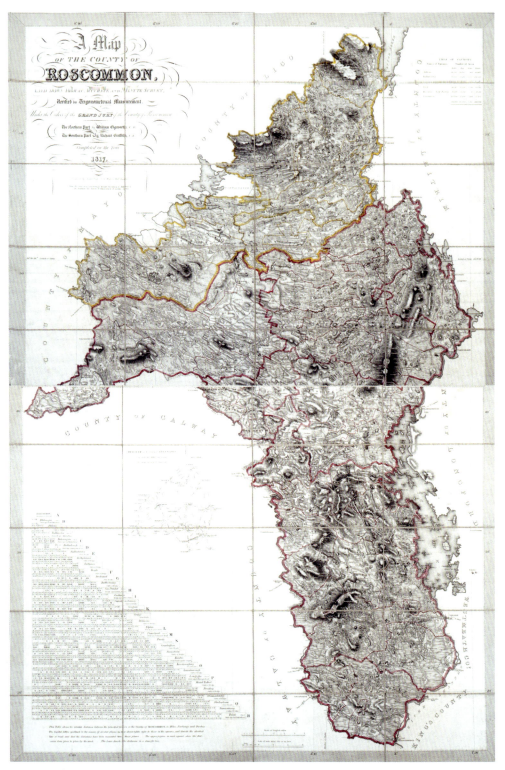

Plate 10. This two-part survey of Co. Roscommon by William Edgeworth and Richard Griffith, helped illustrate to the Spring Rice committee the quality of county maps produced in Ireland. William Edgeworth and Richard Griffith, *A map of the county of Roscommon, completed in the year 1817* (London, 1822) (courtesy of The Placenames Committee/An Coimisiún Logainmneacha).

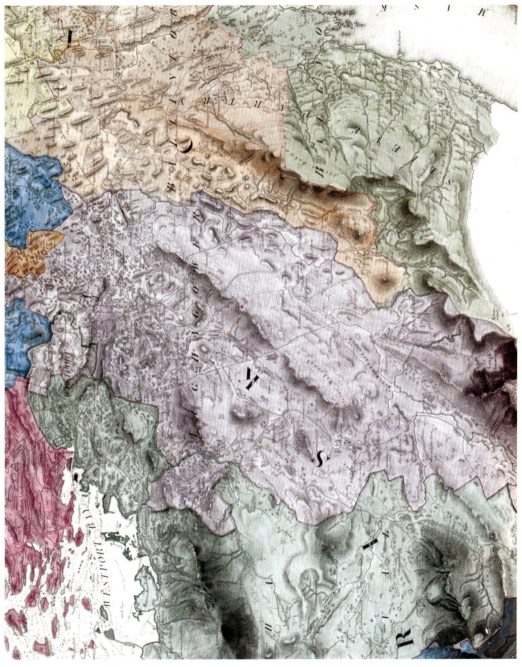

Plate 11. William Bald's acclaimed multi-part map of Mayo was a prime example of what the elite of Irish topographic surveying could produce. Pictured is part 18, featuring Croagh Patrick and Westport (Clew) Bay. William Bald, *Map of the maritime county of Mayo, Ireland, commenced in 1809 and terminated in 1817* (Paris, 1830) (courtesy of The Placenames Committee/An Coimisiún Logainmneacha).

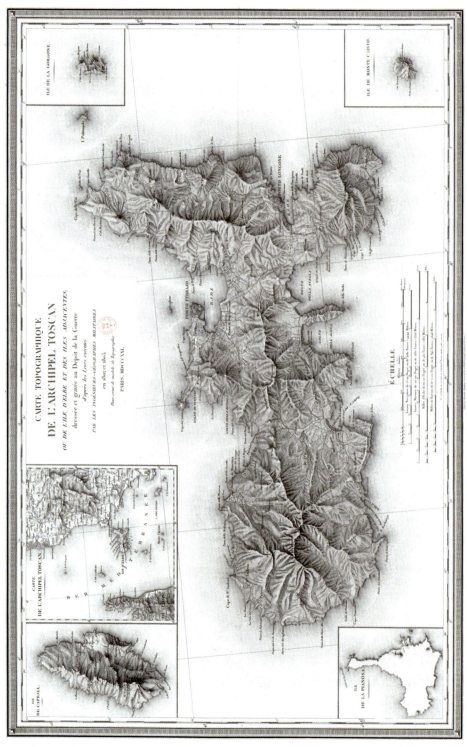

Plate 12. Alexandre Blondeau's 1821 map of the island of Elba and the Tuscan archipelago was shown to the committee as an example of high-quality topographic surveying emanating from France. Alexandre Blondeau, *Carte topographique de l'archipel Toscan* (Paris, 1821) (Bibliothèque nationale de France).

Plate 13. A four-pole (Irish measure) surveyor's chain. Chaining remained the most common form of distance measurement for land surveyors, though care was needed to avoid errors inherent to the instrument (by author).

Plate 14. Scottish engineer Alexander Nimmo spent years surveying the west and north coasts of Ireland, giving him exceptional insight on the island's landscape and its people. Jaspar Rober Joly, *Leenane and the Killary harbour, Connemara* (London, *c*.1850) (courtesy of the National Library of Ireland).

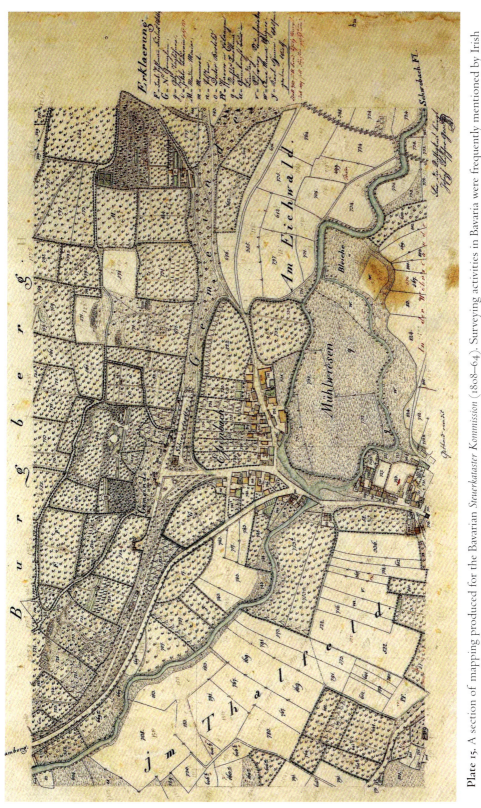

Plate 15. A section of mapping produced for the Bavarian *Steuerkataster Kommission* (1808–64). Surveying activities in Bavaria were frequently mentioned by Irish engineers as an example of the detail needed for Ireland (courtesy of Bayerische Vermessungsverwaltung).

Plate 16. An officer of the Royal Engineers (foreground) and an enlisted Sapper
(background). Each would become an indelible part of early Ordnance Survey operations
in Ireland. Colnaghi & Co., *A field officer of Royal Engineers and a private sapper* (London, 1812)
(courtesy of National Army Museum, London).

to identify these boundaries. An all-military solution to the survey of Ireland would, therefore, not be possible if cess reform remained its main goal. As Wellington did not appear before the committee we are denied a better understanding of his concerns or comprehension of the needs of the survey. However, his brother's presence on the board ensured he was kept abreast of proceedings, and Wellington's shadow overhung the second half of the committee meetings to a far greater extent than it did the first.

CHAPTER FIVE

Enter the engineers, May 1824

The Spring Rice committee reconvened after a month's break. This second portion of meetings would continue until mid-June and had a notably different character than earlier sessions. More witnesses would be interviewed per meeting than before, with many travelling from Ireland to attend. This Irish cohort mainly comprised of well-established civil engineers, capable of advising on a variety of the proposed survey's elements. In this manner, they were able to supply some alternative ideas to Colby's plan. Many had previously produced county-sized surveys with some hoping to become involved with the management of the new survey. As such, discussions became increasingly technical, focusing on how the survey could be executed rather than why it was needed. Other witnesses during the post-April break had more diverse backgrounds, such as existing Ordnance staff, and the Irish constabulary, each adding, in their own way, to the committee's increasingly sophisticated insight.

Most of those called during May were new to the committee, though Colby returned to add to his initial testimonies. It can be safely assumed that he was present for many of the meetings given their relevance to his immediate future and the value of the information presented. Of note were discussions about working conditions in Ireland, supplied by those with first-hand experience. Accordingly, the committee's minutes during May and June provide greater depth of the role of surveying and engineering in Ireland alongside expectations of what awaited Colby.

Richard Griffith, civil engineer

Richard Griffith (b. 1784, d. 1878) was first among the new batch of witnesses. The son of an MP, Griffith was one of the leading figures in early-nineteenth-century Irish engineering. Born in Dublin and educated in Edinburgh, he came to prominence as an engineer for the Bogs Commission, gaining renown as a talented geologist in the years that followed.

---

1 *Report from the select committee on the survey and valuation of Ireland*, pp 42–6.

Griffith's understanding of county surveying was of particular significance to the committee. In early 1819 he had composed a memo on the proposed role of 'county surveyors' as part of a parliamentary bill on Grand Jury tax reform.[2] In it, he had recommended that all Grand Juries be supplied with a baronial map, drawn at eight inches to a mile (larger than the later Ordnance six-inch series). Each was to display a wide variety of artificial structures and natural features and include 'the boundaries of all the *parishes* and *townlands* …'. Trigonometric methods were to be used to ensure accuracy and it would be conducted under the supervision of official surveyors chosen for the task.[3] Unfortunately, this recommendation was not implemented, and the position of county surveyor would not become a reality until the 1830s.[4] By then, the cartographic landscape of Ireland had changed radically, primarily due to Colby's efforts, thus neutralizing Griffith's suggestion. However, his practical experience in sub-county level surveying was eagerly sought by Spring Rice and he was a regular witness throughout May and June.[5]

Griffith began his testimony by describing his professional background, informing the committee that he had worked in Ireland since 1808 and had been a supervisory engineer with the Bogs Commissions. He had since been employed for the Dublin Society as a geological specialist, as well as a civil engineer in Munster.

Griffith commenced his review of the new survey by focusing on its triangulation element. He had extensive experience in this field and outlined problems this portion of the survey could encounter in Ireland. Of note was the frequent poor weather, which would make this task much more complicated than the more amiable English equivalent. While often falling victim to the climate, Griffith had also encountered sporadic vandalism from local farmers, which would delay his work. On one occasion, he had caught them 'throwing down my [triangulation] marks, but I think merely from ignorance', as once he explained their purpose the sabotage stopped. This point highlighted the importance of clear communication with locals to reduce unwanted attention or suspicion. Many of the Irish engineers would frequently mention similar

2 *A bill to provide for the more equitable assessment of sums required to be raised off the several counties in Ireland in pursuance of presentments by Grand Juries or otherwise* (BPP 1819 [570], vol. 1, mf 20.15).   **3** Wilkins, *Alexander Nimmo*, p. 142.   **4** Brendan O Donoghue, *The Irish county surveyors, 1834–1944* (Dublin, 2007), p. 13.   **5** Unsurprisingly, Griffith's career continued its ascent after 1824. He was appointed head of the Ordnance Survey of Ireland's boundary department in the late 1820s. This was a rare senior position for an Irish engineer, given most of his contemporaries were excluded from the organization at the urging of Wellington. He later surpassed this accomplishment through his work on the *Primary valuation of Ireland* (1847–68), also known as *Griffith's valuation*, achieving a baronetage in 1858 as a result.

stories over the coming weeks, undoubtedly being lessons they wished Colby to heed.

The committee then moved to civil divisions. Though the use of townlands as the foundation of the new survey had been discussed before the April/May break, the committee had yet to finalize the smallest administrative area of the survey. In the course of his duties Griffith had become familiar with most forms of administrative boundaries, from counties, baronies, parishes, townlands and, in Cork, an even smaller archaic division called a 'gneeve'. Apart from boggy areas, he had found county boundaries most straightforward to locate. Identifying sub-county bounds, however, frequently required outside assistance. When making a map of Co. Roscommon, for example, he had called upon the aid of local surveyors to identify baronial boundaries and the clergy for parishes. He had not yet incorporated townlands into any of his county projects. The engineer noted that townlands frequently consisted of one single property or estate, their bounds, therefore, being well known to locals. As such, Griffith argued in favour of their use for the new survey though he warned more than once that to obtain an accurate valuation, it would be necessary 'to go further', i.e., field level (see plate 10).

When asked if his Roscommon map could be expanded for future valuations, he responded that 'it would not bear enlarging' due to accuracy concerns. Griffith believed that a scale of six inches to a mile would be sufficient for the proposed Ordnance Survey, remarking that it was similar to the traditional scale of forty perches per inch used for property mapping. This scale alignment was more coincidental than any adherence to standard Irish cadastral practice, though it would undoubtedly make the project easier to integrate into the Irish mindset.

Griffith cautioned that some townlands would consist of multiple 'varieties of soil', e.g., bog/arable/pasture/etc. It would therefore be necessary to establish variable sub-classes for an accurate valuation. He argued that such assessments should be based on soil samples grouped under more encompassing terms. Rental values would be less valuable than this strategy, as rents were often set decades earlier and were frequently no longer related to the value of agricultural output. Of note, Griffith counselled that a valuator would first need maps to work from, a point later repeated by several other witnesses, and that any valuation should be 'made subordinate to the ... survey'. The survey of Ireland, therefore, must be completed *before* its valuation.

Griffith would appear again before the committee at their next meeting.

IRELAND'S GEOLOGY AND 'PEASANTRY', 12 MAY 1824[6]

Richard Griffith returned for his second testimony. While his previous session five days earlier had focused on administrative boundaries and valuations, his second appearance would cover a more comprehensive range of topics.

Richard Griffith, civil engineer

The committee began by bluntly asking how a general survey of Ireland could be executed. Griffith was more than capable of answering, presumably collating his rationale over the previous days. He presented a balanced argument concerning the role of civilian specialists and Ordnance staff, noting areas where each would be best suited. In his opinion, the civilian's camp's most significant weakness was their lack of technical experience:

> I am of opinion that there are very accurate surveyors in Ireland; but none who have had the same degree of practice in trigonometrical surveying that the engineers of the [Board of Ordnance] have had, and they do not possess instruments of equal accuracy.

Conversely, Griffith believed that while seasoned military engineers could execute an island-wide triangulation, they would be poorly suited to measuring civil bounds. Their civilian equivalents, by contrast, would be very comfortable with this element as they were used to 'discovering those boundaries' by various means. He reinforced this point by stating that civilian surveyors were authorities in cadastral surveying, being, in essence, property specialists. In contrast, the military was more accustomed to topographic surveying, such as the measurement of 'natural features' like hills. The new survey would be an amalgamation of both areas, thus leaving room for both groups. Civilians and military staff also differed regarding payment. Griffith estimated that the detail portion of the Irish survey would take around six to seven years. Local surveyors 'could not afford to lie out of their money' if asked to wait until the work had been completed before being paid. Military surveyors, by contrast, would be paid throughout.

Griffith's relevance as a witness was emphasized by his knowledge of valuation, a topic that had been mostly sidelined to this point. Like others, he felt that separate teams should undertake the survey and valuation. He also warned that there were potential benefits to landowners if they bribed a surveyor. Valuers, by contrast, would easily recognize and highlight such

---

6 *Report from the select committee on the survey and valuation of Ireland*, pp 42–57.

deceptions if teams were split. In his opinion, Ireland's top valuation firm in 1824 was Messrs Sherrard and Brassington, based on Blessington Street, Dublin. Disciples of John Rocque's French School of Surveying, Thomas Sherrard (b. *c*.1750, d. 1837) (the senior partner) had begun his career as an estate surveyor in the 1770s, drifting into valuation around 1800.[7] Much of his success had been gained through his work with Dublin's Wide Streets Commission, resulting in Sherrard's close connections with some of the country's most influential politicians. Spring Rice would interview neither Sherrard nor Brassington, nor would they be associated with the later Ordnance Survey of Ireland. However, their firm would remain prominent in commercial surveying until the early twentieth century.[8]

The questioning then turned to geology, which was another area where Griffith's polymathic knowledge came to bear. He had been appointed professor of geology to the Dublin Society in 1812 and since then had 'examined a large portion of every county'. Though a detailed geological map of Ireland had yet to be produced, he had made do by substituting data from general surveys produced by Aaron Arrowsmith (1811) and Major Alexander Taylor (1793). He had found both 'imperfect'.

The committee's real objective with the geology line of questioning was to understand Ireland's coalfields. This deviation in the topic was typical for the parliamentarian's erratic examination technique, the subject having little to do with tax reform. It was also indicative of the pressures they were coming under from outside sources to explore the adaptation of the survey to other disciplines. Griffith explained that there were eight Irish coalfields, the most valuable near Lough Allen. By his estimates, Irish collieries were of the same extent as those in England though their material was of poorer quality. The Lough Allen deposit piqued the committee's attention, wanting to know more about its local transport infrastructure, such as canals. They were also concerned about the local populace and if 'the peasantry in the vicinity ... were a quiet and well-behaved set ...'. This concern arose from a potential loss in investment if the region was prone to rebellion. Griffith considered the population 'well-behaved', and that they would not threaten investment. Inquiries followed about various aspects of Irish geology and mineral reserves, Griffith masterfully answering each in turn with succinct and clear responses. His only stumble occurred when asked about the cost and time it would take to complete a geological map of Ireland, the engineer requesting more time to consider his answer.[9]

7 O'Cionnaith, *Land surveying*, p. 169.   8 John Andrews, 'The French School of Dublin land surveyors', *Irish Geography*, 5 (1965), 280.   9 *Freeman's Journal*, 2 Oct. 1824; *Belfast Newsletter*, 8 Oct. 1824.

5.1. The temporary nature of homes for the rural poor meant their inclusion in the proposed Irish survey was not guaranteed. James Henry Brocas, *A thatched cottage* (n.d.) (courtesy of the National Library of Ireland).

In another random change in their investigation, the committee returned to 'the peasantry'. They wished to know if including rural housing in the proposed survey would be expedient. Griffith believed that housing should only be recorded if above a particular class, noting that some of the poorest huts were frequently replaced and could only be considered temporary structures.

Regardless of radical shifts in the committee's themes, Griffith's knowledge of valuation and geology had proven immense. He responded with accuracy and confidence, doing much to promote the work of his professional class in the process. Despite Wellington's concerns, he had proven that Irish engineers were capable and well-experienced in various fields. However, Griffith was also sensible enough to recognize his profession's limitations. Over the coming days, many of his former Bogs Commission colleagues would further add to this evidence as Spring Rice and his committee delved deeper into the practicalities of surveying Ireland.

A WESTERN PERSPECTIVE, 13 MAY 1824[10]

Following Griffith's two consecutive appearances, the committee heard from another Bogs Commission veteran: William Bald. Bald was a Scottish engineer and land surveyor who, in his late teens, had been apprenticed to famed cartographer John Ainslie (b. 1745, d. 1828). Moving to Ireland in 1809, the young engineer had been initially hired by the Bogs Commission before basing himself in Mayo. Still in his mid-30s when he appeared before Spring Rice, he was justifiably considered an expert in medium-scale cartography and had acquired a near-encyclopaedic knowledge of surveying in his adopted homeland.

William Bald, civil engineer

Bald began, like others, by bringing the committee up to date with his portfolio. This included his time with the Bogs Commission and his acclaimed trigonometric survey of Mayo (at a scale of four inches to a mile) created over the preceding years. The resulting multi-part map was, by 1824, in Paris awaiting engraving, indicative of Bald's pride in his work. He also had begun a similar project in Clare while continuing with valuation surveys across Connacht and Scotland (see plate 11).

Bald had taken inspiration for his map of Mayo from the Ordnance Survey of Britain. This map concentrated on topographical features such as mountains, rivers, and bogland, though it also included baronial boundaries. Hydrographic data had been referenced from the work of acclaimed maritime surveyor Murdock McKenzie (b. 1712, d. 1797). Bald obtained height information from his old Bogs Commission maps.[11] Asserting his technical authority, he informed the committee that he had been the first surveyor to use a theodolite in Connacht. However, this claim is doubtful as the instrument was present in Ireland since at least 1724 and likely arose from the prevalence of the older and less accurate circumferentor among rural surveyors.[12] Such was the extent of his

10 *Report from the select committee on the survey and valuation of Ireland*, pp 57–73.   11 McKenzie's data was subject to criticism later in the Spring Rice committee's investigations, evidence of Alexander Nimmo, 27 May 1824, *Report of the select committee for the survey and valuation of Ireland*, p. 92. For this substantial project, he had sourced a surveyor's chain from the famed London instrument maker Edward Troughton, this device being calibrated directly against the British brass standard found in the Tower of London.   12 Thomas Burgh, *A method to determine the areas*

efforts in Mayo that Bald duly submitted a paper about the project to the Royal Irish Academy.[13]

Given Mayo's rugged landscape, the committee wanted to hear his ideas on including topography. Bald was able to explain different schools of thought on the cartographic representation of terrain in use in Germany, England, France and Italy. To support his arguments, he referred to topographic maps of Lombardy by Giovanni Bordiga (d. 1799) and of the island of Elba by Alexandre Blondeau (fl. 1798–1828). He had recently purchased each of these for further study, indicating that Ireland's surveyors and engineers kept abreast of industrial developments from across Europe. The German technique of shading based on the steepness of terrain was, to Bald, of greatest interest. The ongoing valuation survey of Bavaria was also one he felt the committee should take note of as their maps included every field – a system that had even inspired the French to redo their famed *cadastre* with the same level of detail in mind (see plate 12).

Allowing for such international interests, it is no surprise that Bald had also drafted his own embryonic project concerning a national survey of Ireland. Written several years before, he proposed dividing the island into four to six divisions, each under the command of a senior engineer, with around twenty-five surveyors assigned per division. When queried about the cost of such medium-scale mapping, the engineer asserted that townlands and parishes cost around 9½ pence per acre to measure. He estimated that a cost of 6 pence per acre for a national townland survey would be reasonable – the first time any witness had put a price on the project. By his assessment, it would take eight years to survey the country at a scale of five inches to a mile, equating to £300,000[14] (excluding the primary trigonometric network). That both Griffith and Bald had composed separate draft plans for a national survey demonstrates that two of Ireland's premier engineers had noticed the need for such a resource, further justifying the timing of the Ordnance's involvement.

Irrespective of his call for a new national survey, Bald differed from Colby on several items. For one, he was adamant that townlands should form the foundation of any new survey and valuation. Adding to this suggestion, he recommended that every field within each townland should be measured (in English, Scotch, and Irish acres) and that maps should be recorded at twelve

of right-lined figures universally (Dublin, 1724), p. 13; O'Cionnaith, *Mapping, measurement and metropolis*, p. 64.   **13** William Bald, 'An account of a trigonometrical survey of Mayo, read 30 Apr. 1821', *The Transactions of the Royal Irish Academy*, xiv (Dublin, 1825), 51.   **14** Colby's estimate for the survey, submitted to parliament in June 1824, requested £300,000, of which £25,000 was to be paid in the survey's first year of operation. Andrews, *Paper landscape*, p. 32.

perches to an inch, again differing from Colby.[15] Like others, he agreed that the survey and valuation should be separate entities, conducted by distinct teams.

The discussion then turned to existing cartographic resources. These had been mentioned early in the committee's investigations, with Bald's presence allowing them to delve further into the practical use of such records. The engineer thought the Down Survey was too old to be relevant, having seen copies in Dublin and Paris.[16] He noted that 'there are many accurate surveys of private property in Ireland, but I fear there would be much difficulty in procuring them [from landowners]'. All counties had been surveyed by 1824, but Bald felt that those of Longford (1813), Roscommon (1822) and Dublin (1816) were executed using the best methods and equipment. This point differed from early British witnesses who mostly dismissed the existing library of Irish county mapping. It should be noted however that Bald had a vested interest in county mapping and did not explicitly say such examples were superior, or on par, to Ordnance mapping.

During this testimony, he sought to assure the committee that determining townland boundaries was indeed possible without historical mapping. Bald suggested '[having] gentlemen of the country send their most intelligent people to point out the boundaries', thus relying on local knowledge rather than records. Given the lack of official records related to such boundaries, this suggestion was likely the most practical, though did expose the project to local disputes between landowners. It was becoming clear that the boundary element was making the project a longer and more haphazard process than the committee may have envisaged initially.

The committee's final line of questioning focused on the quality of Ireland's surveying community. While touched upon by Griffith, the subject would soon become a standard talking point for each engineer interviewed in May and June. Bald was able to list nine individuals who he felt were the top practitioners of the era, several of whom the committee had, or would shortly, examine.[17] Each of those named was also noted as having 'valuable assistants connected with them' and could thus be considered representatives of distinct survey teams.

Given his experience in Britain and the Continent, Bald was further questioned on this point:

> [*Committee*] Do the surveyors of England, Ireland, and Scotland differ much either in ability or the manner in which they execute their work?

15 Andrews, *Paper landscape*, p. 24.   16 O'Cionnaith, 'Piracy, property, and politics', 96.   17 Bald mentioned the following engineers: John Killaly, Alexander Nimmo, Richard Griffith, William Edgeworth, David Aher, William Duncan, John Longfield, John Brassington and Clarges Green. *Report of the select committee on the survey and valuation of Ireland*, p. 66.

[*Bald*] The surveyors of England, Ireland, and Scotland differ in their mode of surveying lands.

[*Committee*] Do they in ability?

[*Bald*] I think there are some as good surveyors of land in Ireland as can be had either in England or Scotland.

Like Griffith before him, Bald had done the Irish engineering and surveying communities much service in Westminster. It was clear from his testimony that there was obvious experience among the profession's elite, both regarding the eccentricities of Irish cadastral surveying, but also in denoting topography. Significantly, he had reinforced the idea that a new survey and valuation had been on the minds of the country's top engineers for several years and they had been well prepared for whatever the committee could ask. His testimony was extensive and well received, especially his points concerning medium-scale mapping at home and abroad. He would appear before the committee the following day to expand on these arguments.

THE SCOTTISH CONNECTION, 14 MAY 1824[18]

The committee was not finished with Bald. His experience of the remotest parts of the island made him familiar with the diverse range of surveyors Ireland had to offer. His training and early career in Scotland also allowed him to assess Irish surveying and engineering from an outsider's perspective. Consequently, he could answer the committee's queries on both topics with authority.

William Bald, *civil engineer*

Bald felt that there were around 50–60 'practical surveyors'[19] in Ireland who could immediately assist with the new survey. This group was 'competent at this moment' to survey townland boundaries only, leaving the more difficult triangulation and topographic element to others (i.e., Colby's team). If new surveying recruits were required, he estimated that it would take between three

---

18 *Report of the select committee on the survey and valuation of Ireland*, pp 73–8.   **19** The term 'practical surveyor' was an unofficial title within the profession asserting an individual's expertise and the quality of their work. Such was this term's strength that it was often used in the titles of relevant texts, such as Robert Gibson's *A treatise of practical surveying* (Dublin, 1752) or Samuel Wyld's *The practical surveyor* (London, 1725). Such an endorsement stood in marked contrast to other unofficial ranks used at the time, describing poor practitioners as 'foppish', 'pretenders' or 'bumbling' surveyors; Peter Callan, *A dissertation on the practice of land surveying* (Drogheda, 1758), pp 12–20.

and four years to train them from scratch, tactfully avoiding the subject of Colby's six-week course for his cadets. He also believed that increased use of theodolites for such work would benefit the wider surveying community. This instrument's mass deployment would highlight the advantages of this more accurate device compared to the outdated circumferentor, which maintained a stubborn grasp on the psyche of local surveyors. Bald quickly noted that a few excellent theodolites were already in use on the island. One such example, owned by his former Bogs Commission colleague William Edgeworth, originated from the famed Reichenbach firm in Germany. This reference may have been a deliberate attempt to reinforce his earlier testimony stressing the connection between the elite of Ireland's engineers with a wider European network.

Despite such encouragement, Bald also harboured doubts. He advised against sending large teams of civilian surveyors into the field as each would need to prove his worth and competency first, or, in his words, 'to acquire a knowledge of those who are to be intrusted'. He too shared Colby's earlier (and well-proven) concerns about the same issue encountered during the Ordnance Survey's Lincolnshire experience. Smaller Irish teams would, therefore, initially be preferred, with an engineer supervising a maximum of twenty-five men. The Bogs Commission used a similar hierarchal model, demonstrating the impact that earlier organization continued to have in Ireland a decade after it was disbanded.

Turning again to topography, the engineer objected to the committee's suggestion that Ordnance staff record the path of rivers. Rightly, he noted these often formed territorial boundaries between counties or baronies. Such features, in turn, would be documented by the proposed civilian teams involved in the territorial survey. Bald observed that if rivers were to be simultaneously considered territorial and topographical, then the effort to record them would be doubled. Instead, he suggested that Ordnance staff undertake the triangulation first, with specific attention paid to the quality of their baseline. To support his argument, he used examples of large trigonometric surveys by Gen. William Roy in Britain, Col. William Lambton (b. *c.*1753, d. 1823) in India and Ferdinand Hassler (b. 1770, d. 1843) in the United States of America.[20] Unfortunately, we do not know if Colby was present for this statement, its potential to sound condescending dependent on the manner of its delivery. Continuing, Bald recommended that details like rivers could be recorded

---

20 The names of the surveys referred to by Bald were the Military Survey of Scotland (1747–55), the Great Trigonometrical Survey of India (1802–71), and the United States Coast Survey (1807–36). Hassler's name was misspelled in the select committee minutes [Heslar].

afterward '. . . by men who have been in the habit of surveying and valuing land' (i.e., civilian surveyors and engineers).

Bald was confident that the territorial element could proceed immediately as 'no difference will be perceptible' if townland surveys were reduced to a general map. If two triangulation reference points were fixed every 100 acres, he judged that any errors in the territorial survey could be detected and adjusted. This same process was later echoed by several witnesses, though was rejected (where possible) in favour of that used in Britain, i.e., a preliminary triangulation followed by the detail and territorial surveys. Once the survey began, however, Colby had a purposeful habit of not informing his topographic teams of the features of these reference points, thus allowing him to examine the accuracy of each surveyor's work more efficiently. Such trickery lay several years in the future.

Bald championed the use of civilian surveyors far more so than many of his colleagues. He was confident that they would be up to the task and that there was room within the new project's scope for civilian management of specific areas. Others would later add to this assessment. Bald would return to provide further evidence in early June.

Alexander Nimmo, civil engineer

The committee welcomed their next expert, engineer Alexander Nimmo. He, like Bald, was Scottish, both men coming to Ireland as part of the Bogs Commission's efforts to find qualified (and cheaper) engineers in Britain. Like many hired in this manner, Nimmo discovered the Irish market eager for his expertise, his beautiful Bogs Commission maps of Kerry doing much to elevate his position within local government circles. Following the cessation of his bog work in 1814 he found great success creating charts for the Fisheries Commission and as a civil engineer, building roads and harbours on behalf of the government.

Nimmo was no stranger to parliamentary committees or members of Spring Rice's group. In 1819, committee member Sir John Newport interviewed him as part of a review of Ireland's labouring community, the MP also being familiar with Nimmo's work in his Waterford constituency.[21] Alongside Griffith and Bald, Nimmo could rightly be considered one of Ireland's top engineering minds and would be called to give evidence before Spring Rice's committee on multiple occasions. His initial foray would focus on the history of similar valuation projects, alongside the state of surveying and mapping in 1820s Ireland.

21 Wilkins, *Alexander Nimmo*, p. 137.

When asked how the proposed survey should be executed, Nimmo launched into an extensive and highly detailed monologue covering a range of subjects and periods. The committee appears to have found this of great interest as he was rarely interrupted, and when so, it was simply to clarify specifics.[22] From the beginning, Nimmo echoed the argument made by many previous witnesses that, if possible, the triangulation, territorial, and valuation portions of the project should remain distinct entities. Despite his obvious experience, he was also keen to alert the committee that '... it would not be in my power to take any active share in the intended survey, even if I was thought qualified', immediately separating himself from the project.

With his professional boundaries set, Nimmo delved back in time to as far as the eleventh-century Doomsday Book, examining the long and intertwined connection between taxation and land measurement. He reviewed a fourteenth-century map of Ireland by Ricardus Corinensis before jumping to the work of William Petty and the 'foot soldiers' who executed the Down Survey. This review was not entirely limited to Irish examples, with Nimmo mentioning other noted surveys conducted in Sweden, France and the Low Countries, all for the same taxation purposes. The engineer held French cartography in especially high regard, noting that 'France [has] given us some very pretty maps'. This stream of thought invariably turned Nimmo's oration to the enduring influence of Rocque, who produced well-received surveys of Middlesex, Surrey and Berkshire and founded the French School of Irish surveying in the 1750s.[23]

The mentioning of Rocque's name raised further questions from the committee concerning his long-term influence in Ireland. Nimmo responded that there were many Irish surveyors trained in Rocque's methods (notably triangulation). Several had been mentioned previously by Griffith, notably Thomas Sherrard, though there had been few advancements within that school of cartographic thought:

> [Rocque's] pupils in [Ireland] form a school of land-surveyors at present, the most respectable in the surveying and valuation of land in the kingdom, but his science not being such as subsequent operations have introduced, these persons still work with the old instruments, the needle or circumferentors, and, in case of canal operations, the level.

22 In 1851 Spring Rice recalled Nimmo's testimony on the history lecture, calling it 'the best history of topography and of maps that is to be found anywhere'. Evidence of Lord Monteagle, *Select committee on Ordnance Survey* (Scotland) (1851), p. 22. 23 Some active French School members named by various witnesses before the committee included Thomas Sherrard, John Longfield, and David Aher. Aher would be the only one to provide testimony (see below, p. 135), John Andrews, 'The French School', p. 280.

Shifting topic, the committee asked if topographic data was of use outside of military and geological purposes. Nimmo replied that it was a vital component for engineers, though only of limited importance in general-purpose civilian mapping. On this point, he clearly distinguished between the needs of traditional land surveyors and the new generation of engineers of which he was a member.[24] The latter held a great affinity with engineering concepts of the Industrial Revolution rather than the former's adherence to traditional proprietary concerns. Beginning in the late eighteenth century, a notable and widening divide emerged between surveyors and engineers, as Nimmo informed the committee:

> I have already observed, that land surveyors and topographical engineers are two distinct classes of person; the latter … when employed in a civil capacity, we call engineering surveyors.

By the 1820s this difference had consigned property surveyors to a lower technical rank than their engineering brethren.

While Spring Rice's committee frequently analysed the capabilities of Irish surveyors, none were ever called as witnesses.[25] As such, they were an ever-present, though voiceless, part of the committee's discussions.[26] Nimmo was, however, keen to state that while Ireland's engineers (including himself) did work of great merit, they would be incapable of executing the primary triangulation network of the survey to the same accuracy as the Ordnance department. This concluded his first day's evidence.

Nimmo and Bald gave the committee a good overview of local surveying capabilities. Nimmo's history lesson had proven popular with the parliamentarians and displayed his evident knowledge of Irish sources. Irrespective, it did little to find an immediate solution to the cess issue. Instead, it demonstrated that Ireland's cartographic history had undertaken a fragmentary journey to date, with many highly regarded records, such as the Down Survey, used out of habit rather than for their accuracy.[27] The country's

---

24 O'Cionnaith, *Land surveying*, p. 206.   25 One surveyor would be interviewed by the Spring Rice committee, though he had spent most of his career in England with only limited experience in Ireland (see below p. 116).   26 Ireland's resident topographic surveyors however were a distinct entity from the well-established French School of surveying. While the latter had looked to France for cartographic inspiration, the former had a strong Scots influence, beginning with the arrival of Andrew Skinner and George Taylor (d. 1841) in the 1770s.   27 This point was echoed by Richard Griffith decades later, noting the Down Survey, 'after a period of 200 years, has been so acquiesced in by all parties, that it is always receivable in evidence, though not conclusive, it is admitted to be evidence'. Evidence of Richard Griffith, *Select committee on Ordnance Survey* (Scotland) (1851), p. 131.

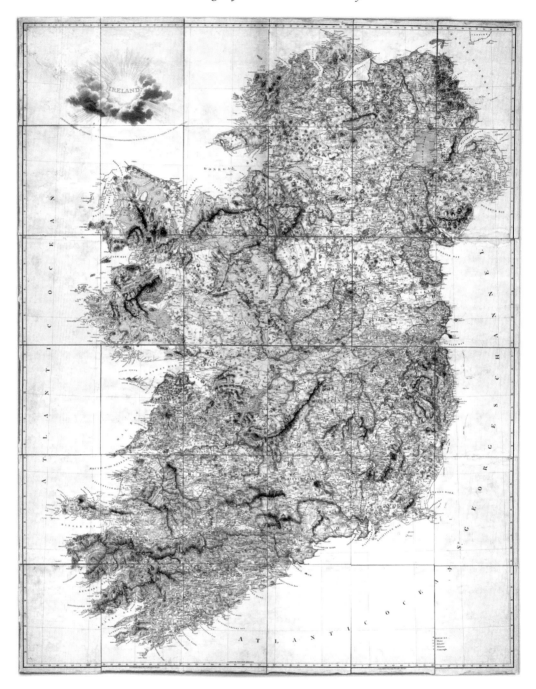

5.2. Aaron Arrowsmith's 1811 Map of Ireland, though well executed, lacked the rigorous control sought for the proposed reformation of county cess. Aaron Arrowsmith, *Ireland* (London, 1811) (David Rumsey Map Collection, David Rumsey Map Centre, Stanford Libraries).

existing surveying population remained of crucial importance to the committee, with Nimmo expanding on this topic at the next session three days later.

'COMMON SURVEYORS' AND 'INFERIOR ARTISTS', 17 MAY 1824[28]

Alexander Nimmo, a civil engineer

Nimmo began his second day of evidence by discussing Ireland's other, lesser-known 'ordnance survey'. Undertaken by Gen. Charles Vallancey in the 1770s, this manuscript series provided a general map of Irish roads and topography for use in case of invasion or rebellion. It was not connected with the later Ordnance Survey of Ireland under Colby and covered only the island's southern half.

Nimmo had consulted this map series and found it accurate in parts, notably, those areas measured by theodolite rather than circumferentor. He observed that Vallancey's use of two instrument types introduced obvious errors throughout the series, thus making it unreliable overall. According to Nimmo, the true legacy of Vallancey's project was its use as a source for better-received maps of Ireland, namely those by Arrowsmith[29] and Taylor,[30] both mentioned earlier by Griffith. Given the convenience of Vallancey's addition of topography, Nimmo felt that it could also be of use to the new survey.[31] Regardless of the utility of Vallancey's work, Nimmo confirmed to the committee that no truly 'correct map of Ireland' existed.

After receiving their grounding in Ireland's cartographic heritage, the committee asked for Nimmo's assessment of the country's surveyors. This was comparable to similar questions asked of Bald (May 14) and demonstrated that the committee still saw some potential for civilian involvement. Nimmo held Irish land surveyors in greater esteem than many other witnesses. Specifically, he advised that they would be excellent in gathering local territorial data for the proposed survey:

> It is clear, the local surveyor would take exceeding [sic] great care, for his character … to be as correct as possible in his representations, and they should not be carried further than his instruments and his science would permit him to go … We have a great many country surveyors, very

28 *Report of the select committee on the survey and valuation of Ireland*, pp 78–82.   29 Aaron Arrowsmith, *Ireland* (London, 1811).   30 Alexander Taylor, *A new map of Ireland* (London, 1793).   31 The new survey could forego any topographic detail if it remained purely devoted to cess reform and administrative bounds. The opportunity for a multi-purpose map, however, was too valuable to miss.

capable of giving us the contents of a townland, and even a tolerable valuation of it . . .

He was also eager to clarify that there was a wide range of surveyors at work and that they should not all be classified as a homogenous group:

> 'The common surveyor' is a very wide expression, because we have them of all degrees of skill; but we have many men in Ireland to whom we may perfectly well trust the survey of a parish, to whom I would with the utmost confidence intrust the survey of a parish, [as] if it were my property. We have also several who have shown themselves competent to more extensive operations.[32]

Despite such support, Nimmo maintained the belief that the Board of Ordnance should be solely responsible for the triangulation due to their 'experience in that particular department'.

Nimmo also echoed Bald's stance regarding the survey sequence, arguing that the territorial and detail survey by 'common' civil surveyors should be conducted *before* the Ordnance-led triangulation. This differed from the sequence of the Ordnance Survey of Britain and contrasted with the order of survey elements applied during the Bogs Commission surveys, in which Nimmo was heavily involved. While Bald had not expanded on his suggestion, Nimmo at least elaborated, explaining that this process could act as a means of measurement quality control. Using this proposal, Nimmo hoped that Ordnance officers would be able to 'check upon the [preceding] operations of the surveyors', continuing,

> It has been customary to fill in the detail of these national maps by inferior artists [i.e. 'common surveyors'] . . . but when it comes to be a matter of value and extent of property, we have no check upon the inferior artist, as the final operation is delivered into the hands of the inferior artist, instead of being delivered into the hands of the superior artists [i.e., Ordnance officers].

Such a procedure would undoubtedly have helped avoid the issues Mudge and Colby encountered in Lincolnshire with civilian surveyors. However, it would still require some triangulation data to compare against. Colby eventually opted for an amended version of this plan when delays in the triangulation network forced him to start topographic work out of his planned sequence.

32 For more on the unofficial classification of land surveyors operating in Ireland see Callan, *A dissertation*, pp 12–20.

Changing subject to valuations, Nimmo believed that such assessments should be recorded in a book with a general map of the area in question on its first page. A master set would be stored elsewhere for referral. This process of providing valuators with duplicate maps would play a significant part in the Ordnance's legacy, eventually leading to the engraving and mass production of printed six-inch maps (see below, p. 166). He also suggested that if the committee also used a set of 'respectable surveyors' for the valuation the results would be:

> … of so superior cast, so very eminent in authenticity, beyond any other valuation that ever has been procured of private property in Ireland … thus I conceive, that every cabin, and every fence, and every tree, should be introduced into the map of the townland.

Showing a level of prudence previously absent, the engineer recommended that the date of valuation references should be set by parliament, with guideline values used regardless of later fluctuations. When asked if 'corn rent' would be a fair price of measure Nimmo responded that it could be used but the Exchequer might as well expect to be paid in corn. Rental values on a parish would therefore be of greatest use for tax assessment.

The worth of Nimmo's evidence on his second day of testimony was mixed. He had clarified that there were indeed suitably skilled surveyors in Ireland who could undertake the detail or territorial parts of the project with some supervision. Neither he nor the committee however had dwelt long on this subject, or on the triangulation element that Nimmo was understandably happy to leave for Colby. His insistence on the boundary section being completed first was nonetheless unusual. This sequence would have produced results for tax reform far quicker than the years necessary for a nationwide triangulation but would have created questions regarding the accuracy of initial results should such maps be later adjusted. Unable to complete their full range of questions, the committee requested that Nimmo join them again the following day.

THE SOLE SURVEYOR, 18 MAY 1824[33]

Nimmo returned for a relatively short session, this being his third consecutive day of evidence. The committee also heard testimony from land surveyor Patrick Kelly, the only commercial surveyor (rather than an engineer) called to appear.

---

33 *Report of the select committee on the survey and valuation of Ireland*, pp 82–6.

Alexander Nimmo, civil engineer

The committee resumed by asking Nimmo about his preferences for parish over townland boundaries in medium-scale mapping. He responded by stating the term 'townland' did not represent a standard administrative space across Ireland as with parishes, and in many places, the word was not used at all. He suggested that sub-denominations smaller than parishes might therefore be surveyed by 'inferior artists', but their work would always need to be checked. Again, he reiterated his belief that the quality of the surveyor, rather than the size or the administrative subdivision measured, would dictate the project's accuracy.

Intrigued by Nimmo's stance, the committee wished to know if 'good [commercial] surveyors … could make measurements upon modern trigonometrical principles?' This, in essence, was asking him for a comparison between the general body of land surveyors in Ireland and the smaller group of topographic engineers. Nimmo replied that he had twelve young surveyors working for him to whom 'I would confidently entrust the trigonometrical measurement of a parish'. Also in his employment were an equal number of 'inferior class' surveyors, the engineer keen to differentiate between the various professional strata. Based on his managerial experience, he recommended that the 'inferior' class could be employed for between six and nine pence per acre measured. In contrast, senior surveyors (capable of managing parish surveys) should receive two guineas per day.

Again, Nimmo had different concepts than other witnesses. For example, he saw no problem with surveyors undertaking the valuation if superior officers could then revise their findings. Earlier commentators had been absolute that both survey and valuation staff should consist of different groups, thus avoiding the potential of bribery by landholders. In contrast, Nimmo instead sought a system of hierarchical inspection for field surveys and valuations, with base data continually refined at each successive stage. Despite such distinctions, Nimmo, like Bald and Griffith before him, had brought the committee up to date with the capabilities of Ireland's surveying population. Should a wider body of surveyors become involved with the detail or territorial element of the project, it would be due to the evidence supplied by these engineers.

Witness: Patrick Kelly, land surveyor

The same level of praise could not be applied to the committee's next witness – Patrick Kelly. Kelly is a virtual historical unknown and, surprisingly, was the only commercial surveyor called to testify. He had worked both as a surveyor and doctor of law in Ireland (presumably in property disputes) but was far more familiar with practice in England. His selection to testify is a mystery. There were many experienced Irish surveyors whom the committee could have called to aid their investigations but either through time constraints, expense, or simple elitism, none were given that chance. Kelly's testimony provided little true insight, the committee missing a significant opportunity to give the Irish surveying profession a voice regarding the task ahead, or to impress Colby and Wellington.

Kelly spent much of his testimony discussing enclosures, an activity he had engaged in while working in England. This form of land management was more common in England's disappearing open field system than in Ireland's well-established estate landscape.[34] As a result, this evidence was of little relevance to cess reform. Yet, he was able to identify several operational differences between the two countries, mainly relating to the variation between the Irish plantation measure and the English statute measure.[35] When asked, he also had quite clear opinions on Irish and England land surveyors:

> [*Committee*] Have you had an opportunity of observing the comparative merits of English and Irish surveyors?
> [*Kelly*] In measuring small farms and fields, the Irish surveyors seem the most rigorously accurate, owing, perhaps, to the greater value attached to land in Ireland, and to the constant rivalship which exists there amongst surveyors; whereas contested surveys in England are very uncommon.[36]

This, however, proved to be the limit of Kelly's expertise, as, when asked directly on how the new survey and valuation should be executed, he responded:

> This is a very important question, on which much may be said in favour of different plans, I, therefore, beg some time to consider it.

It would be over a week before the committee would hear again from Kelly, the above question, unfortunately, remaining unanswered.

INDIAN INFLUENCE, 25 MAY 1824[37]

Richard Griffith was summoned for his third appearance. On this occasion, the committee intended to cross-examine him on his previous testimony, based on their increased knowledge gained from Nimmo and Bald over the previous days.

34 Nick Hayes, *The book of trespass* (London, 2021), p. 36.   35 Gibson, *Practical surveying*, p. 129.
36 O'Cionnaith, *Mapping, measurement and metropolis*, p. 33.   37 *Report of the select committee on the survey and valuation of Ireland*, pp 86–91.

Richard Griffith, civil engineer

The committee had recently heard a significant amount concerning the proposed roles of Ordnance staff and civilian surveyors. This invariably raised as many questions as it had answered. Some, such as Nimmo, seemed convinced civilians would play an obvious part by gathering data in the field. Others, notably Colby, had concerns, but maintained some flexibility should the project's timeline require expedience. The committee, therefore, began their questioning by asking Griffith for his stance on the Ordnance's role in the upcoming survey. He responded that it would be preferable if the Ordnance's highly skilled staff should avoid being used to chart 'civil divisions', and local civilian surveyors should be employed instead. Knowing the bad habits of some practitioners Griffith, like Nimmo and Bald, also advised that the triangulation portion should not be conducted first. His reasoning was based on concerns that if local surveyors were supplied with Ordnance reference points they would 'make their survey agree with it', whether their surveys were correct or not. Larger areas, such as counties, should be measured by civil engineers, such as himself, using triangulation methods. These, in turn, could then be checked against Ordnance points. Paradoxically, though Griffith repeatedly stated that detail surveys should proceed first, he also noted 'it would be advantageous to have the great trigonometrical points given as a foundation [for detail survey]', contradicting his previous statement.

Griffith was keen to voice some of his concerns about the traditional measurement methods used by rural surveyors given their potential role in the new survey. These primarily related to the use of graduated chains to physically determine distances. Overreliance on chain measurements could result in an incorrect acreage per townland compared to the more accurate triangulation methods previously described.[38] For the benefit of the committee he listed the reasons why, namely,

> … the inaccuracy of the person employed in chaining …
>
> … the chain itself becoming short, by the insertion of dirt between the links in wet weather [changing the length of the chain and thus the distance measured]
>
> … the inaccurate method of ascertaining the horizontal surface on ascending a hill [using longer slope instead of correct horizontal distances]

---

38 Graduated metal chains were used as a form of measuring tape by surveyors well into the twentieth century.

Concluding this particular point, Griffith stated:

> I have no doubt if the whole of Ireland were surveyed by the common methods, that the island would appear to contain more acres than would be given as its area by the trigonometrical surveyors.

Comments about exaggerated land sizes were nothing new, especially when traditional methods were used for national mapping. This was especially true when comparing such customary approaches with new, scientifically based techniques used by Colby and others of his status. Allegedly, when presented with the trigonometrically-correct *Carte de France corrigée* in 1684, King Louis XIV (b. 1638, d. 1715) was rumoured to have responded that he had lost more land to his surveyors (due to their more accurate measurements) than he ever had to his enemies.[39] Griffith's concerns were, therefore, well founded, the cumulative effect of localized errors making any national survey incorrect if non-scientific procedures were used (see plate 13).

Again, the engineer felt that if an Ordnance triangulation survey could determine two points per square mile, then civilian engineers (referred to as 'men of character and ability in their professions') could use them for their own local baselines. Still debating the pros and cons of which part of the survey to complete first, Griffith continued by noting that any detail or territorial surveys could be delayed until the early 1830s if the full, island-wide triangulation was to occur first. Thus, he advised the committee that if they wanted a swift resolution to the cess issue, territorial and details surveys should begin using civilians. Conversely, if they chose a more accurate overall product, then they would have to wait for the triangulation element. Regardless of what order was chosen, Griffith insisted that civil engineers should 'be placed at the head of the detailed survey' rather than land surveyors, with the Ordnance performing the triangulation work.

Captain Henry Kater, physicist

The committee had heard extensive evidence from Irish engineers for several weeks. The timing of the next witness was thus fortuitous given the points raised by Griffith. Henry Kater (b. 1777, d. 1835) was a former army captain with great experience in scientific-grade surveying in British India. He was, therefore, more akin to Colby than either Griffith, Nimmo, or Bald, and one whose testimony would thus prove a valuable counter to that of the Irish engineers.

39 O'Cionnaith, *Land surveying*, p. 210.

Kater had been stationed in India during the late 1790s, assisting in the Great Trigonometric Survey of the sub-continent (begun 1802). Returning to England, he became a specialist in physics, working with the Board of Longitude and becoming a Fellow of the Royal Society in 1814. Of particular interest to Spring Rice's committee was his research with Colby on the difference in longitude between the Paris and Greenwich observatories, elevating his opinion on the upcoming survey of Ireland to the highest levels.[40] His contribution to the Spring Rice committee also exposed the prominent link between India and Ireland as areas of imperial interest for Britain, regarding the use of geographic science for governance.[41]

Kater began by informing the committee that he was aware of their proposed Irish project and had already submitted a methodology to Marquis Wellesley on how he thought it should be executed. His thesis followed the operational sequence laid out by Colby, namely the measurement of a highly accurate baseline, two hierarchal nationwide triangulation networks, and the acquisition of detail in the field. This final point again exposed the large gap in technical expertise required for the triangulation and detail elements, Kater stating:

> … those secondary operations would require only common trigono-metrical calculations, and therefore may be executed by inferior persons, inferior in point of science.

Overall, he felt the entire operation could be run by one organization, preferably military, and valuations should only occur once accurate reference maps had been produced. Detail surveys would also need to be regularly scrutinized as '… you must confide in a considerable degree to the persons employed … I certainly would leave no part of the operation unchecked.' Part of this scrutinization would be intentionally withholding information about triangulation reference points from surveyors gathering detail, as mentioned earlier by Nimmo. Such redaction would force them to calculate the distances between reference points themselves, thus allowing the quality of their work to be checked against known values. To aid this explanation, he recounted a triangulation survey he had supervised in 1804 between Mangalore [Mangaluru] and Madras [Chennai] in India, cities separated by around 400 miles, which had used similar methods.

---

40 John Connolly, *The history of the corps of royal sappers and miners* (London, 1855), p. 237.   41 Barry Crosbie, 'Ireland, colonial science and the geographical construction of British rule in India, c.1820–1870', *The Historical Journal*, 52:4 (2009), 963–87.

Kater's lack of confidence in civilian surveyors echoed many of the concerns raised earlier by Colby. Likewise, he dismissed the idea of an immediate commencement of local surveys to aid 'the proceedings of the scientific body of the Ordnance', stating such work would be no more useful 'than a map drawn by a countryman would'. This position was prudent given his background, though was delivered harshly. Such dismissiveness was apparent throughout his testimony. Kater frequently disagreed with earlier witness statements – in fact, his commentary on ideas suggested by others (except Colby) was often curt, bordering on arrogant. For example, when asked for his remarks on the positioning of reference points every few hundred acres by the Ordnance team, he replied sharply that:

> [it] would be an utter waste of time, it would be occupying the time of scientific men in obtaining a degree of precision, which would here be quite useless.

He also advised against the use of existing features (such as prominent parts of buildings) for triangulation as '… the operations are so nice [i.e., accurate], that no church steeple would be found sufficiently firm to enable us to observe upon it with the requisite accuracy …'. Instead, he recommended a type of large, purpose-built stone marker he had seen used in London, Paris, and India, fashioned specifically for the project.

To conclude, the committee asked what scale an accurate map of small civil divisions such as townlands could be accurately projected. Kater was aloof in his response, stating, 'I am really not prepared to answer that question …', admitting he had never 'gone into that particular line of detail'.

FISHERIES AND FRIENDLY LOCALS, 27 MAY 1824[42]

Like Griffith, Nimmo had quickly become a favourite of the committee. So far his testimony had ranged over many subjects. However, his fourth and final appearance on 27 May was more focused, concentrating on the Irish fisheries industry. Specifically, the committee wanted to understand his assessment of existing hydrographic data and whether this data could be added to the new survey. While well outside of their original cess remit, it was clear that Croker's earlier testimony (7 April) on the needs of the Royal Navy had resonated with the committee. Therefore, they remained keen to understand how the project

42 *Report of the select committee on the survey and valuation of Ireland*, pp 91–5.

could be extended from a valuation to a general survey of the island (and its seas). As usual, Nimmo's experience and knowledge proved extensive.

Alexander Nimmo, civil engineer

For many years Nimmo had been employed to 'examine' the coast of Ireland through his role as an engineer with the Fisheries Commission.[43] This included the creation of maps and the construction of relevant infrastructure, namely piers, and harbours, to protect fishing fleets. Beginning in Sligo and working northward around Ulster, by 1824 he had mapped the coast down the Irish Sea as far as Wicklow. An equivalent map of the southern portion of the coast was based on earlier work he had conducted in Munster, some under the auspices of the Bogs Commission.

Nimmo informed the committee that the coastal charts of Ireland by the great Scottish hydrographer Murdock Mackenzie were still in use by the Admiralty. He found these '… in general tolerably correct, [but they] contain a variety of egregious errors …'.[44] For example, he noted a serious incident where three fishing vessels were lost in Strangford Lough due to Mackenzie placing submerged rocks in the wrong position on his charts, a mistake Nimmo subsequently corrected. Apart from artificial harbours, Nimmo had also plotted natural ones such as Carlingford, Howth and Killala Bay using trigonometric methods. He intended to produce prints of Galway Bay and four or five other prominent coastal locations through a publisher in London, but this had yet to occur (see plate 14).

Throughout his fisheries work he had used a 7-inch theodolite made by English instrument maker Edward Nairne (b. 1726, d. 1806). These measurements were supported by sextant readings using a device constructed by the Troughton company – both considered state-of-the-art for the era. The theodolite had initially belonged to engineer Major Alexander Taylor, who subsequently gave it to Nimmo, indicative of the long-term value placed in these items.

The committee concluded this short meeting by breaking from their usual technical questions and asking Nimmo about the rural population of Galway. Of particular interest were incidences of vandalism and what resistance, if any, he had met. This line of questioning was similar to queries asked of Bald and Griffith, the committee still curious about the attitudes of rural 'peasantry' to the presence of surveyors. Like his colleagues, Nimmo had occasionally met

---

43 The Fisheries Commission (1819–30) was responsible for promoting the fishing industry.
44 Wellesley to Wellington, 17 Feb. 1824, *Dispatches*, ii, p. 219.

with suspicion, however his reputation with the Fisheries Commission did him much good:

> [*Committee*] Having stated, for the purpose of making a trigonometrical survey of Galway, you found it necessary to establish artificial points and stations; had you any difficulty, from the nature of the country and the population, in establishing those points and stations, and preserving them for the purposes you required?
>
> [*Nimmo*] None whatever, for the inhabitants knew perfectly well who I was, and the object I had in view.
>
> [*Committee*] Were the population of the country friendly to the object that you had in view, and anxious to promote it?
>
> [*Nimmo*] Friendly; when they first saw us begin, there was a report that there was going to be a war immediately, for the officers of the army were fortifying the hills, which gave great satisfaction, as they expected the price of corn would rise directly.
>
> [*Committee*] But when the real object of your survey was known, were they friendly to it?
>
> [*Nimmo*] Perfectly so; I have built so many piers and other works in that neighbourhood, that they knew perfectly well who I was.[45]

A SCIENTIFIC REFLECTION, 29 MAY 1824[46]

As the committee's knowledge increased, so too did their range of experts. Their 29 May meeting saw four witnesses testify, the largest number called in a single day to date. Each was questioned on specifics of the survey or valuation rather than an overview of the entire project, with several supporting core ideas the committee had, by this stage, come to embrace. None of the interviews were as extensive as those with Griffith and Nimmo over the preceding days, this session marking the beginning of the final stages of the group's investigations.

---

45 During the eventual survey Colby would frequently have to call upon police protection. His complaints were mostly related to the theft of surveying equipment rather than organized resistance to the Ordnance's work. Likewise, Colby was reprimanded in 1834 by Lt Col. Sir William Gosset (b. 1782, d. 1848), undersecretary of Ireland, for using Ordnance officers to aid the high sheriff of Co. Fermanagh. Gosset felt cause to remind Colby that such activity was 'highly detrimental to the important service [of the survey]'. 15 Mar. 1830, Colby to William Gregory (NAI CSO/RP/1830/280); 9 June 1834, William Gosset to Colby (NAI CSO/RP/1834/2567).   46 *Report of the select committee on the survey and valuation of Ireland*, pp 96–100.

Major George Warburton, police inspector general, Connacht

First before the committee was Major George Warburton (b. 1781, d. 1845). Warburton had been chief magistrate of Co. Clare from 1816 to 1823,[47] before his promotion to inspector of police in Connacht.[48] He was among the very earliest police officers in Ireland, being a forerunner of the Royal Irish Constabulary (RIC) and serving at a time of great rural disturbance.[49] He would eventually retire in 1838 as inspector general of police. As one of the few public officials interviewed by the committee, Warburton's insight was of importance.

The committee began by asking the officer if the boundaries of the townlands were well-defined. Warburton wholly agreed, adding to his response with a colourful story of a police raid:

> I recollect an instance [when an illegal alcohol] still was thrown over a hedge, and lay upon the bank of the hedge, and so accurate was the definition of the [townland] boundary, that it was argued that the bank of the hedge was in one townland, and the gripe of the hedge was in the other. That particular instance shows me it is a very accurate definition.

As a non-surveyor, Warburton's confidence in the identification of boundaries did much to soothe the committee's anxieties. He also felt that the added expense 'to the public of a minute survey' would be very welcomed if it included field and property boundaries. The inclusion of such data, along with an accompanying valuation, would act, according to him, as a stimulus to estate owners to improve their lands. Overall, he was highly supportive of cess reform and had seen first-hand the problems it was causing across the country. He had repeatedly witnessed how unfair the existing cess system was, with some areas virtually exempt from tax while others were 'more severely taxed than they ought to be'. If tax was equally applied, people would be more eager to pay it as 'there would be less taxation on individuals ... [and] there would be a more equal partition of the burden'.

Patrick Kelly, surveyor

Surveyor Patrick Kelly returned to add to his previous evidence. Kelly, the only commercial surveyor interviewed by the committee, had provided testimony ten

47 House of Commons Committee, Disturbances (Ireland) (1825), p. 162; Michael MacMahon, *George Warburton: Co. Clare's first professional policeman*, published via Clare County library, https://www.clarelibrary.ie/eolas/coclare/people/george_warburton.htm, last visited 31 Mar. 2023. 48 Lords Committee, *State of Ireland* (London, 1825), p. 77. 49 Ray Warburton, 'Warburtons of Garryhinch', https://warburton.one-name.net/clandocs/GarryhinchClan.pdf, p. 50.

days earlier; however, his information was of little relevance to cess reform. His first session had ended with him requesting more time before he coud outline how the new survey should be executed. On his return he backed the sequence favoured by Colby and Kater, suggesting that an initial triangulation survey would be most helpful, with detail filled in later by others. He also suggested that speed would be of great importance for the detail portion, '... before the [triangulation] stations should become obliterated', echoing the committee's earlier concerns around vandalism, intentional or otherwise.

Kelly had spent most of his career in England and was asked how regularly were parochial maps consulted there. He responded that their use was widespread, even in major cities like London, and that it was rare not to see a local map displayed in a vestry. Continuing this point, Kelly felt that each parish in Ireland should submit its map for valuation purposes which could then be combined to form county maps. His high regard for the Board of Ordnance's department's skill was also apparent, suggesting, as had others, that they avoid undertaking the territorial survey:

> ... it seems wholly out of [the Ordnance Survey's] province to measure fields or lay down minute divisions, where every hedge and offset must be traced with the chain.

William Hyett, professor of military drawing, Woolwich

Kelly's evidence was followed by that of military surveyor William Hyett. Hyett had served as part of the Board of Ordnance's survey wing since 1805 under Colby's predecessor. In 1817 he had taken a position at the Royal Military College, Woolwich, as a professor of military drawing, which included topographic surveying.

Despite having served with the Ordnance Survey for over a decade, the professor disagreed with Colby's proposed sequence of events in Ireland. Instead, he followed the concept preferred by many of the Irish engineers, namely, that the territorial surveys should occur before the triangulation. He felt that this would be more advantageous, to reduce 'from a larger to a smaller scale than vice versa'. Hyett also thought that this order would allow supervisors to identify errors in fieldwork more easily, a point echoed by Griffith, Bald and Nimmo. It should be noted that neither Hyett nor others had mentioned the possibility of concurrent topographic and triangulation surveys, with the survey's total workforce remaining open for debate and dependent on civilian involvement.

Regarding survey detail, the professor believed that measuring to field level would be of greatest advantage for the valuation, but that townlands would be adequate. Unlike others, Hyett had little issue with employing civilians. He had spent time in Ireland during his career and met many 'country surveyors' who were fully competent. He did, however, warn of their limitations:

> [*Committee*] Do you think the common [Irish] country surveyor, would be qualified, without previous instruction, to make a map of a larger extent than a townland?
>
> [*Hyett*] Perhaps not, in some instances.

In his opinion, such technical weaknesses could be overcome if these surveyors were '… placed under the direction of some person of science, who would put their plans together, and under whose direction the survey should be made'. He also warned, that such 'country surveyors' would need to abandon the traditional use of circumferentors and adapt to theodolites from a perspective of accuracy.

Hyett's examination was significant not because of the questions asked but rather those that were avoided. His knowledge of cartography was evident given his employment in one of England's top military academies. Yet, he was never questioned on map design or content (outside the depth of detail). Additionally, the committee failed to enquire on the progress of Colby's cadets training, the topics they were studying, or Hyett's assessment of their capabilities. This was a significant missed opportunity, given the prominent role this same corps would soon play in Ireland. This absence also stands in marked contrast to the repeated questions asked about the qualities of Ireland's civilian surveyors. There is no evidence that such omissions were intentional. Instead, they reflected the often-haphazard nature of the committee's interrogations, with members obsessing on one detail at the expense of another. This brief discussion marked Hyett's only appearance.

Davies Gilbert, member of parliament for Bodmin

The final witness for the day was Davies Gilbert MP (b. 1767, d. 1839), mathematician, MP for Bodmin, Cornwall, and part of Spring Rice's select committee. As a member of the Royal Society with a talent for engineering, Gilbert's opinion continued the narrative of what his colleagues had heard earlier that day.

The MP's interview gives the impression of a self-imposed sense-checking exercise by the committee. Undoubtedly his contributions to the Royal Society elevated Gilbert's position among the witnesses to a par with Colby's or Kater's, though it should be noted he had limited knowledge of land

5.3. Davies Gilbert was one of the few members of Spring Rice's committee with scientific and mathematical knowledge. He helped sense-check much of the evidence presented to him and his colleagues. Henry Howard, *Engraving of Davies Gilbert* (London, n.d.).

surveying.[50] These three men were, however, in a different academic league to previous interviewees, and reflected the character both the committee and Board of Ordnance wished to project about the new survey. While Gilbert could add

50 Much of Gilbert's research was based on the history and culture of his native Cornwall,

little new information, he could instead help publicly verify ideas already suggested to Spring Rice.

For example, his initial point of evidence was in direct contrast to one made by Hyett. Agreeing with Colby and Kater, Gilbert firmly believed the triangulation should occur first, followed by the topographic survey. This point had acted as a wedge between two camps of technical witnesses. The Irish-based engineers preferred an immediate start to detail surveys while those aligned to scientific surveying preferred to wait until the triangulation network was established. Each stance had a self-serving element based on their respective goals, with the engineers likely to benefit most should their argument find favour. However, the combined force of Colby, Kater and now Gilbert certainly fell more in line with Westminster's vision of scientific mapping. In a fresh suggestion, Gilbert also proposed that townland surveys would be best taken independently of each other. This would avoid any propagation of error between neighbouring administrative areas and demonstrated his obvious understanding of the topic at hand.

Like Kelly, Gilbert felt that the detail measurement should take place as soon as possible after the triangulation, to avoid the 'great inconvenience' of the removal or vandalism of markers. The MP insisted that the surveys should be conducted using only theodolites and chains and that less accurate circumferentors be excluded entirely. Of note, he was also able to identify three large and highly accurate theodolites which he understood were suitable for the primary triangulation network – one already in Colby's possession, one in the Royal Society (that had originally belonged to General William Roy), and another owned by the Troughton company. The availability of such devices would help the survey of Ireland keep within budget by avoiding the expense of commissioning new instruments, at least initially.

Though admitting he 'was never [previously] concerned in surveying', Gilbert supported the hierarchical approach of engineers supervising a greater body of 'inferior surveyors'. Regardless, he displayed genuine concern about hiring a large number of junior civilian surveyors, commenting that 'it would be impossible for the greater part of these gentlemen to obtain any employment in their profession after the survey was completed'.

Gilbert's real expertise lay in mathematics. His knowledge of trigonometry was well in advance of his parliamentary colleagues. He therefore knew the

though he was highly active in parliamentary investigations on a wide number of subjects, as ascertained by his obituary. 'The numerous parliamentary investigations (particularly those connected with the arts and sciences) in which [Gilbert] took a prominent part, will form lasting memorials of his profound learning and indefatigable perseverance; and the application of his knowledge to practical purposes was attested by the active interest he took in most of our great national works.' *The Gentleman's Magazine*, 13 Jan. 1840.

influence baselines could have on the accuracy of a triangulation network. When asked directly if the length of a baseline could be determined more accurately through physical measurement than calculation, Gilbert responded that:

> I imagine a line can be measured, provided it is perfectly accessible, with more accuracy than it can be computed, but with enormous trouble and labour and expense. The baseline on Hounslow heath [measured in 1784 by Mudge] ... required several months in measuring and it was under five miles in length, whereas that line being accurately measured, other lines of equal or of manifold greater length might be computed, through the medium of trigonometry, in a very short time, and with, an accuracy ... as precise as that of the original line.

Gilbert's contributions provided the committee with a summary of the evidence heard over the previous days. He was likely the only committee member knowledgeable enough to provide such a service, his lack of direct surveying experience being of little hindrance compared to his familiarity with practical sciences and mathematics. Though the committee was nearing the end of its investigations such revision remained valuable.

EDGEWORTH'S INTERNATIONAL NETWORK, 31 MAY 1824[51]

With May drawing to a close, the committee welcomed up-and-coming civil engineer William Edgeworth (b. *c.*1794, d. 1829). Edgeworth, a native of Longford and the committee's youngest witness, was the son of scholar and engineer Richard Lovell Edgeworth (b. 1744, d. 1817), and brother of famed novelist Maria Edgeworth (b. 1768, d. 1849).[52] Like his fellow Irish engineers, he had much to say to Spring Rice concerning the upcoming survey, with the committee equally eager to hear about his acclaimed work in county surveying.

William Edgeworth, civil engineer

Like others before him, Edgeworth commenced his testimony by informing the committee about his professional background. He had begun his career as a junior surveyor with the Bogs Commission, working under his father who was

51 *Report of the select committee on the survey and valuation of Ireland*, pp 100–8.   **52** Maria Edgeworth and Spring Rice were frequent correspondents for over thirty years, Maria describing the MP as 'someone I like very much'. She would also meet Henry Kater and George Warburton, both of whom were also interviewed by the Spring Rice committee. Maria Edgeworth, *The life and*

one of its senior engineers, on par with Bald, Nimmo and Griffith. Since the mid-1810s he had used his father's academic connections to travel widely in England and Europe, taking every opportunity to expand his technical knowledge, including corresponding with Colby and Kater on their respective work. He had also been equally active at home, helping create well-received Grand Jury maps for counties Roscommon and his native Longford. Thanks to such projects, he was recognized as an up-and-coming star within Irish engineering and one whose experience would prove of great value to Spring Rice.

Edgeworth's work on Grand Jury maps was of particular interest. Each was conducted using triangulation techniques and with the best available equipment. Edgeworth had used a Troughton-made six-inch theodolite for his county maps, with his primary triangulation network points based 5–10 miles apart and measured to within 20 seconds angular tolerance.[53] This mention of measurement tolerance was one of the few times this critical aspect of surveying was cited during the entire course of the committee's investigation, its absence being notable for modern technical readers. The Roscommon project had been shared with Richard Griffith, Edgeworth being responsible for charting the northern portion of the county while his colleague took the southern half.

The young engineer was understandably proud of the results of both surveys. With some justification, he boasted to the committee that the Longford map had proven worthy of publication and that the Roscommon map was currently with engravers. Also, unlike many earlier witnesses, he was able to put a precise value on the cost of each project. Longford, for example, equated to 1½ pence per acre, resulting in an overall bill of £1,000 for the county.[54] Additionally, in a piece of foresight, Edgeworth's Roscommon survey had been connected to Bald's concurrent survey of Mayo, resulting in a high accuracy, pre-Ordnance triangulation network across a large part of Connacht. Such information was beneficial to the committee, with this network, alongside the inclusion of sub-county boundaries and estimated costs acting as a precursor to the work they envisaged would take place over the following years. Despite such enthusiasm, Colby had made it clear that he would conduct the triangulation independently, ignoring any pre-existing networks. Regardless of this hard line, Edgeworth had successfully impressed the committee with his experience in this field and the quality of his output.

---

letters of Maria Edgeworth, 2 vols (New York, 1895), ii, p. 426.   53 In Longford, for example, Edgeworth had used a triangulation network using prominent hills, windmills, and stately homes as reference points.   54 Paid for by parliament, 46 Geo. 3, c. 134.

5.4. William Edgeworth's 1813 four-part map of Co. Longford was a substantial achievement for the youngest engineer interviewed by the Spring Rice committee. William Edgeworth, *A map of the county of Longford* (London, 1813) (courtesy of The Placenames Committee/An Coimisiún Logainmneacha).

Questioning then moved to scale, a topic that had appeared intermittently over the past several weeks. Edgeworth suggested that 20 to 30 perches to an inch would be sufficient to present townlands, translating that to twelve inches to a mile – double that set by Colby. Subsequent questions from the committee attempted to steer Edgeworth back to using a six-inch scale, asking if it would be sufficient for valuation. Their witness agreed it would, though he believed that the larger the scale, the more accurate the final valuation. He also assured that doubling the scale would not equate to a doubling of costs.

Next in line for investigation was Edgeworth's use of local surveyors. This question had been asked of each Irish-based engineer so far, with Edgeworth adding his own opinion. He had employed a team of four surveyors for his county maps. Each had previously worked under his father and had been tasked with measuring to barony level in Longford and parish level in Roscommon. This group had found most territorial boundaries easy to determine in both counties, except when working in boggy terrain. The bishop of Elphin had also been highly cooperative by providing a helpful list of townlands per parish, which was then in use for local tithe collections. The committee was particularly curious as to how Edgeworth checked the accuracy of his surveyors' work. He replied that he had asked his surveyors to 'intersect all the principal and minor points that I was at the time trigonometrically determining'. If his and the surveyors' points did not align, then errors were easily exposed and their work adjusted accordingly. Accuracy was also reflected in the scale of the final map, Edgeworth clarifying that skill was as important in the office as in the field:

> [*Committee*] Is not a large scale easier for the surveyor [to draw]?
>
> [*Edgeworth*] If he is not a very neat draughtsman it is.

The committee remained keen to hear Edgeworth's advice as regards topography. He informed them that his county surveys had measured rivers, as they frequently acted as territorial boundaries. The exact height of hills or mountains had been avoided, but terrain had been represented by symbolic shading. He was, however, able to add some of his international experiences to this topic, being acquainted with the respective heads of the Neapolitan and Bavarian topographic surveys. Edgeworth had even visited Bavaria and had seen their near-finished survey in print, reinforcing Ireland's connection to a wider, pan-European surveying community. Producing a sample Bavarian map, Edgeworth described how it was used for both the sale of land and taxation purposes. Each map showed minuscule detail, including fields, houses, and even house numbers where available. It was produced at twelve inches to a mile, explaining his previous inclination toward that scale for Ireland. The Bavarians had also employed both a primary and secondary triangulation network similar to that intended by Colby, but had used an instrument called a plane table to fill in detail. Edgeworth was so impressed with the theodolites used for their triangulation network that he had purchased one from the prominent Reichenbach firm in Munich. A stronger recommendation for a foreign survey would be hard to find. A similar line concerning the survey of the Kingdom of Naples followed inquiries about Bavaria. Edgeworth was in correspondence with the Neapolitan survey's chief, Ferdinando Visconti (b. 1772, d. 1847), and described how their techniques differed from the Bavarians, namely calculation methods (see plate 15).

Given this experience, the committee asked what parts of an equivalent Irish survey Edgeworth would feel comfortable executing. He responded:

> I am competent to undertake any part of them; but I should prefer undertaking the secondary triangulation, and overseeing the accurate execution of the interior of a portion, say one province, for I am convinced the great triangulation can be in no hands, so good, as in Major Colby's, and the military engineers employed in the English and Scotch survey.

Edgeworth's comment echoed his peers, each of whom had openly recognizing Colby's expertise. However, he seems to have had a greater interest in participating in the survey than others.

Returning to Irish surveying, the young engineer felt that any local surveyors employed would need further instruction and better instruments to complete the detail. He disagreed with an idea proposed by the committee of using multiple baselines to speed up the project, stating that it would only be added effort without the same level of reward.

The tone of Edgeworth's responses changed notably when probed about existing survey resources in England and how quickly the Irish project could be completed. His answers became much shorter and sharper, as he wished 'to be clearly understood'. This likely came from his assertion that he could not vouch for the other men's work, being cautious of making potentially erroneous statements before a group of politicians and on public record. He reaffirmed, though, that wherever he had worked in Ireland he had received no resistance from the local populace. Admittedly sometimes cattle of 'an idle inhabitant' would damage his triangulation markers but he had felt safe in his day-to-day duties. Deploying a similar public relations approach as Nimmo, he generally found people left him alone:

> … but I must state, that I never went into the country with any force, never carried any firearms, always explained to them how far my works were likely to tend to their benefit.

The mention of weapons may have been indirect advice to Colby's officers to emphasize the scientific and social benefits of their work rather than its military nature. Despite such guidance, Edgeworth acknowledges that working in Ireland had inherent difficulties. These mainly were weather-related, as conditions were often worse than in England. This was especially true of the west coast where 'you must cover your instruments' due to the rain.[55]

As a concluding point, Edgeworth submitted a paper he had written for the Royal Irish Academy the previous year, based on a letter to Nimmo discussing his triangulation survey of Roscommon (see Appendix D).[56]

This was Edgeworth's only appearance before the committee, apart from a concise session in early June. It seems a pity that the talented engineer was interviewed in such depth only once, so late in the hearings, and that he had no opportunity to expand on his extensive local and international experience. His observations of equivalent European surveys were a rare gift matched by few witnesses, with his surveys of Longford and Roscommon being relevant to the upcoming project. Regardless, the committee had already heard much from Edgeworth's colleagues (namely Nimmo, Bald, and Griffith) and may have felt that any more would have led to repetition. Additionally, whatever measurements other European countries took within their borders was of topical interest, though it was not pivotal to the Irish cess question.

The committee had made substantial progress by the end of May. A wide range of practical and scientific-based topics had been reviewed, with some of Ireland's most prominent engineers proving their worth. The qualities of Ireland's land surveyors had been emphasized, though it was clear that some up-skilling and re-equipping would be necessary. Alternative sequences of the survey's execution had been proposed and rationalized, with several civilian witnesses understandably holding out hope for senior positions. The extent of Ireland's administrative and cartographic record, both ancient and modern, had also been assessed, being as much use to modern readers as it was to the committee. While impressive, Colby's original assertation meant that such records would only be used for consultation. At this stage, the same could also be argued for the services of Ireland's engineers, irrespective of whatever personal expectations they held.

---

55 Once the survey began, Colby soon developed methods of ensuring his men did not let adverse weather damage fragile equipment, as mentioned by one of his subordinates; 'When the survey first commenced, the wind was continually blowing down instruments, which led General Colby to say that if the wind blew down any more the men should pay for them. Such was the sympathy between the wind and the men that it ceased, and did not blow down any more.' Captain G.A. Leach to Captain B.A. Wilkinson, 20 June 1855, quoted in Andrews, *Paper landscape*, p. 63. 56 Alexander Nimmo, 'A letter from William Edgeworth to Alexander Nimmo, 1823', *The Transactions of the Royal Irish Academy*, xiv (Dublin, 1825), 63.

CHAPTER SIX

The survey and valuation of Ireland, June 1824

June marked the final month of the committee's investigation. Only three meetings were held before their report was published on the 21st with many open subjects resolved in the intervening days. Several recent witnesses would return during this period, though there was still sufficient scope to hear from new engineers, cartographers, and, at last, a professional valuer.

As they began this final phase of interviews, the committee turned to two surveying experts from radically different theatres: Irish civil engineer David Aher (b. 1780, d. 1842) and triangulation specialist and Ordnance surveyor James Gardner. Each had valuable experience and was well-regarded within their respective professional communities. By this stage of the investigations, however, Spring Rice and his colleagues appear to have formulated (though not vocalized) a high-level plan for the survey and valuation of Ireland. Gardner and Aher's evidence would help reinforce this master plan.

David Aher, civil engineer

David Aher was the first to present for the day. He started with the usual summary, explaining that he had commenced his career as a land surveyor before drifting into civil engineering. Despite this shift in interest, he remained proud of his surveying roots, namely his association with 'the French school of [John] Rocque'. The engineer was thus able to trace his professional lineage to the elite of Irish commercial surveying, while demonstrating his capabilities in the increasingly prominent field of engineering.

Expanding on his network of connections, Aher described how he had worked under the distinguished engineer Major Alexander Taylor[2] before being

---

1 *Report of the select committee on the survey and valuation of Ireland*, pp 108–14. 2 Taylor was an engineer, surveyor, and cartographer who was part of a group of Scot's surveyors that established themselves in Ireland during the 1770s. An officer in the Royal Engineers, he worked on numerous projects around Ireland, often in partnership with other officers such as Andrew Skinner and Charles Vallancey. Taylor and Skinner produced a popular book, *Maps of the roads of Ireland in 1788*. Andrews, *Plantation acres*, p. 356; O'Cionnaith, *Land surveying*, p. 171.

hired by the Grand Canal company around 1803. Like many of similar professional rank, he had later found employment with the Bogs Commission, though had failed to achieve the acclaim of his colleagues Nimmo, Bald or Griffith. At the time of his interview, he was still working as an engineer and was employed at the Castlecomer Collieries in Kilkenny.

When asked if he had ever been involved 'in any considerable territorial surveys,' Aher recollected his 1812 Grand Jury survey of Co. Kilkenny. Still incomplete by 1824, this survey had cost around 2 pence per Irish acre (£2,480 for the county) and had been funded through private and public means. Of particular relevance was this map's inclusion of townlands, which Aher felt were the key to administrative mapping. During this survey, he found most townlands to be around 300 acres in size, though some extended up to 2,000. Aher also observed that their boundaries frequently matched those of estates, reflective of confiscation and settlement patterns of the seventeenth century. Accordingly, he believed such boundaries should be well-known to local bailiffs, except in bog and mountain regions.

Aher preferred a blank slate from which to work during his Kilkenny survey, matching Colby's approach to historical data. Accordingly, he had not used the Down Survey as a guide. Unusually, he had initially avoided triangulation methods due to 'not having at the time an instrument of sufficient accuracy'. This was later rectified when he was sent a more accurate instrument by Taylor. Overall, the engineer felt that this mixed measurement process worked well and that he could ascertain the quality of his earlier measurements by comparing them to his later-surveyed triangulation points. Throughout, Aher had been assisted by his surveyor brother-in-law, Hill Clements (and Clements's two sons), emphasizing the long-established familial nature of surveying in Ireland.[3]

The semi-application of triangulation control ensured that Aher's Kilkenny survey would not meet the committee's requirements. His valuation work near Castlecomer, however, piqued their interest. This subject had so far received little attention in the committee's meetings despite being the ultimate goal of the Irish survey. Aher was particularly proud of the efficiency of his valuation methods. For example, he avoided surveys of individual fields if the total area of a townland was of the same quality of land (and therefore the same value), making his efforts more efficient. The committee pushed him further on this point, likely stemming from Spring Rice's own evidence given in March on the changeable nature of fields in Ireland. Aher admitted that much of this cadastral work was based on pre-existing surveys, which were supplied to him (with some reluctance) by tenant farmers:

3 O'Cionnaith, *Mapping, measurement and metropolis*, p. 17.

[*Committee*] Were the farmers always willing to produce their maps?

[*Aher*] In some instances they were unwilling to produce their maps until we sent persons to make surveys of the small farms [and thus correct any historic errors]; in a few days after this the other occupiers gave us every information and produced their maps and leases.

Aher's threat to re-survey holdings may have explained the greater resistance he experienced compared to Nimmo in Galway and Edgeworth in Roscommon. Such opposition may have also been due to underlying regional differences rather than solely due to his approach. For instance, he regularly found his triangulation markers disturbed as he 'commenced my operations at a period when the minds of the lower classes were much agitated', indicative of the localized rural strife that frequently occurred across the country. However, like previous interviewees, he believed that local paranoia could be combatted through patience, as 'the peasantry imaged that it was some military operation that [he] was preparing against them'.

Aher's testimony touched on many points previously heard by the committee. There were obviously elements of his work that they disliked, notably his patchy triangulation efforts in Kilkenny, though his inclusion of townlands was a welcome rarity. The fact that he was not examined on the minutia of his county survey work compared to Edgeworth or Griffith indicated that, by this stage, the committee felt they had been sufficiently briefed on the topic.

James Gardner, trigonometric surveyor, Ordnance Survey

James Gardner was next to present evidence. A sixteen-year veteran of the Ordnance Survey, Gardner was a specialist in triangulation networks and served as Colby's senior assistant. Furthermore, he had been granted licence in 1823 to become the official retailer of Ordnance mapping in England, his appointment in thanks to strong recommendations from Colby. In addition to this expertise and close association with Colby, he also seems to have guessed (or was briefed on) what the committee's line of questioning would be, preparing answers accordingly. Such suspicious clarity was obvious from the outset of his interview. For example, he easily proposed eighty primary triangulation control points for the entire island, an unusually precise figure that no other witness had volunteered to date.

This precision was also evident in responses to other queries. For instance, Gardner advised that reference points should be spaced up to every five hundred acres if townlands were to be included. The greater the spacing between points, the less time would be necessary to compute the entire network. As many witnesses had stated that townlands were usually around three hundred acres in size, Gardner's suggestion did much to ease the committee's mind by balancing the need for accuracy against speed. When asked in a follow-up question if the placement of such points could be extended down to townland level, he responded that such an incredibly dense network would require an individual 188 years to complete (projected to end in 2012). Of that time, eight-and-a-half years would be required to fill out the calculations if written at the phenomenal rate of 18,000 words per day. In essence, including a triangulation point per townland would be impractical, and his suggested lower-density network would still be sufficient.

Gardner spoke with confidence on all subjects raised about triangulation. He helped clarify that the survey's initial baseline measurement could not be accurately measured without specialized equipment and that a standard surveyor's chain would not be sufficient. If standard chains were used for this critical measurement, they would introduce an error fifteen times larger than by 'the most improved instrument'. Echoing other Ordnance witnesses, he also wanted to avoid using 'common field surveyors' where possible and encouraged the employment of those familiar with the complexities of triangulation measurements only. His reasoning was logical, arguing that the entire project depended on the accurate execution of a nationwide network, which would facilitate the survey's topographic and territorial elements. The baseline alone would take an extended period to measure and require methods not normally associated with commercial surveying. It was thus best left to Colby's supervision. That the Ordnance Survey would manage the primary triangulation network was certain at this stage of the investigation. No witness had argued against this point, confirming Wellesley's initial request in February. This was highlighted in recent evidence over the previous days, with its focus on how topographic and territorial data could be gathered rather than concerns over triangulation. Gardener's input reinforced such opinions.

With the committee nearing the end of its inquiry, Spring Rice and his colleagues now began to concentrate on the survey sequence and to what depth the Ordnance involvement would go. Gardner would return to continue his evidence the following day.

ONE ORGANIZATION, ONE SURVEY, 2 JUNE 1824[4]

Continuing his testimony, Gardener returned to delve further into the intricacies of triangulation. This meeting would also prove pivotal in exposing

4 *Report of the select committee on the survey and valuation of Ireland*, pp 114–16.

the committee's intentions regarding Colby's staff in Ireland, one that had so far only been implied rather than stated clearly. Of immediate concern was managing the twin pillars of triangulation and topographic detail. Gardner's evidence would prove authoritative on the former, with subsequent witnesses reinforcing the committee's views on the latter. Once agreed, the more topical issues of who would record townland bounds could then be resolved.

James Gardener, trigonometric surveyor, Ordnance Survey

Spring Rice resumed by asking Gardner how long the primary triangulation of Ireland would take if conducted in a 'masterly manner'. Gardener's response was succinct, much like Colby, replying that it would be completed 'in eight to ten years'. Per his previous day's evidence, his suspiciously accurate response indicates that he was aware of what questions he would be asked, working out technical details and accompanying timelines beforehand. When questioned about resources needed for the triangulation element, for instance, Gardener felt it would take 'ten persons about 35 years to fix two reference points per 100 acres across Ireland'. He also warned that the risk of error would increase if more teams were employed to speed up this process, as supervision would undoubtedly be weakened. Following this theme, the committee then enquired what would happen if such points were established at a parochial (approx. 6–7,000 acres) rather than townlands (approx. 1–300 acres) level. Again, Gardner believed this would require a significant number of calculations but that parochial points could be determined faster.

With these parameters in place, a detailed exploration of various scenarios followed, including the potential of the Board of Ordnance also taking charge of the topographical element. To date, it was generally agreed that Colby's men would execute the triangulation. However, as to who would be tasked with filling up the triangles with physical detail was more open-ended. The committee had spent significant effort over the previous weeks ascertaining the qualities of Ireland's resident surveying community and their ability to assist in this task. Yet, from the outset, Colby had muddied the waters by raising concerns about including non-Ordnance survey data at any point in the project. A single management system for the entire survey, therefore, was of interest to him. Gardner openly agreed with what his superior had hinted at, stating that if the Ordnance took complete charge of the topographic survey, then the resulting maps would be as accurate as the triangulation element. This pivotal point concluded Gardner's testimony. While his second day of questioning proved much shorter than his first, Gardner again demonstrated his value as one of the most informed experts on large triangulation networks. Perhaps of greater importance, the topic of sole ownership of the project falling to Colby was now out in the open.

William Edgeworth, Major Thomas Colby, William Bald, David Aher, various roles

After completing their interview with Gardner, the committee then conducted several short discussions with previous interviewees, namely Edgeworth, Colby, Bald and Aher. The selection of the three Irish engineers was probably due to pragmatic reasons rather than a reflection of their seniority over their colleagues. Each had been recently interviewed, with earlier witnesses such as Griffith and Nimmo likely no longer present in London. It fell to them to voice their profession's final conclusions.

The committee's line of questioning led from where Gardner had left off, revolving around the nature of the Ordnance's future role. In this manner, it was more concise than the usual meandering repertoire; each witness was asked semi-standardized and comparable questions in turn. Going first, Edgeworth was questioned on the evolution of the Ordnance's role from pure triangulation to overall control of the project. He reaffirmed his belief that the Ordnance's existing staff were so specialized and in such high need (both in Britain and Ireland) that the decision of their level of involvement should be left to them:

> If the ordnance could spare an adequate time for the determination of the [townland] boundaries, and for surveying the natural features of the country, it would certainly be a saving of expense.

Next came Colby. He remained as dismissive as ever of the idea of including survey data outside of his control as part of a general scientific map. This stance left little option but to have the Ordnance conduct the topographic elements themself. Bald fully agreed, arguing that if non-coordinated local surveys were incorporated, both the price and difficulty of the entire project would increase. When asked if it would be cheaper if both triangulation and topographic portions were combined under one organization, he responded 'Of course'. Last to comment was Aher, echoing Bald's response on reducing difficulty and cost by having a single authority in charge of the project.

Overall, the Irish engineers displayed immense trust in the Ordnance's capabilities, with their only concern being the available workforce. Colby's path toward management of the survey was clear. The following day, the committee announced in newspapers that a trigonometrical-based survey of Ireland 'should be forthwith vigorously carried into effect', advising their fellow MPs to take 'adequate measures' accordingly.[5] Mention of civilian contributions to the boundary element were notably avoided, but Colby still had more to add.

---

5 *Freeman's Journal*, 3 June 1824.

This meeting proved to be the penultimate of Spring Rice's committee. Over the previous months, the parliamentarians had heard expert testimony covering various subjects. The importance of the 2 June meeting lay in its line of questioning, the committee giving clear hints as to where their conclusions concerning Ordnance's role lay. The final meeting would take place over a week later, giving each committee member the time to collect their thoughts before giving their (now) informed opinion on the entire project.

THE FINAL MEETING – OPINIONS, CONCLUSIONS, 10 JUNE 1824[6]

The last meeting of the Spring Rice committee's investigations took place on 10 June 1824, a day that would see the final pieces of evidence entered and, ultimately, expose each committee member's views. Admittedly, the testimonies given on this final day had little impact on overall conclusions, though it gave each member, as well as Colby, a chance to clarify some outstanding issues. However, before the superintendent of the Ordnance Survey could share his last thoughts, the committee surprisingly called a new witness, valuer Adam Murray.

Adam Murray, valuer

Despite valuation being the aim of the new survey of Ireland, it had yet to be discussed in meaningful detail. By June, it was obvious to all that the valuation of Ireland would have to wait until the topographical and territorial surveys were complete. Murray's appearance, therefore, allowed Spring Rice to legitimately say he had interviewed at least one professional valuer, irrespective of his eleventh-hour addition. While others, notably Griffith, had been able to outline valuation techniques, this information had been part of a broader testimony. By contrast, Murray focused exclusively on this issue.

Little is known of Murray outside of his testimony. By this point in his career, he had been a surveyor with the Land Revenue Commissioners in England for around six years and had worked in valuation since the 1790s. Despite this extensive experience, his testimony to Spring Rice frequently wandered, and his opinions seemed less expert than the committee hoped for. Regardless, the members remained interested in his views.

His previous involvement in Ireland was limited to one valuation project on the Locke estate in Co. Kerry.[7] Working on behalf of the owner, Murray

6 *Report of the select committee on the survey and valuation of Ireland*, pp 117–25.   7 This estate was located near Tralee, Co. Kerry. In 1840, the Ordnance Survey noted that Murray was the estate's agent, on behalf of its owner, William Locke. At the time, Locke was living in Paris, with Murray running the lands remotely from London. *Ordnance Survey name books, Co. Kerry*, vol. 2, p. 102.

divided the estate into four classes, including two different types of arable land. In total, this valuation took him six weeks and covered thirteen thousand acres. Throughout, his efforts to determine townland boundaries proved fruitless as no local would assist him. This was in marked contrast to the experiences of others working with rural communities, such as Nimmo or Edgeworth. They had found assistance forthcoming once they had explained what they were doing, though Murray failed to outline the cause of resistance to his queries. He did, though, have access to older maps of the estate, which he used to base his valuations, as 'I was not directed by my employer to make a survey and measurement of all his estate'.

Murray's expertise slowly diminished as questioning continued. His unusual opinions on surveying equipment raised eyebrows among committee members – notably, his unconventional stance that angles taken with a theodolite were nowhere near as accurate as those taken with a surveyor's chain. He was, however, familiar with the Ordnance Survey of Britain, correctly noting that its format would be unsuitable for valuation due to the lack of local boundaries. On a practical note, Murray deemed that a smaller scale would be of greater use to valuers as 'you have less paper to carry with you into the field'. Conspicuously, he did not mention the resulting generalization of map detail, which would make the valuers work harder, a point that underlined the proposed six-inch to a-mile scale for Ireland. This logic also conflicted with his following argument, telling the committee that he liked to assess land on a field-by-field basis to value an estate. Thus, he wanted smaller-scale maps with more information crammed into them.

Despite his apparent limited experience in Ireland, Murray felt confident to give the committee his opinion between Irish and English work conditions. Most conspicuous was the prevalence of local country surveyors in Ireland:

> [There] are men to carry your instruments; in every parish there are surveyors; people, that if they are not accurate surveyors have been accustomed to survey land, which would be a great assistance in running your lines, and you measure a line much cheaper than if you could only get people that have never had any practice.

When follow-up questions were asked regarding the quality of these local surveyors, Murray responded that he found their work satisfactory but, in the intervening years, had entirely forgotten their names.

Major Thomas Colby, Ordnance Survey

The committee then called Colby back for his final interview. This would be the last evidence they would hear before adjourning to compile their report. Colby's interview was required to clarify several outstanding issues before each committee member publicly gave his final opinion on the project. As usual, the Major was direct, informed, and confident throughout.

To begin, he was against the idea suggested by several witnesses that detail surveys should start before the triangulation network, believing the results would require 'considerable examination and additional expense'. He observed that if townland surveys were to be produced as standalone maps, then the triangulation element would be of little use. He was also reluctant to incorporate recently executed (though admittedly high-quality) survey data for Mayo by Bald and Roscommon by Edgeworth and Griffith in case there were any underlying issues not immediately obvious. This stance emphasized Colby's unwavering caution surrounding non-Ordnance data.

When asked if fields could be included if the survey's scale was increased from six to twelve inches, Colby replied:

> I should think it would either increase the time very much or be attended with another inconvenience, namely, the creating [of] a large body of surveyors, who would, when the work was completed, be thrown entirely out of employ.[8]

The committee pursued this point by asking how the French could complete a twelve-inch survey for the same purpose in just seven years? Colby shot back that the French had made use of an extensive pre-prepared network that was entirely missing in Ireland. Suitably corrected, they continued their comparison with foreign surveys, by asking how the Bavarians could complete an even more detailed survey in just twelve years. Knowing his limits, Colby answered that he was not familiar with the 'general nature of the surface of Bavaria to answer the question'.

The committee then laid before Colby their two primary options for the survey. The first combined a scientific survey (triangulation) with the measurement of townland boundaries and topographic detail, all under the command of one organization. The second would see two distinct operations under unconnected management. In this latter scenario, the Board of Ordnance would undertake the triangulation and topographic portions, as they had in Britain, with a new civilian organization responsible for the territorial and

8 This was a similar concern as Gilbert's, see above, p. 128.

valuation elements. As the second option would require boundary information to be fitted into existing mapping, Colby explained that replotting data from original field books would simply double the effort. The paper on which the original surveys were drawn would invariably expand and contract over time due to changes in heat and moisture, causing even further potential for error. This, when also combined with expected inaccuracies with the initial fieldwork, would reduce precision to such an extent that errors could not be compensated for by adjusting the triangulation network. Given the scientific desires of Colby and the committee, it was obvious that the MPs were in favour of the first option and were looking for a clear argument as to why the second, split-command alternative would be more time-consuming, complicated, and expensive.

When asked if the proposed survey should follow the Bogs Commission method of dividing the country into separate divisions, Colby again clarified that this too would require extensive reworking to fit a national model. Ireland would need to be surveyed as one entity to ensure equal accuracy. He also stressed that even if divided into districts, an island-wide triangulation survey would still first be needed.

Major Colby had laid out his vision of the entire project falling under one command: his. Admittedly this was a different standpoint from the one he had initially taken in March where he had shown less interest in the territorial aspect. The evidence of other witnesses however had done much to assure him that townland bounds were generally well known. Though Wellington had concerns, Colby would have no problem in measuring townland boundaries, but he would need someone (i.e. civilians) to identify them first. With these final remarks, Colby had yet again proven himself to be the leading witness examined, evident in the attention the committee paid to his statements.

COMMITTEE MEMBERS' CONCLUSIONS

Following Colby's appearance, each committee member was asked to give their opinion, for the record, on how the survey and valuation should be managed. These judgments were not necessary for the eventual parliamentary report, later published on 21 June, but were a very brief sense-check of the evidence heard over the previous months. The statements, given by each member in turn, can be divided into two separate categories: thoughts on the primary territorial division to which the survey would be conducted (parish, townland, etc.) and how the project should be managed. The subject of valuation did not feature in these short reviews, nor did the sequence of triangulation versus detail surveys (evidently giving way to Colby's stance earlier that day).

The use of townlands as the smallest territorial division received broad support. Committee member William Fitzgerald thought they were 'indispensably necessary', a point echoed by Dominick Browne and Lord Oxmantown. Spring Rice felt that if any other division was used, the entire project would be '… utterly incomplete for the purposes for which the Committee has been appointed'. Croker altered his initial position given in March, based on the use of baronies, to one more in line with his colleagues' opinions. No mention was given as to how the boundaries would be identified, only that they should be included in the final mapping. Therefore, the Irish landscape's immediate future was provisionally set at townland level (though field detail would eventually supplant it once the survey began).

Management of the project (triangulation, topographic and territorial surveys combined) also met with near-total agreement, though there remained some disparity. Browne wanted the Board of Ordnance 'by all means' to be in charge, a view echoed by fellow committee member James Grattan. The lord lieutenant of Ireland, Richard Wellesley, unsurprisingly had 'no hesitation' in Colby's overall command with Spring Rice and Newport both stating that the Board of Ordnance would be efficient, economical and accurate. By contrast, Oxmantown felt there was scope for topographic surveys to be kept independent of Colby. Croker believed that Ordnance teams would require the assistance of 'local surveyors, and even of the local magistrates'. He was last to give his opinion, providing a clear answer in support of Colby and his staff:

> [*Committee*] When the boundaries of parishes and townlands are so ascertained, you would still recommend the laying down of those boundaries under the authority of the Ordnance?
>
> [*Croker*] Certainly.

This position was in clear contradiction of Wellington's opinion regarding the use of his men. The Field Marshal's priority remained fixed on a duplication of the British survey, with local concerns, such as townlands boundaries, not to involve Colby. Despite such stipulations, Colby had proven he would not follow Wellington's lead mindlessly. He was an experienced officer with a proven capability of taking charge when it came to the needs of the Ordnance Survey in Britain. From the outset of the Spring Rice committee, Colby had stated that he was willing to measure territorial boundaries in Ireland if he could be suitably persuaded that others could correctly identify them.[9] The

---

9 12 Nov. 1824. Colby to Goulburn (NAI CSO/RP/1824/1950). Colby mentioned that he would not 'direct the surveyors to insert any parts of boundaries which are not definitely marked on the ground.'

weight of evidence, provided by engineers such Nimmo, Bald and Edgeworth, along with that of police constable Warburton, had convinced him that this element would be possible, though would have to involve non-military staff.

The future of Irish surveying and mapping was thus permanently changed. The path was virtually cleared for the Board of Ordnance, under Thomas Colby, to conduct a six-inch townland survey of the entire island. The involvement of Irish engineers and surveyors was kept on the table, though the likelihood of them being part of Colby's plan remained unknown.

REPORT FROM THE SELECT COMMITTEE ON THE SURVEY AND
VALUATION OF IRELAND, 21 JUNE 1824

After four months of interviews and questioning, Spring Rice could finally bring his findings before parliament. The published document consisted of a primary ten-page overview, various supportive appendices, and a substantial archive of the committee's minutes. The report summarized all relevant evidence that had been presented, thematically condensed based on how it aided the committee in reaching its conclusions. Though parliamentary support was Spring Rice's ultimate target, there also remained one additional obstacle: Wellington. The Field Marshal remained in charge of Ordnance resources and was Colby's commanding officer. His direct backing was still required for tangible success in Ireland.

Accordingly, Spring Rice decided to approach Wellington directly in the days before the report's publication. If the two men could resolve any of the misunderstandings face-to-face, then the likelihood of the report's success would increase significantly. It was a gamble by Spring Rice. However, it was wiser to resolve any difference in private than on the floor of the House of Commons. Wellington had probably been kept abreast of the committee's proceedings by Colby and Wellesley, so undoubtedly had a better-formed idea of the problem than in February. Likewise, Spring Rice was also in a far stronger position than before, supported by the testimony of his expert witnesses.

Recalling his visit to Wellington many years later, Spring Rice stated that he was 'kindly' received by the duke. The territorial element continued to be the main topic of concern between the two men and was, understandably, the centre of their conversation. Wellington began by re-explaining his issue with Ordnance officers being asked to record features 'of a territorial nature rather than the natural geography of the country'. Should their measurements differ from that of landowners, then Wellington feared that his department would be dragged into the undesirable legal minefield of property disputes. Understandably, this was a realm professional soldiers were 'little fitted for'.[10] He also reminded Spring Rice of Wellesley's concerns over civilian surveyors and that his men could not take orders from private practitioners. To counter Wellington's arguments, Spring Rice presented him with the committee's findings, being the opinions of those 'whose knowledge of Ireland he placed … full reliance'. The committee, and Colby, had been convinced that information on townland bounds was readily known throughout the country. Unfortunately, this information was so poorly documented in historical maps, or official records, that local knowledge was the only suitable alternative. Civilians would thus be more suitable for this task than Ordnance officers. Though the discussion was likely more heated than Spring Rice chose to recall, Wellington eventually relented, swayed by the weight of evidence supporting the inclusion of townlands.[11] The format of the Ordnance Survey of Ireland was thus set.

The report sets the scene

With the duke suitably placated, the report was officially presented to parliament on Monday, 21 June. It opened with a summation of the cess issue, referring to various testimonies to explain the problem and showing how a lack of accurate mapping amplified its impact. This synopsis included an outline of the different types of territorial divisions in Ireland, describing the archaic system of townlands, ploughlands etc., and the lack of suitable records concerning their bounds. The recommended solution, as stated, was a new survey conducted to townland level using the latest scientific methods and technology.

An overview of national surveys was conveniently provided in the report's opening pages. This was intended to show that Ireland had been frequently mapped in the past but that such historic information was no longer suitable. It also assured readers that the new survey would not be punitive, in contrast to earlier schemes. The opening outline also included details of similar surveys in France, Bavaria and Naples, demonstrating that the creation of a scientific-grade national survey had, by the 1820s, become part of good governance.

The solution, as reached by the committee, was given in two central themes: first, recommendations on the survey in its entirety (triangulation, topography, and territorial bounds), and second, the valuation.

---

10 Portlock, *Memoir*, p. 195.   11 Evidence of Lord Monteagle, *Report from the select committee on Ordnance Survey* (Ireland), p. 26.

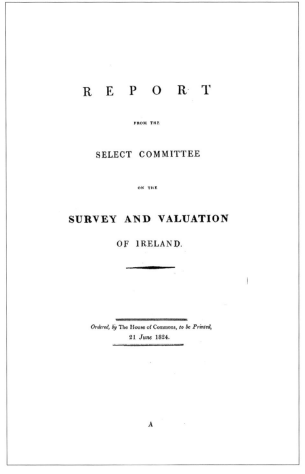

REPORT

FROM THE

SELECT COMMITTEE

ON THE

SURVEY AND VALUATION

OF IRELAND.

Ordered, by The House of Commons, *to be Printed*,
21 *June* 1824.

A

6.1. The cover page of
the *Report from the select
committee on the survey and
valuation of Ireland,*
presented to the House
of Commons on 21 June
1824 (private collection).

The report noted that the new survey should be conducted to townland
level. This conclusion was felt to be the best solution, providing information
detailed enough for accurate valuation but not so complex that the project's
timeline would become extravagant:

> It is obvious, that if a baronial or even a parochial subdivision were alone
> to be affected, sufficient data would not be furnished for the
> apportionment of the local taxes; and if, on the other hand, a survey by
> fields were to be undertaken, as in France and Bavaria, the expense of such
> a work would be augmented, and its completion postponed. A Survey by
> Townlands appears to your committee to be the rational medium between
> these two extremes.

Evidence from Griffith, Nimmo and others, as well as, those familiar with national surveys, such as Colby, had convinced the committee on the use of these small administrative areas. The collective argument, put forth by multiple witnesses, that an Ordnance Survey of Britain-style map for Ireland would prove 'insufficient for the purposes of valuation' had clearly been heard. The intended survey would therefore be a very different entity from its British equivalent.

The committee reassured readers that the process of correctly identifying townland boundaries was achievable. This would invariably involve local civilian assistance though the report did not dwell on this potentially sensitive issue. It did, however, explicitly refer to Colby's confidence that such divisions could be included in the mapping, 'provided the boundaries were set out'. The report also emphasized that should delays and difficulties in identifying townlands become apparent, then that concept would be abandoned.

An Ordnance Survey of Ireland

Management of the entire project by the Board of Ordnance received a glowing recommendation in the report. The committee could not 'conceive any other authority so well calculated to ensure the scientific accuracy and unity of principle which ought to distinguish a great national work'. The existing Ordnance team, though small, was experienced and well-equipped. It also fell under military command, thus creating accountability more than could be expected from civilian management. Due to Wellington's last-minute concession, the mapping of townlands would now fall under the Ordnance's control though others would first have to identify them. The report emphasized that consulting townland surveys of non-Ordnance origin would be 'a sacrifice of time, convenience and economy', thus cementing support for Colby.

The report urged that relevant legislation be enforced (46 Geo. III) to aid the project, requiring each Irish Grand Jury to tabulate townlands within their respective districts. This information would create a reference guide for Colby and his subordinates to work from. Efficiency could also be gained if the Ordnance was given access to existing cartographic records, including the Down Survey, 'however imperfect' such sources were. Hope also remained that private landlords and local authorities would provide 'zealous cooperation' once the goals of the project were understood.

It was noted in the report that the survey of Britain had been in operation for over three decades but was only two-thirds complete. Though clarifying that some of this delay was due to the Napoleonic wars, the same time frame could obviously not be taken for Ireland. As a result, the committee advised that the

Ordnance Survey of Ireland should have greater scope to hire whatever staff they needed to expedite the project, including civilians. They also observed that due to the efforts of the Bogs Commission, Ireland had an established 'school of scientific topography'. If their expertise was needed, these specialists would make ideal candidates. No mention was made of triangulation work previously conducted by the Bogs Commission across large parts of the island, this aspect was, evidently, of insignificance to the new survey. Regardless, recognizing the Bogs Commission and its positive impact was an important acknowledgment of Ireland's engineering community, and a substantial endorsement of Nimmo, Griffith, Edgeworth and others.

The report's recommendations on final mapping were surprisingly brief. The series was to be based on a scale of six inches to a mile for the entire island and doubled to twelve inches for cities and 'great towns'. Nothing was mentioned regarding the similarity, and convenience, between the proposed six-inch scale and the forty perches to an inch traditionally used. Instead, the rationale for this recommendation came from the Ordnance's previous large-scale work in Kent, where six inches had been applied in preference to the usual two-inch scale. Additional topographic features, such as the altitude of mountains, 'as well as the boundary of the enclosed [sic] lands, whether bog, mountain or rock', were also to be included. Other decisions on cartographic content were left entirely to Colby.

In an uncharacteristically negative tone, the report found existing maritime charts of the Irish coast 'inaccurate and unsatisfactory'. To this end, the committee believed that further cooperation between the Admiralty and the Board of Ordnance would be in the public interest and result in improved shipping safety. This point was due to Croker's ongoing calls for improved charts and the Admiralty's follow-up letter, the potential for expanding the survey to an ever-wider field of interests being evident.

The survey was intended to be the beginning of a new era in Irish mapping. To emphasize its authority, the committee believed it 'should supersede all local topographic proceedings, whether under the authority of Grand Juries or otherwise'. In short, the Ordnance Survey of Ireland was to be the official cartographic resource for the country. Despite noting the quality of work of some county surveys, such as in Roscommon (Griffith and Edgeworth), Mayo (Bald) and Kilkenny (Aher), the committee believed that all other county maps were imperfect and unfit for purpose. The mix of scales, styles and accuracies found between these records would therefore be replaced by a single, homogenous, centralized source, under the remit of one organization. This statement would have significant implications for the involvement of Ireland's civil engineers in county mapping, with near immediate effect.

To support his conclusions, Spring Rice also included several appendices to the committee's findings.[12] These included an abridged copy of an 1815 investigation on Grand Jury tax returns, which added context to the issue of cess inequalities. Similarly, appendices on the Down Survey, the *cadastre* of Savoy, and even the Doomsday Book linked the historical importance of mapping with good governance. Of greatest use to readers, however, was the inclusion of Griffith's plan for a survey of Ireland. As mentioned during his 12 May testimony, Griffith demonstrated that he had a firm understanding of how sub-county boundaries could be incorporated into a large-scale survey. Though relatively short, Griffith's thesis proved he had spent considerable time studying this issue. The remaining statistical data contained within the appendices outlined the extent of Irish civil administration and emphasized the size of the task awaiting Colby.

As the project still required parliamentary sanction, the report's authors remained eager to note the new survey's potential commercial benefits. They drew attention to the Bavarian system, where landowners could purchase maps relevant to their property, calling it 'not an ineligible one'. The future Irish survey was anticipated to have even greater potential for 'private utility' if valuation and census data were also included, the committee being:

> … inclined to hope they may furnish individual proprietors, at a moderate price, whether inhabitants or absentees, with valuable information respecting the condition of their estates, and the best means of improving them.

Irrespective of its detail, there were many areas where the report remained glaringly vague. Andrews rightly notes that the true limits of the report were 'narrow', with a marked difference in focus between the minutes and final submission.[13] As a result, little had been clarified concerning the survey's expected accuracy or design of mapping. While Colby had been assigned the measurement of townlands, he had been given no clear instructions on how to perform this task or how he was to interact with those expected to identify these bounds. Regardless, this once thorny issue had at least reached a compromise suitable to Wellington, Spring Rice and Colby.

---

12 The report's appendices included —'*Extracts from a report of a parliamentary committee on Grand Jury tax presentments (1815)*', pp 126–7; '*Report of the committee of the commissioners on the Public Records of Ireland, concerning the condition of the Down Survey (1813)*', pp 128–35; a short overview of the '*Cadastre of Savoy*' (in French), p. 137; '*Extract from the Saxon Chronicle, respecting the Doomsday Book*', p. 137; '*Mr* [Richard] *Griffith's plan for executing the proposed survey and valuation of Ireland*', pp 138–9; an extensive record of '*county tax returns of Irish baronies, parishes and townlands*', pp 156–374; and sample forms for a '*general statistical return*' and '*county returns*', p. 381.   13 Andrews, *Paper landscape*, p. 29.

Rather more alarm could be portioned to the report's brief conclusions concerning valuation. A general topographic survey would keep both the Admiralty and Whitehall happy but reform was still needed for the Irish landholder. In an almost remorseful tone, the report openly admitted that there was yet no detailed plan in place for the eventual valuation, but the committee members could 'suggest some leading general principles'. These would be based on a fixed and uniform standard, allowing seamless assessment under the mandate of a single central authority. Once established, valuations would undergo frequent checks to ensure that the system remained up-to-date, thereby avoiding the problems that had plagued previous methods. It was obvious to all involved that the mapping and territorial aspects of the survey would take several years, with the committee hoping that further investigations on valuation would have the input of the Grand Juries, and landowners.

Ending his review, Spring Rice again stated how different this new venture would be compared to earlier surveys of Ireland. It was intended for reform rather than the 'violent transfers of property' that had dominated Irish history. As Europe was now at peace, the expertise of the Board of Ordnance could be fully brought to bear on such pressing civil matters, helping calm growing social pressures on the island:

> Your committee trust that the Survey will be carried on with energy, as well as with skill, and that it will, when completed, be creditable to the nation, and to the scientific acquirements of the present age. In that portion of the empire to which it more particularly applies, it cannot but be received as a proof of the disposition of the legislature to adopt all measures calculated to advance the interests of Ireland.

The Spring Rice committee had achieved many of its goals during the spring and summer of 1824. The ease with which the report was heard in parliament demonstrated that Spring Rice 'had caught and expressed the drift of public opinion',[14] the committee pursuing its objective with vigour and expedience. The years of work Spring Rice, Newport and Croker had spent assessing the need for an accurate survey prior to 1824 was obvious, doing much of the groundwork themselves. The range of witnesses called had been sufficient to justify their conclusions, with the depth of the investigation touching on all aspects of the survey (though admittedly, some topics received only the briefest of study). Meetings held during May and June were of greatest practical importance, the improved standardization of questioning. This logic ensured

14 Ibid., p. 31.

that Irish expertise had a voice, though not all involved in the surveying profession were offered a seat at the table.

The report's greatest immediate success was persuading Wellington. Yet, the defiance Spring Rice and his fellow members of parliament had shown to him was tempered by their reliance on Board of Ordnance resources and Colby's guidance. Wellington had tried his best to intimidate the committee into restricting the project's brief, but this had been deflected through the weight of evidence gathered and Colby's own reassurances. As a result, the committee had successfully asked an organization with three decades of experience to significantly adjust its *modus operandi* for their reformative needs. The long-term significance of this change was likely not realized by many in this group.

For Colby, all matters related to reform and British rule in Ireland were secondary to practical concerns. Once assured that assistance would be provided, he was happy to include townland boundaries as just one of a range of features his team would measure. The ghosts of civilian involvement in Lincolnshire still haunted his approach to Ireland, however. This stance would change over the coming years, again differentiating the Irish survey from its older British sibling.

Undeniably the report provided Irish engineers an opportunity to dispel doubts over their expertise. Collectively, they had demonstrated their competence and rightly buried Wellesley's February statement about them as deep as they could. There had been no descension among them to Colby's control as the true emphasis for the survey came from Westminster rather than Dublin Castle. The odds for an Irish-managed project were, therefore, virtually nil from the outset. As with other aspects of the Union, the report showed that an individual's Irishness (or overt association with Ireland, in the case of Bald and Nimmo though not Wellesley or Wellington) could be detrimental, limiting their usefulness to the Ordnance Survey. While some engineers had initially requested senior roles from Goulburn, they soon relented once it became clear it would not be a repeat of the Bogs Commission and would offer only limited opportunities. The project would be a survey of Ireland rather than an Irish survey. The engineers had, nonetheless, received greater acknowledgment than those who felt the true burden of cess inequalities. The 'peasantry' of Ireland would have to wait many years before the results of such reform were felt on the ground but could, at least, be assured that change was coming.

CHAPTER SEVEN

Epilogue: 'This great national undertaking'[1]

Events moved swiftly following the report's publication. On 22 June, the day after it was presented to parliament, Colby received orders from the Board of Ordnance to accelerate his deployment to Ireland:

> The report of the committee of the House of Commons on the survey of Ireland having been made to the house, and the master general having consented that such a survey shall be made by this department, I am directed to acquaint you, ... that you will immediately take the necessary steps, by providing instruments and making the proper additions to persons employed under your direction, so that the work may be proceeded without a moment's delay ...[2]

By September, Colby had arrived in his new theatre, accompanied by his subaltern, Lieutenant Thomas Drummond (b. 1797, d. 1840).[3] The two men spent the remainder of the year touring the country, selecting the most suitable mountains for the survey's primary triangulation.[4] For the most part, Colby was left alone to conduct his work as he saw fit, with only one short communique from Wellington relating to the scale to be used.[5] In response, Colby recommended that counties Antrim, Derry/Londonderry and Down offered 'the greatest facilities for beginning the work', being physically closest to the existing British network.[6] Recommendations were duly submitted to Wellington that a company of sixty-two non-commissioned officers and men be formed to aid with the survey's execution. This unit (the 13th Survey Company of the Royal Sappers and Miners) was assembled at Chatham and placed under the command of Major William Reid (b. 1791, d. 1858), Royal Engineers. Reid would serve as Colby's deputy and proved an able administrator during his time

---

1 *Freeman's Journal*, 6 May 1824. 2 Board of Ordnance to Colby, 22 June 1824, quoted in Andrews, *Paper landscape*, p. 31. 3 *Freeman's Journal*, 17 Sept. 1824. 4 Portlock, *Memoir*, p. 122. 5 '... the map must be drawn and filled up on the scale of six inches to a mile. It can be reduced afterwards to any scale that may be thought expedient, and may be engraved on such scale, or on the original scale of six inches. But the record must be complete on that scale', quoted in Andrews, *Paper landscape*, p. 32. 6 Colby to Goulburn, 12 Nov. 1824, National Archives of Ireland

with the survey. The sappers he commanded would work as auxiliaries to Colby's specialist staff, conducting measurements with surveyor's chains and taking rudimentary angular observations.[7] The 13th Company would later be joined by two similarly sized and newly formed companies the following year, swelling Colby's resources.[8]

With his units taking shape, he was able to present an estimated budget for the entire survey to parliament. The triangulation and topographic costings for the survey equated to £200,000 (€31 million in 2024),[9] with the boundary element coming to £100,000 (€15.7 million). This combined value was close to Bald's evaluation given on 13 May, equating to 1½ pence per acre, with Colby requesting £25,000 for the survey's initial year.[10]

Reactions in Ireland to the new survey were mostly positive. The *Freeman's Journal* referred to it as 'a highly popular undertaking, and one which must invite the active assistance of every native of the country who may be able by labour or head or hand to promote it.'[11] Others recognized the benefit of having a standardized and accurate map series of the island. Commentator William Monck Mason, for instance, felt that it provided 'the groundwork of all other' projects connected with reform in Ireland, which would 'depend upon the stability of this foundation'.[12]

Colby, now a Lieutenant Colonel, had a virtually free hand in how the survey was to be conducted and staffed. This proved both beneficial to his plan but equally left him exposed to criticism. The Spring Rice report provided him with high-level parameters and established a clear requirement for topographic and territorial elements. In this regard, all involved were fortunate to have a superintendent capable of independent and decisive choices, as Colby 'thread

(NAI CSO/RP/1824/1950). **7** Portlock, *Memoir*, p. 226. **8** 'By the end of the year [1825] the effective men on the survey [of Ireland] counted 109 of all ranks, who were chiefly dispersed in the field. Several were employed in offices as draftsmen and computers, but at this early period, very few were entrusted with any particular responsibility. Civilian assistants, for the most part, were second to the officers, and aided in superintending the management of the districts; but in the field, the sappers took the lead as surveyors, never working as chainmen, or subordinately to the civilians. As the duty was new, their qualifications required tact and practice before a fair return of progress could be realized. In August very few had proved themselves of sufficiently matured acquirements to merit advancement to Colonel Colby's classes, and five only of the number had graduated as far as 1s. 4d., a-day [pay]'. Connolly, *The history of the corps of royal sappers and miners*, p. 247. **9** This value was the same as that provided by William Bald's testimony to the Spring Rice committee on 13 May of £300,000 and that provided by John Foster MP in 1819 on the same topic, *Hansard*, xl, 805 (26 May 1819). **10** Andrews, *Paper landscape*, p. 32. **11** *Freeman's Journal*, 29 Sept. 1824. **12** William Monck Mason, *Suggestions to the project of a survey and valuation of Ireland* (Dublin, 1825), p. 5. Monck Mason's assessment would soon prove correct, with various interested parties ranging from private landowners, geologists, public bodies and the post office requesting and receiving Ordnance data before its official publication. Andrews, *Paper landscape*, p. 137.

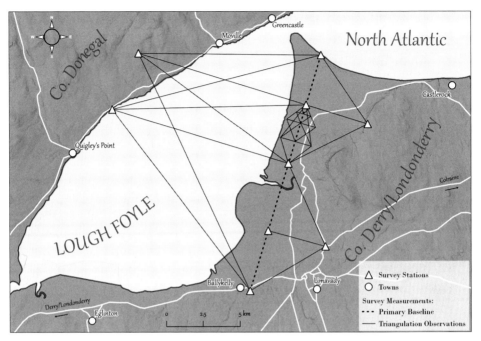

7.1. The Lough Foyle Baseline measurement occupied much of the Ordnance's early surveying operations in Ireland but was vital to the project's overall success. By author.

his way … through most of the ambiguities of the committee's report'.[13] Wellington, for his part, was content to leave Colby to his work.[14] When petitioned by the private secretary of King George IV to arrange a post for a young officer, the duke responded that he was reluctant to do so as:

> Major Colby is at the head of the [survey] and is responsible to me for the due conduct of its details; and accordingly, I have allowed him to select every individual who is to be employed under him. I have not named nor even suggested one.[15]

Ordnance Survey personnel began to arrive in 1825. This initial group included Colby's class of cadets as well as most of his existing staff. The remaining Ordnance staff were left in London and tasked with revising the existing mapping of Britain. The Ordnance Survey's efforts would remain focused in Ireland until the 1840s.

---

13 Andrews, *Paper landscape*, p. 32.   14 Owen and Pilbeam, *Ordnance survey*, p. 27.   15 Wellington to Sir William Knighton, 6 Nov. 1824: Wellington, *Despatches*, ii, pp 332–3. Portlock, *Memoir*, p. 257.

Mountjoy House,[16] secluded in Dublin's leafy Phoenix Park, became the organization's new Irish nerve centre. Colby, however, preferred to spend much of this initial period on-site in north Ulster. It was here that one of the first Ordnance contingents disembarked, consisting of a captain and three lieutenants of the Royal Engineers, accompanied by a detachment of Royal Sappers and Miners.[17] They were soon at work, conducting preliminary observations on Divis Mountain near Belfast, linking Ireland with the established British triangulation network in Scotland. The Irish survey's hyper-accurate baseline measurement would later be measured along the shores of Lough Foyle in 1827, setting the foundation of the island's triangulation network.[18] This network would eventually extend island-wide.

Unfortunately, not everything went according to plan. Delays in the baseline measurement resulted in the pragmatic decision to begin topographic work without full triangulation control. This went against Colby's initial vision of the survey but he had few other available options.[19] Several of the Woolwich cadets recruited in March 1824 were also found to be poorly trained, or even incompetent, despite the entire batch receiving the same instruction. Within three years, only half of this initial intake remained in Colby's service, the remainder either being transferred or leaving the military entirely.[20] Despite such irritations, Colby's willingness to get involved with all aspects of the survey had a positive impact on the remainder of his men. One noted that he was:

> … [willing] to lend his own hand to the raising of stones and building objects for observation, or to make houses to shelter the soldiers in camp; he would occasionally join with the men in a game of quoits[21] … and was a warm promoter of their feast at the close of each trigonometrical season.[22]

As expected, there were incidents of local resistance to the Ordnance's initial work. The suspicion and petty vandalism warned of by Bald and Nimmo invariably followed the sapper's progress around the country. Violence was rare, but a uniformed military force's appearance did little to ease tensions in the complex social environment of pre-Famine Ireland. In one instance, Reid, writing on Colby's behalf, informed Dublin Castle about the removal of a survey pole on Kippure Mountain in Co. Dublin by locals. This had been erected 'at considerable expense' by Colby's men and its disappearance had

16 Close, *The early years of the Ordnance Survey*, p. 89. Built in 1728 as a lodge of influential estate owner Luke Gardiner, Mountjoy sat on sixteen acres within the Phoenix Park and had served as a barracks since 1812.   **17** *Freeman's Journal*, 6 May 1825.   **18** Portlock, *Memoir*, p. 123.   **19** Hewitt, *Map of a nation*, p. 252.   **20** Andrews, *Paper landscape*, p. 36.   **21** A throwing game similar to 'Horseshoes'.   **22** Portlock, *Memoir*, p. 7.

caused notable delays. Though the incident was being investigated by constabulary, Reid assured Dublin Castle that he had also reported the incident to the parish priest as 'the inhabitants of this mountain [were] all Roman Catholics'.[23]

CIVILIANS STAFF AND THE ORDNANCE SURVEY

Despite early attrition among Colby's cadets, he was soon able to shore up his initial staff with his fresh companies of sappers. Their use appealed to both Colby's and Wellington's original vision of the Irish survey, and by the end of 1825, he had three entire companies at his disposal. There was, however, some grumbling among the ranks about their new duties. One issue was Colby's orders relating to the removal of sidearms. In July 1825, Col. Charles Pasley (b. 1780, d. 1861), of the Chatham School of military engineering, warned Colby that the affected soldiers would be 'completely lower in public estimation unless their arms be restored to them'.[24] Colby eventually relented.

The term 'Sapper' was also proving detrimental to Colby's search for recruits. Many within the military saw this title as being inferior to that of 'engineer', with Colby openly acknowledging this unusual titular situation:

> ... it cannot be doubted but the means of obtaining good recruits is greatly diminished by this apparently trivial circumstance of having to bear a long and obscure name which has no reference to the greater part of their duties.[25]

Pasley went further, lamenting: 'I wish to God, that *vile labour-like* name could be abolished'.[26] The corps of sappers and miners would eventually be merged with the Royal Engineers in 1856 (see plate 16).

By 1826 the Ordnance Survey of Ireland remained a near-universal military organization. With the exception of one clerk and two draftsmen in Mountjoy House it had no civilian staff in Ireland. This situation soon changed.[27] Throughout the Spring Rice investigation, Colby had remained theoretically open to using civilians for less technical elements, though he maintained his reservations. He continued to show a preference for a military-only survey during his first years in Ireland:

---

23 Maj. William Reid to William Lamb, Chief Secretary, 30 Nov. 1827 (NAI CSO/RP/ 1827/1917); 'public notices' (NAI CSO/RP/1825/1298); 'good will of the people' (NAI CSO/RP/1825/1253).   24 Col. Pasley to Colby, 23 July 1825, quoted in Close, *The early years of the Ordnance Survey*, p. 110.   25 Quoted in ibid., p. 114.   26 Ibid.   27 Ibid., p. 110.

When this survey was proposed, a large portion of the Engineering Corps was unemployed, and I conceived that the whole of the soldiers in the Corps of Sappers had gone through a course of practical geometry, etc … The formation of this military body from the Corps of Engineers and Sappers during a period of profound peace … seemed to me to possess great advantages with regard to the corps themselves.[28]

This stance gave ammunition to several of Colby's detractors. The Colonel had an innate caution around the accuracy of his measurements, which resulted in slow but gradual progress. Criticism was common during the Ordnance Survey's earliest years in Ireland. Most grievances related to its expense and unhurried methodology, 'but only a few Irishmen complained in public about the way it chose its personnel'.[29] By 1826 however, several of Colby's officers were calling for the employment of civilian surveyors to expedite the project. One was Major Reid. Colby's relationship with his deputy had grown increasingly frayed during these initial years. Reid had come into Colby's service with little surveying experience but had a solid record of administrative skill and personal bravery, demonstrated during the Peninsular War (1807–14). An obvious quick learner, he had begun to express concerns with Colby's 'unfashionable' chain measurements between reference points in place of the faster method of traversing using theodolites[30] Reid was also one of the main proponents of employing civilian draughtsmen, labourers and surveyors to alleviate pressures on the survey's military staff. Unbeknownst to Colby, Reid quietly began this process while his commander was away on business in Britain, directly undermining his orders. Subsequent newspaper adverts during the winter of 1826–7 to fill these roles met with a glut of applicants. As expected, Reid's actions greatly irritated Colby, who referred to the new hires as 'an influx of uninstructed civilians'. Reid somehow managed to retain his post.[31] Unfortunately matters between the two men did not improve. Reid continued to protest at the survey's techniques, going over Colby's head on one occasion and complaining directly to Dublin Castle. Such criticisms eventually reached Wellington, who was now prime minister. Formal investigations followed regarding the survey's progress, in which Colby ably defended himself. Reid was subsequently dismissed from Colby's service.[32]

Regardless of Reid's departure, the change in recruitment policy did begin to pay dividends. Bolstered by civilian staff, by 1830 nearly six million acres had

28 Quoted in Close, *The early years of the Ordnance Survey*, p. 108.   29 Andrews, *Plantation acres*, p. 382.   30 Owen and Pilbeam, *Ordnance Survey*, p. 30. Heavy use of chaining had also been cautioned against by Griffith, see above, p. 118.   31 Close, *The early years of the Ordnance Survey*, p. 111.   32 Owen and Pilbeam, *Ordnance Survey*, p. 31.

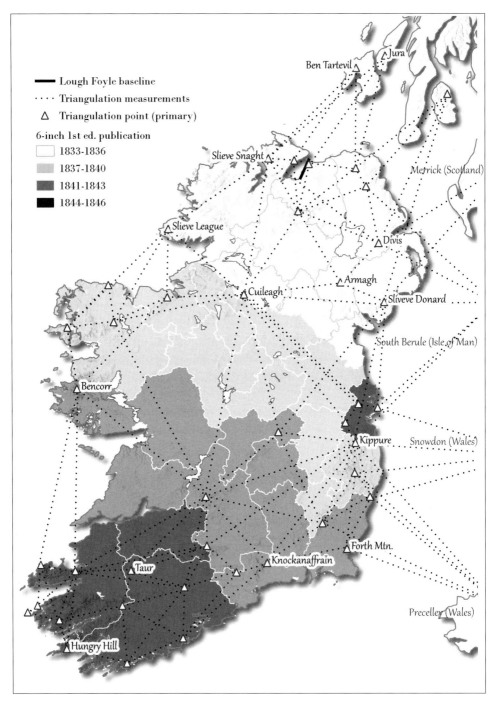

7.2. The Ordnance Survey's initial primary triangulation network, overlaying the production date of first edition six-inch mapping at county level. By author.

been surveyed, with the survey's staff ballooning to nearly two thousand. Civilians comprised the majority of this number, with most being Irishmen (and many being Irish-speaking Catholics).[33] Their involvement proved vital to the survey's advancement, parliament being duly advised that such headway could only be maintained if sufficient funding could be found.[34]

Most civilians worked within a compartmentalized system devised by Colby. This ensured that each man remained dedicated to a specific task. Those taking measurements, for example, would not be responsible for calculating the results, nor drawing the same measurements on maps. This approach was duly noted by fellow cartographer George Everest (b. 1790, d. 1866) during a visit to Ireland in 1829. Everest's time with Colby would later influence his survey work in India, incorporating methods first established in Ireland into yet another sphere of the British empire.[35] Though such processes proved tedious for his Irish staff, Colby was pleased with their performance. He was comfortable extolling their qualities in public and even transferred some to aid the revised six-inch survey of Britain in the 1840s.[36] Notwithstanding civilian involvement, the initial years of the Irish survey would eventually become inseparable from the sappers, who formed a nucleus for this well-disciplined body.[37]

Of notable absence in Colby's ranks were the Irish engineers who had received compliments from the Spring Rice committee. Their exclusion can be traced to the earliest communications between Wellesley and Wellington in February 1824. While the duke had eventually been forced to give ground to the committee on the territorial aspect of the project, his influence ensured that the organization's command remained military in nature. Invariably, the survey proved commercially disruptive to the country's civil engineers, forcing the abandonment of several county surveys already underway. The 'few crumbs of praise' they had received in Spring Rice's report did not translate into new, paying roles within Colby's organization, forcing them to look elsewhere.[38] Nimmo, for example, halted his work on coastal charts due to the growing scope of Colby's work.[39] He instead withdrew to areas where the Ordnance would offer little competition, such as public infrastructure projects and early rail lines.[40] His compatriot William Bald followed suit, finding employment on similar schemes in Ireland, England and France. In 1830 Bald also published his large-scale map of Mayo, which had been frequently referred to during Spring

33 By comparison, Colby's British team comprised of just thirteen officers in 1852, Andrews, *Paper landscape*, p. 36.   34 *Statement of progress of Ordnance Survey of Ireland*, Parliamentary papers, 54 vols, xxxix (1837), p. 281; Hewitt, *Map of a nation*, p. 280.   35 Hewitt, *Map of a nation*, p. 260; Crosbie, *Irish imperial networks*, p. 113.   36 *Dublin Evening Post*, 18 Oct. 1838.   37 Portlock, *Memoir*, p. 226. 38 Andrews, *Paper landscape*, p. 33.   39 Ibid.   40 *Dictionary of Irish biography*: 'Nimmo, Alexander', https://www.dib.ie/index.php/biography/nimmo-alexander-a6214 (last accessed 15 Feb. 2023).

Rice's investigations. Deservedly, it met with much acclaim upon publication.[41] Nimmo and Bald employed their younger colleague William Edgeworth following the committee's investigation, though the promising young engineer's life was cut short only five years later due to illness.

The engineers were not shy in voicing their disdain of the disruption the survey had caused. An 1828 committee of inquiry into the Ordnance Survey of Ireland, for example, noted the impact the project had on the private sector. This was supported by one Ordnance officer who wrote:

> I do believe that the greater part of the civil engineers of Ireland are hostile to our having the survey: that from the intercourse they have with the gentlemen of the country an opportunity is afforded of poising their minds as to its accuracy, and that the idea of employing soldiers to execute what they alone imagined themselves qualified to undertake is a disparagement which they cannot well brook.[42]

Colby took offence at such attitudes from civil engineers, noting the 'irksome and invidious' task of assessing his growing team's work to ensure exactness. Ironically, much of this burden he had brought upon himself.

Though Colby had been initially reluctant to involve civilians, by the 1830s, he had a growing menagerie of non-cartographic specialists attached to his work. This included linguists, historians, artists and geologists, each busily collecting data for the Ordnance's topographic department archives. Such ancillary reporting grew operationally, and financially, cumbersome as Reid's replacement, Lieutenant Thomas Larcom (b. 1801, d. 1879), collated 'every species of location information relating to Ireland'.[43] An 1837 memoir of the parish of Templemore, Derry/Londonderry, for example, exceeded 300 pages and cost £1,700 to produce.[44] Irrespective of Colby's justifications, such expense and effort could not be extended to the entire island, and he was soon instructed to reign in his scientific curiosity.[45]

FROM MEASUREMENTS TO MAPS TO MEMORIES

The first six-inch Ordnance map of Ireland was produced in 1833, with Colby having the honour of personally presenting it to King William IV (b. 1765,

---

41 *Dictionary of Irish biography*: 'Bald, William', https://www.dib.ie/index.php/biography/bald-william-a0331 (accessed 15 Feb. 2023).   42 Capt. Water to Colby, 28 Mar. 1828, quoted in Close, *The early years of the Ordnance Survey*, p. 121.   43 *Memoir of the city and northwestern liberties of Londonderry: parish of Templemore* (London, 1837), preface. See Appendix E.   44 OSI/OSNI, *Ordnance Survey in Ireland: an illustrated record* (Dublin, 1991), p. 24. See Appendix E for Colby's justification and methods.   45 Hewitt, *Map of a nation*, p. 268.

d. 1837). He found the king to be 'very gracious' and was gratified 'that the first Irish map [had] been so well received'.[46] Colby's selection of this scale had proven apt, with the maps capable of showing the townland boundaries needed for cess reform, alongside parishes for tithe calculation.[47] By 1846 the entire island had been charted.

The six-inch parameter had initially been intended only for the use of valuers in the field. As in Britain, a condensed one-inch variate was planned for general and public use, with the Board of Ordnance having no solid intention of creating a commercial six-inch series.[48] Eventual engraving and printing of the now famed six-inch series would come about almost by chance. Civil engineer Richard Griffith proved pivotal in this transformation from manuscript to print.

Griffith had been the only member of the engineers (or Irishmen) interviewed in 1824 to find a prominent role within the new survey. In 1825 he was appointed commissioner of a boundary department, identifying and naming the maze of townlands across Ireland while defining their borders.[49] This body was not part of Colby's direct command but rather reported to the lord lieutenant. The territorial element had caused significant concerns in Westminster during Spring Rice's investigation but progressed relatively smoothly under Griffith's management. His team were required to mark the locations of boundaries but not to measure them, thus laying the groundwork for Colby's surveyors who would follow afterwards. Regardless of his remit to note rather than measure, Griffith's experience of practical land surveying, especially relating to property bounds, proved to be of great benefit to this exercise:

---

46 Quoted in Close, *The early years of the Ordnance Survey*, p. 92. 47 The decision to exclude field boundaries proved costly and was soon reversed by Colby. An 1856 review of Ordnance Irish operations identified that 'it is … regretted that the examples of France and Bavaria had not been followed: the neglect of so doing has led to that very augmentation of expense and postponement of the completion of the work, which was feared if the survey had been made in complete detail as in those countries, in the first instance. It was in consequence of the instructions which were issued … that the northern counties of Ireland, which were first surveyed, were made without that detail, which has subsequently been found to be essentially necessary for the local valuation and assessments, and hence it is that we are now revising those northern counties at a great additional expense.' *Report on the Ordnance Survey of the United Kingdom for 1855–56* (South Hampton, 1856), p. 11. 48 Speaking in 1846, Griffith felt that 'I do not think there was anything settled' during the Spring Rice committee regarding the use of the six-inch series outside of valuation, *Report from the select committee on Ordnance Survey* (Ireland), p. 19. Spring Rice would later recommend that the one-inch map of Ireland was necessary to conform with the British original. He also noted that the minute detail required for the six-inch Irish base data would make it more accurate than the British version. *Report from the select committee on Ordnance Survey* (Ireland), p. 27. 49 5 Geo. IV, c. 112 (1825).

The admirable manner in which the boundary department performed its
duty, and the value of that harmony between proprietors, who had been
before disputing about mere trifle, which was one of the results of the
prudence and patience which were exhibited in the enquiries [*sic*] of its
members, cannot be over-rated.[50]

However, like so many aspects of the Survey's early years in Ireland, progress
was often countered with condemnation. Griffith's relationship with Colby was
frequently strained. Each man was, at times, openly critical of the other's work.
Griffith's feedback on Ordnance mistakes proved irritating to the perfectionist
Colby. Though he had produced a highly accurate survey, the scope and scale
of the project invariably introduced errors into the minutia of Colby's first
maps. Minor issues, such as unmarked features or mispositioned buildings,
drew pointed disapproval from Griffith.[51] In turn, Griffith's work was far from
perfect. William Gregory (b. 1762, d. 1840), undersecretary of Ireland,
frequently received letters from Colby complaining of Griffith's methods. These
objections included the engineer being based in Mallow, Co. Cork, when he
should have been in Ulster[52] or Colby's fear of lawsuits should Griffith make
errors in marking property boundaries.[53] Colby later commented that, at times,
he felt the boundary department was 'in a peculiarly defective state'[54] due to
Griffith's management, with linguist John O'Donovan remarking that:

> I am inclined to believe that Mr Griffeth [*sic*] frequently divided parishes
> into townlands, more from his fancy than from the authority of the people[55]

Given the complexity of the task assigned to Griffith, perfection would have
been near impossible. An 1828 investigation led by Sir James Carmichael Smyth
(b. 1779, d. 1838) largely exonerated Griffith and, instead, encouraged him and
Colby to improve inter-departmental communication.[56]

Alongside his management of identifying townlands, Griffith would also
become the survey's valuation commissioner in 1829.[57] He advised that his
valuers would require several copies of each six-inch Ordnance map to conduct
their work in the field. As these maps were intended as manuscripts, a decision

50 Portlock, *Memoir*, p. 195.   51 Hewitt, *Map of a nation*, p. 267.   52 '… the gentleman appointed
to conduct the setting out of the boundaries in the north of Ireland is occupied in making
roads in the south.' Major William Reid to William Gregory, 7 June 1826 (NAI, CSO/RP/
1825/673).   53 Major William Reid to William Gregory, 17 Apr. 1826 (NAI, CSO/RP/1826/
2216).   54 Close, *The early years of the Ordnance Survey*, p. 112.   55 John O'Donovan to Thomas
Larcom, 8 Oct. 1834, quoted in Hewitt, *Map of a nation*, p. 267.   56 William Smyth, 'Sir Richard
Griffith's three valuations of Ireland, 1826–1864' (PhD, NUIM, 2008), p. 85.   57 Goulburn to
R. Byham, Ordnance Office, 20 Mar. 1826 (NAI CSO/RP/1826/2648).

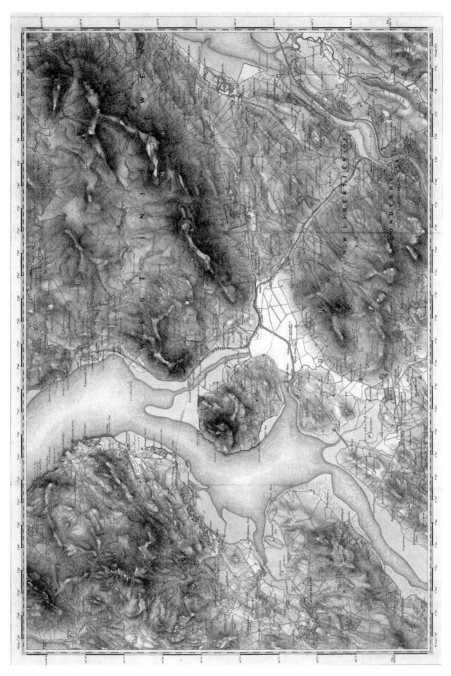

7.3. An 1879 sample of Ordnance Survey mapping for the Inishowen peninsula, Co. Donegal. The mass production of such maps was a feature that helped distinguish the Ordnance Survey of Ireland from earlier manuscript series. Ordnance Survey, *Londonderry, Sheet 11* (Dublin, 1879) (David Rumsey Map Collection, David Rumsey Map Centre, Stanford Libraries).

was therefore needed on how best to supply an adequate number to the valuation teams. Colby could either order them traced multiple times, thus keeping them in manuscript form, or have them engraved and printed. Ultimately, printing was the cheaper option, with the fiscally-conscious Colby approving.[58] The compilation of one of Ireland's best-known historic map resources can thereby trace its origin to 'a mere economical accident' spurred by Griffith's needs.[59]

Griffith's valuation began in May 1830, with the first full county valuation (Derry/Londonderry) published in 1834. By 1844, a total of eighteen counties had been completed.[60] Overall, Griffith's assessments were considered very accurate, though some complained he knew 'no more of farming than engineers usually do'.[61] Regardless, his work did much to rebalance the cess system. As the century progressed, Griffith would also further expand his involvement in Irish geology, helping found the Royal Geological Society of Ireland and ultimately obtaining a knighthood for his polymathic efforts.[62]

Though cess reform remained the valuation's primary objective, Griffith, with support from officials in Dublin Castle, also made his results suitable for tithe restructuring. By the mid-1830s, sporadic violence to the tithe system had become increasingly common and is remembered as the Tithe War (Cogadh na nDeachúna) (1831–6).[63] The subsequent Tithe Commutation Act for Ireland (1838)[64] eased this situation by radically reducing rates. Complete relief, however, did not come until 1869 and the disestablishment of the Church of Ireland.

The future careers of Colby, Wellington and Spring Rice also contained similar triumphs, coupled with difficult setbacks and defeats. These three men held the most significant influence over the foundation of the Ordnance Survey of Ireland in the spring of 1824. Wellington had ordered the project, Colby had designed it, and Spring Rice reorientated its goals. Each had also been forced to compromise on their initial stances due to the evidence uncovered during the investigation. Admittedly, Wellington had been required to make more significant compromises than Spring Rice, such as the inclusion of townland

---

58 *Report from the select committee on Ordnance Survey* (Ireland), p. iii.   59 *Report from the select committee on Ordnance Survey* (Scotland), p. 24. Other series of Ordnance six-inch mapping in Ireland would follow with revisions: First edition (1833–46), Second edition (1846–62), Third edition (1900–7), Fourth edition (1905–57). PRONI Historic map viewer, https://www.nidirect.gov.uk/services/search-proni-historical-maps-viewer (last accessed 25 May 2023).   60 Smyth, 'Sir Richard Griffith's three valuations of Ireland', p. 142.   61 *Morning Chronicle*, 20 Apr. 1848.   62 *Dictionary of Irish biography*, 'Griffith, Sir Richard John', https://www.dib.ie/index.php/biography/griffith-sir-richard-john-a3649 (last accessed 15 Feb. 2023).   63 Stephen McCormac, 'The tithe war; reports by Church of Ireland clergymen to Dublin Castle', *History Ireland*, 13:4 (2005).   64 6 & 7 Will. IV, c. 71. (1836).

borders and the likelihood of civilian involvement. But the duke had also had his way by ensuring the upper echelons of the survey would remain firmly in military control. Despite his lower social, political and military status, Colby had proven the most influential of the three. Wellington and the committee had followed his outline for the survey with little argument or objection, with both parties content to leave the many technical vagaries of the investigation in his capable hands. Throughout, Colby had demonstrated the confidence, clarity of purpose, and scientific know-how to retain the duke's and the parliamentarians' trust. Those of the British survey interviewed by Spring Rice had willingly fallen in line with their superintendent's wishes, further cementing Colby's authoritative standing. The survey of Ireland was to be his.

Ireland was as new for Colby as it would be for the Board of Ordnance survey department. In Britain, he had inherited his command, along with its practices and problems from others. By comparison, Ireland was a blank slate, indelibly linked to his standards and vision. The role would bring many annoyances, including budget issues and human resources problems, each, at times, intruding into the intricacies of complex scientific fieldwork. Mistakes in early mapping, when identified, were ruthlessly pursued. Coupled with this vigour were the cultural and political complexities of early nineteenth-century Ireland, which were equally new entities to the Englishman. As mentioned in the introduction of this book, the Ordnance Survey was a reformative act within a wider imperial system. Undoubtedly it played a positive and practical role in accurately charting Ireland, though the ghost of William Petty remained close, especially in its early years. In this regard, Colby was mostly successful in shedding any association with the earlier forfeiture surveys.

It is also important to note that, like other aspects of imperialism, the Ordnance's Irish venture was a two-way street. Lessons learned there were, by the 1840s, conducted back to Britain. Methods were improved, scales increased, and the survey of Britain began to look increasingly like its Irish relative. In turn, such trends were disseminated to other spheres of the empire, similar to the impact Stuart surveys of sixteenth-century Ireland had had in Virginia or the Caribbean. Under Colby, Ireland once again became Britain's cartographic test ground, with the ambitious scope of the Ordnance Survey in Ireland, as set out by the Spring Rice committee, affecting its creator as it did its subject.

For his part, Colby continued to split his time between Ordnance operations in both Ireland and Britain. Dublin, however, remained his family home. In 1828 he married Elizabeth Hester, with the couple initially residing in Dublin's fashionable Mountjoy Square. He soon moved his growing family to the more convenient Knockmaroon Lodge in Castleknock, close to the Ordnance Survey's headquarters, though he was often absent at work around the country.[65] Colby led from the front, and frequently visited his officers and men in the field. Such was the case when he visited a team at the summit of Knockanaffrain in Wexford:

> From this noble and rugged mountain crag, Colonel Colby looked over the varied and vast expanse of mountain, plain, and the sea before him with a fervid enthusiasm, and it was from the readiness and warmth with which he thus on all occasions identified himself with the feelings of his officers, and made himself one with them in thoughts and acts, that his visits were so welcome, so encouraging, and so profitable.[66]

Colby's immense devotion to duty was frequently noted. This was most obvious in his pedantic stance toward the quality of his mapping, though it also expanded to his role as an officer. Ever conscious of operational costs, he frequently went without pay, though, this sacrificial policy ultimately backfired when he was refused his arrears.[67]

Colby would remain in charge of the survey of Ireland for the next two decades. During his tenure, he would transfer many of the insights learned in Ireland back to a reinvigorated British survey, including aiding the development of the Scottish equivalent in 1838. Alongside his surveying duties, he found time and energy for multiple academic pursuits. He became a fellow of the Royal Society and Royal Irish Academy, and the Geological, Geographical, and Statistical Societies of London. He received a doctorate from the University of Aberdeen, alongside other awards and acknowledgments. He retired from the Ordnance Survey in 1846, the same year the last Irish county was published, with the rank of major general. Following several years in Germany, he returned to England, dying, aged sixty-nine, in New Brighton, near Liverpool, finally free 'of so much bodily and mental exertion'.[68]

While Colby had been the dominant force behind the Ordnance Survey's work, Wellington's opinion (and ego) most obviously hung above the events of 1824. His prompt decision to deploy Colby had initially triggered the formation of the Spring Rice committee, and it remained his mind that the committee ultimately wished to change. Had they been unsuccessful, or if another had

---

65 Close, *The early years of the Ordnance Survey*, p. 96. With fieldwork underway in Ireland, many of the resulting calculations were completed under his supervision in his new British headquarters in Southampton. Colby had moved his primary headquarters there from the Tower of London following a fire in 1841. Again, like many aspects of the survey, these vital calculations were done on Ireland's behalf, but without its involvement, triangulation measurements being assessed by British mathematicians. Irrespective, Dublin's Mountjoy House, the command centre of the Irish survey, continued to act as a repository for the volumes of material generated such as field books, sketches, copper plates, etc.   66 Portlock, *Memoir*, p. 129.   67 Ibid., p. 258. His widow was eventually granted a life pension upon his death, ibid., p. 314.   68 Ibid., p. 313.

been in his place, the history of the Ordnance Survey of Ireland may have been radically different. Wellington became commander-in-chief of the British army in 1827 though he resigned when he was appointed prime minister the following year. Initially building his administration around a 'neutral' approach to catholic emancipation, he hoped to walk an increasingly fine line on this controversial issue. This stance collapsed with the election of Daniel O'Connell as MP for Clare, Wellington's subsequent support for the Catholic Emancipation Bill (1829) causing the defection of several Tory ministers.[69] The same personality traits that had bolstered his military success proved less suitable for his premiership, earning him the nickname the 'Iron Duke' due to his stubbornness and drive. His unpopularity with the public, and within his party, ultimately caused the collapse of his cabinet in 1830. Wellington remained active in politics until the mid-1840s, serving as foreign secretary to Prime Minister Robert Peel (b. 1788, d. 1850) and later sitting in the House of Lords. He also continued to play a military role, serving as a colonel for several regiments well into later life. He died in 1852, aged eighty-three, receiving a state funeral at St Paul's Cathedral in London.

Likewise, Spring-Rice's career proved turbulent. Becoming secretary to the treasury during Earl Grey's (b. 1764, d. 1845) Whig administration, his resistance to O'Connell's reform efforts cost him his Limerick seat in 1832. He was subsequently returned as MP for Cambridge, though he struggled in his treasury role due to the wider economic recession affecting Britain.[70] Eventually ushered out of office in 1839, he was elevated to the peerage as Lord Monteagle, leaving behind 'the much-abused name of Spring-Rice'.[71] Partially redeeming his public image in Ireland during the famine, he was remembered in parliament as 'a tedious speaker ... neither a very strong nor a high-minded man, [but] we must do him justice as a shrewd one and a good partisan.'[72] He died in 1866, aged seventy-five.

Outside of politics, Spring Rice's legacy is also perpetually linked with that of Colby and the Ordnance Survey. His vision of the survey and its role in Ireland proved vital in shaping its primordial days. He had led resistance to the initial outline of the project as set by Goulburn, Wellington, and Wellesley, aided by his staunch political allies and the reforming zeal of the early nineteenth century. Large-scale mapping in Ireland would be forever changed thanks to his actions. Just as Ireland and Britain had been politically joined two decades earlier, they would, until Irish independence in 1922, be cartographically united under one organization.

---

69 *Dictionary of Irish biography*, 'Wellesley (Wesley), Arthur', https://www.dib.ie/biography/wellesley-wesley-arthur-a8961 (last accessed 16 Feb. 2023).   70 *Dictionary of Irish biography*, 'Rice, Thomas Spring', https://www.dib.ie/biography/rice-thomas-spring-a7661 (last accessed, 16 Feb. 2023).   71 *The London Times*, 9 Feb. 1866.   72 Ibid.

APPENDIX A

Principle of triangulation

The accuracy of a survey covering a large portion of land depends on a network of control points established by the surveyor. These act as a mathematical frame onto which geographical detail is projected. Ascertaining the location of each of these control points, or stations, relative to each other is therefore of vital importance and can be determined using a method known as triangulation.

A triangulation network comprises of a series of known points visible from at least two other points within the same network. In its simplest and most stable form, the triangles between three stations are as equilateral as possible, allowing for the best geometric stability. Though only three stations are needed to create a network, adding more stations allows for redundant observations resulting in higher precision and better positional checks.[1]

In the case of the Ordnance Survey of Ireland, these points were marked by pillars placed on top of prominent mountains across the island, allowing observers to see other points in the network many miles away. These formed a primary triangulation network consisting of dozens of stations whose positions were known relative to each other. In turn, each station could be used to create secondary triangulation networks within each primary triangle, allowing field surveyors to take their measurements of roads, buildings, townland boundaries and natural features based on a stable, national reference system. It was the size and accuracy of this network that distinguished the Ordnance Survey's work from earlier national or regional surveys of Ireland, ushering in a new era of scientific quality mapping.

In the example below, surveyors wish to identify the location of point C. In turn, a secondary network of control points is required within the triangle ABC, from which surveyors can record local geographic detail. The locations of hilltop stations A and B are known, as is the distance between both. Placing high-precision theodolites at each point, the surveyors record the interior angles between each – CAB, ABC and BCA (figure A1).

This angular data is combined with the predetermined distance between stations between AB. Such information allows the surveyors to apply the 'law

1 Arthur Bannister, *Surveying* (Pearson, 1998), p. 206; John Uren, *Surveying for engineers* (Macmillan, 2006), p. 243.

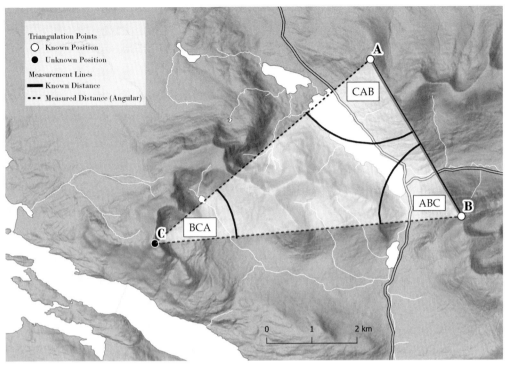

A1. A basic triangulation network.

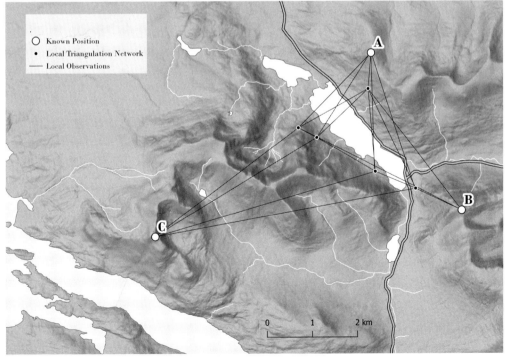

A2. A secondary triangulation network, established within the primary network.

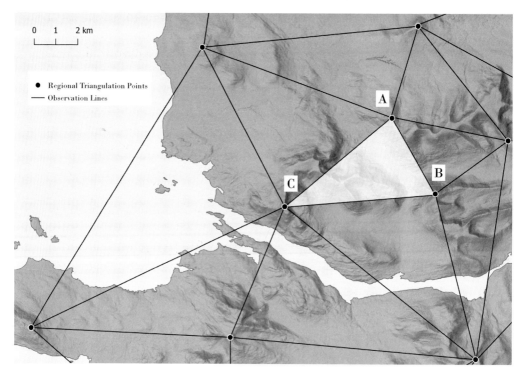

A3. Triangulation networks could be expanded as far as necessary, based on a survey's requirements.

of sines',[2] which will allow for the calculation of the length of lines AC and BC, thus identifying the location of point C.

With point C identified, the same method can be used to establish a local, secondary triangulation network within the triangle ABC. Surveyors would then be able to physically measure the location of the lake shore and roads within the triangle ABC to a higher degree of accuracy than if no control network was used. The Spring Rice committee would frequently discuss the density of this secondary network in 1824, with members hoping to balance accuracy and expediency.

In addition to establishing the secondary network within ABC, the successful position of station C would permit the extension of a regional network of primary triangulation points. If any of these points were known before the measurement of C, observations from each could be used to refine the further positioning of C. Any small measurement errors within this wider

$$2 \; \frac{\sin \alpha}{a} = \frac{\sin \beta}{b} = \frac{\sin \gamma}{c}$$

network could be diffused across the whole, meaning their local impact is minimalised. In this manner, the wider network of triangulation points becomes geometrically sound, ensuring that any physical detail recorded within the survey area is to a standard and high level of accuracy.

Correspondence between Richard Wellesley and the duke of Wellington, Spring 1824

Lord Wellesley to Field Marshal the Duke of Wellington[1]

Dublin, 17 Feb. 1824

My dear Arthur,

You must be fully acquainted with the various considerations (almost of every description, and involving every public and private interest) which render an accurate survey of Ireland an object of primary importance to the government and to the nation. The matter has been attentively viewed and earnestly recommended by Committees of the House of Commons; and I believe that on this subject of Irish concern, all parties are united. In the first notes which I sent to [Prime Minister] Lord Liverpool respecting the improvement of the system of valuing the collection tithe, I adverted to the utility of an accurate general survey, to which all valuations might be referred, and which might serve as a permanent standard of reference not only for tithes, but for all charges on the land, and might operate as a perpetual corrective of the numberless abuses now existing in the local and municipal taxation in the provinces of Ireland.

I really consider that no greater practical benefit could be conferred on Ireland than the accomplishment of an accurate general survey of the country, and the present moment seems to me favourable to the commencement of so great and useful an undertaking. I am, therefore, anxious that the attention of government and of Parliament should be directed to the subject, and that the mode of carrying the plan into execution, as well as the means of providing for the expense, should be soon determined.

It is too certain that such a plan cannot be executed by Irish engineers and Irish agents of any description. Neither science, nor skill, nor diligence, nor discipline, nor integrity, sufficient for such a work, can be found in Ireland. I am therefore satisfied that the only source from which the means of executing the survey can be derived is the Ordnance; and that you are the only authority capable of infusing the spirit which such an operation would require into the

1 *Dispatches* [357], p. 218.

agency which must be employed. The accuracy of the Irish engineers has largely been exhibited most glaringly in the charts and maps of the Irish coast, executed under the direction of the Irish Commissioners for the Fisheries.[2] At the Admiralty, you will learn what enormous and dangerous errors have been discovered in those official charts.

I have mentioned this plan of an Irish survey to Mr Goulburn, but I have not made it the subject of a despatch to government, thinking it would be more successful under your protection and countenance. If you should approve the general idea, it cannot be mentioned too soon in Parliament, and I should be glad if on any favourable occasion, you could refer to it in the House of Lords.

Ever, dear Arthur, yours most affectionately,
Wellesley

Wellington to Wellesley[3]

London, 23 Feb. 1824.

My Dear Wellesley,

I have received your letter of the 17th instant, and I quite agree in your opinion of the importance of an accurate survey of Ireland. Before I had heard from you, I had had two conversations upon the subject with Mr Goulburn, and had agreed to undertake the work, which I will endeavour to render as complete as possible. But Mr Goulburn will most probably have informed you that owing to the want of persons properly trained, I was apprehensive that I could not undertake to make much progress in the course of the year 1824; but we will make all our preparatory arrangements in this year, and commence next year with such force as will enable us to complete the survey of the whole of Ireland in five or six years. We should only mislead you if we were to promise to do more.

I was very happy to learn from Campbell[4] that you were so well.

Believe me, &c.,
Wellington

2 See Nimmo's testimony, p. 109.   3 *Dispatches* [359], p. 220.   4 Sir Colin Campbell (b. 1776, d. 1847), British Army officer, a veteran of Wellington's Peninsular campaign and future lieutenant governor of Tobago (1828), Nova Scotia (1833), and Ceylon (1840).

APPENDIX C

Report from the select committee on the survey and valuation of Ireland, June 1824

(HC 1824 (445) viii, 79)

The select committee appointed to consider of the best mode of apportioning more equally the local burthens collected in Ireland, and to provide for a general survey and valuation of that part of the United Kingdom; and who were instructed to report their observations and opinions from time to time, with the minutes of evidence taken before them, to the house; have, pursuant to the order of the house, considered the same accordingly, and agreed to the following report:

In considering the subject referred to them, your committee have not felt themselves called upon to enter into a prolonged examination of witnesses to prove the necessity of a new survey and valuation of Ireland. Such a measure has been recommended by former committees, and its expediency admitted by the house. It has formed the subject of various petitions to parliament, and has been looked to by the people of Ireland as a remedy for the inequalities of the present mode of apportioning the taxation levied under the authority of grand juries and vestries. The expediency of proceeding in this great national work, is apparent from a consideration of the sums annually levied under the presentment laws. By returns laid on the table of the house during the present session, it appears, that the amount of the grand jury taxes imposed in the last year, has exceeded £750,000. The obscurity and want of uniformity of the general system, as well as the inequality incidental to the mode of apportioning these local taxes, have been admitted by the parliament of Ireland at remote periods. In some parts of Ireland, the assessment is made by the civil division of ploughlands, varying in size and value, but rated at an equal sum. In other cases, a division by townlands has been established, each townland contributing according to its assumed area, which bears no defined proportion to its actual contents. Gneeves, cartrons, tates, and other sub-denominations of land, are recognised in other parts of Ireland; but, however, the names may vary, the evil seems universally the same; and the inequality complained of in the middle of the last century by Sir William Petty, continues, without correction, to the present times. This subject has frequently occupied the attention of the legislature. A select committee, in the year 1815, after a minute investigation, reported, 'that some mode should be taken to render grand jury assessments more equal, by correcting the defects arising from apportioning the county rate according to old surveys, calculated on the measure of land formerly deemed profitable, and not comprehending the great improvements which have subsequently taken place'. Extracts from the evidence taken before the select committee of 1815, will be found in the appendix to the present report. In the following year a second report was presented to the house, stating 'that the various modes of levying the grand jury presentments, from the inequality of their pressure, arising out of the distant periods of time, and unsettled state of the country where such arrangements were made, require immediate and complete alteration'. In 1819, a bill was introduced to provide for the survey and valuation of Ireland; but the measure was not persevered in. During the present session, a vote of £5,000 was agreed to, for the purpose of a trigonometrical survey, and the house resolved 'that it is expedient, for the purpose of apportioning more equally the local burthens of Ireland, to provide for a general survey and valuation of that part of the United Kingdom'. The utility of the proposed measure, as well as the necessity of its immediate commencement, appear, on a review of the records of parliament, to be established beyond the possibility of doubt.

Your committee have considered it important to inquire into the proceedings taken, both in the British empire and in foreign countries, in the execution of territorial surveys and valuations; such an inquiry appearing likely to supply useful information on the subject referred to them by the house. One of the earliest as well as the most minute of these surveys, is that transmitted to us under the name of the Domesday Book. This ancient record, like the other earliest surveys, was not laid down as a map on paper, but as a catalogue or terrier of property. This inquest, properly called 'the most important financial operation' of that period, was intended to contain a survey of 'every hide of land in the kingdom. Commissioners were sent down into the counties, with authority to impannel a jury in each hundred, from whose presentments and verdicts the necessary information might be obtained. They directed their inquiries to every important particular: the extent of each estate; its division into arable land, pasture, meadow and wood; the names of the owners, tenants and subtenants; their condition, whether free or servile; the nature and obligation of the tenures, and the estimated value.' The extraordinary precision and minute details of this ancient work have scarcely been surpassed in modern times; and the mode in which it was effected, appears to your committee not wholly inapplicable to the intended survey of Ireland.

The Survey of Forfeited Lands [Civil Survey, 1654–6], made under the authority of Lord Strafford, in Ireland, is considered to have been executed in like manner as a terrier, though accompanied by outline maps. These original documents have unfortunately been destroyed.

The most extensive and valuable survey of Ireland was undertaken by Sir William Petty [the Down Survey], under a commission dated December 11, 1654; it was executed in consideration of a payment of 20s. by the day, and of 1d. an acre for the grantees obtaining possession of the lands. This survey was laid down with the chain, and with wonderful accuracy, considering the period at which it was executed; it consists of county maps, containing the boundaries of baronies and parishes, and of baronial maps on a scale of forty perches to the inch; the latter distinguish the boundaries of parishes and townlands; many of these maps have been destroyed by fire, but are replaced by copies taken from the originals deposited at the Royal Library at Paris. Of 1,430 maps, about 260 are of the baronies, and the remaining 1,170 of the parishes; about 67 of the baronial maps are burned, with more or less injury, 130 are fully preserved, and two are stated to be lost: of the parochial maps, about 391 have suffered from fire, and about 780 have altogether escaped. These maps are deposited among the records in Birmingham Tower [in Dublin Castle] and are evidence in courts of law as between the Crown and those deriving under it, as also between two persons both deriving title under the Crown.

The last official survey of an extensive nature, made in Ireland, was that of the Forfeited Lands, in the reign of William III; it is preserved in the vice-treasurer's office, and comprises about 2,000,000 of acres.

In France, the great territorial survey or cadastre, has been in progress for many years; it was first suggested in 1763, and after an interval of 30 years, during which no progress was made, it was renewed by a decree of the government of that day, and individuals of the highest scientific reputation, M.M. Lagrange, Laplace and Delambre, were consulted, with respect to the best mode of carrying into effect the intention of government. Subsequent events suspended any effectual operations in the French cadastre till the year 1802, when a school of topographical engineering was organized. The operations now in progress were fully commenced in 1808. The principle adopted, is the formation of a central commission, acting in conjunction with the local authorities; the classification of lands, according to an ascertained value, is made by three resident proprietors of land in each district, selected by the municipal council, and by the chief officer of revenue. 'In the course of thirteen years, one-third only of each department had been surveyed, having cost the state £120,000 per annum. At the rate at which it is carried on, it may be computed as likely to require for its completion, a total sum of £4,680,000 or an acreable charge of 8¾d.' The delay of the work as well as the increase of expense, seem to have been the result of the minuteness of the survey, which extends to every distinct field; a minuteness which, for many reasons, your committee consider both unnecessary and inexpedient to be sought for, in the proposed survey of Ireland.

The survey of Bavaria is of more modern date, but of equal minuteness. It is commenced by a primary triangulation, and principal and verification bases; it is carried on to a second triangulation, with very accurate instruments, so as to determine 'all the principal points; the filling up the interior is completed by a peculiar species of plane table; and in order to do away with the inaccuracies of the common chain, the triangulation is carried down on paper to the most minute corners of fields'. The map is laid down on a scale of 12 inches to the mile, or $\frac{1}{5000}$ part of the real size; and as it contains all that is required in the most precise survey of property, it is used in the purchase and sale of real estates.

The cadastre of Savoy and Piedmont began in 1729; and is stated to have at once afforded the government the means of apportioning justly all the territorial contributions, and to have put an end to litigations between individuals, by ascertaining, satisfactorily, the bounds of properties.

The Neapolitan survey under Visconti, and that of the United States under Heslar [*sic*], are both stated to be in progress; but your committee have not had the means of ascertaining on what principles they are conducted. The practical subject referred to your committee may be considered, as it relates, §1. To the survey; and §2. To the valuation. Each of these demands consideration, with the view of defining the duty to be done, and the means by which that duty is to be performed.

1. The surface of Ireland consists of about 12,000,000 Irish acres, or nearly 20,000,000 acres in English measurement, divided into 4 provinces, 32 counties at large, 8 counties of cities, towns or other independent local jurisdictions; 252 baronies, about 2,400 parishes; and a further civil subdivision, already alluded to in this report, generally known as townlands, but bearing different names in the several counties in Ireland. These sub-denominations, which may be generally expressed by the word townland, are the ancient and recognised divisions of the country; they form the basis of the Down Survey; they have been long used in the apportionment and collection of county and parochial rates. The county surveys executed in all cases, except two, are admitted to be useless as a basis for taxation, because the boundaries and area of the townlands have been omitted; and in the latest county survey contemplated, the grand jury acted upon a conviction that a survey by townlands was indispensable. It is

obvious, that if a baronial or even a parochial subdivision were alone to be effected, sufficient data would not be furnished for the apportionment of the local taxes; and if, on the other hand, a survey by fields were to be undertaken, as in France and Bavaria, the expense of such a work would be augmented, and its completion postponed. A survey by townlands appears to your committee to be the rational medium between these two extremes; sufficiently close for practical purposes, without aiming at any extreme minuteness of detail. Your committee have closely examined this important branch of the subject, and after having placed, upon their minutes, the evidence of those who from local knowledge and professional experience were qualified to form an opinion, they feel it their duty to express their decided conviction, that a survey which did not include the boundaries and contents of townlands, would be insufficient for the purposes of valuation. Your committee are of opinion, that, could the counties of Ireland be furnished with a map as perfect in its execution and as accurate in its details as the ordnance survey of Great Britain, it would not answer for the purposes of the grand jury taxation, unless a minute subdivision, namely, that of the separate townlands, were superadded to the boundaries of counties and of parishes.

Your committee conceive, that the difficulty of tracing and of surveying these boundaries of townlands is not so considerable as might at first be apprehended.

They have learned with satisfaction from Major Colby, that 'the additional time it would require would not be very considerable, provided the boundaries were set out'. Mr Griffith considers 'that there would not be any great difficulty in ascertaining the boundary of the townlands'. Mr Bald is of the same opinion. Mr Edgeworth states, that it would not have added materially to the expense of the survey of Roscommon, executed by him and Mr Griffith, if he had laid down these subdivisions; and Mr Aher, whose survey of Kilkenny actually includes the boundaries of townlands, has informed your committee, 'that these boundaries are less difficult to trace than those of parishes'. Had the result of their investigation been different, and had the possible delays and difficulties connected with the representation of these subdivisions appeared greater than they really are, your committee would not have felt themselves at liberty to abandon a principle essentially necessary for the success of the measure to which their attention has been directed.

It has given your committee great satisfaction to think that the direction. of the survey can be undertaken by the board of ordnance; they cannot conceive any other authority so well calculated to ensure the scientific accuracy and unity of principle which ought to distinguish a great national work. The high character of the officer who conducts the trigonometrical survey of

England, the advantages derivable from military organization, and the command of the best instruments, afford a sufficient security for the successful completion of the work. Your committee feel a perfect confidence, that the map, about to be furnished, will comprehend the local subdivisions, without which it would not answer the peculiar purposes of valuation. Were the boundaries of townlands to be omitted, the counties would be obliged to supply the deficiency by independent efforts; and the experience of the past, with the state of too many of the existing local surveys, sufficiently prove, that it would be in vain to expect to obtain through the medium of the grand juries such separate maps as could be compared and combined for any useful national purpose; the expense of such double operation would also be considerably increased, and an inferior work would be produced at a sacrifice of time, convenience and economy.

Your committee fully agree in the opinion of Major Colby, that steps should be taken without delay to facilitate the tracing of the townland boundaries, a measure which that officer conceives would reduce, by one half, the time required for this particular branch of the survey. With this view, your committee have already instructed their chairman to bring in a bill, which they trust may pass into a law during the present session, requiring the several grand juries to carry into effect the provisions of the 49th Geo. 3, so far as respects the tables of townlands and their acreable contents. They also conceive, that every other aid and facility should be afforded to the officers of the ordnance, both by placing at their disposal an enlarged supply of improved instruments, and by giving them a free access to all the existing public maps and records which bear upon the subject. The Down Survey, that of the Forfeited Lands, the county and baronial maps, however imperfect in themselves, may be of some service. When the objects with which the intended survey is undertaken are understood, your committee are convinced, that not only will all the local authorities in Ireland afford their zealous cooperation, but that many private individuals will, on public grounds, allow access to such maps and other documents, as can be of service in tracing the boundaries.

In the survey of Roscommon, the bishops and clergy afforded every facility in settling parochial boundaries; your committee trust, that such aid every will in the present instance be renewed, and assisted by the magistrates and the police throughout Ireland. They are happy to learn, from the evidence, that so far from there being any reason to apprehend obstructions on the part of the peasantry, a reliance may be placed on their good will and cooperation. It is however, important, that the nature and object of the proposed work should be thereby explained and understood; when that explanation is given, there can be no doubt but that the proprietors and occupiers of land in Ireland, will feel that the completion of the survey and valuation is likely to conduce to the general good, and add to the value of property.

Whilst your committee express their belief that the execution of the survey cannot be placed in better hands than in those of the ordnance officers, they cannot but add, that it is expedient to give much greater dispatch to this work, than what has occurred in the trigonometrical survey of England. That great work, highly creditable as it is to the individuals by whom it is conducted, has already been 33 years in progress, and yet it still wants one-third part of its completion. It ought to be added, however, that the operations of the ordnance suffered interruption during the war. The Irish survey is of the most urgent necessity, and no effort should be omitted to accelerate its completion. It may be observed, that the ordnance survey of Ireland must, in the course of a few years, have been undertaken by that department, and that by hastening the period of its execution for the important purposes of the Irish valuation, there will be ultimately no greater expense borne by the public. A limitation of the number of persons employed, appears a questionable policy on the principles of economy, as the directing staff must be maintained no less for the control of a limited, than for the guidance of a more extended operation. It is satisfactory to your committee to report, that the former surveys carried on under parliamentary authority, have established in Ireland a school of scientific topography. Whether it may be expedient that any of the respectable civil engineers of Ireland should be employed, under the authority of the ordnance, it is altogether for that board, in its discretion, to determine; but your committee perfectly agree with Major Colby, that a central and effectual control is indispensable to the successful termination of this undertaking. The best scale for effecting the intended survey, appears to your committee that of six inches to the English mile; this will afford sufficient means to the engineers to enter into all the detailed information requisite; it is the scale on which the ordnance survey of Kent was originally commenced. With respect to the engraving, it may be advisable to follow the same scale adopted in the British maps.

A protraction upon a double scale of 12 inches to the mile, for cities and great towns, where the valuation must necessarily be more minute, has been recommended, and appears desirable. The altitudes of the principal mountains should also be given, as well as the boundary of the unenclosed lands, whether bog, mountain, or rock. The latter will correspond to the distinction traced on the ordnance map, between cultivated lands, commons, and woods.

Your committee have learned, that the hydrographical charts, now extant, of the coasts and harbours of Ireland, are inaccurate and unsatisfactory. Combined operations between the admiralty and the ordnance, for the purpose of furnishing information so important to the public interests, have already been suggested, and your committee trust that the views of the admiralty, contained in the secretary's letter of the 22d day of April, may be carried into effect. The soundings of the harbour of Plymouth have been laid in with advantage, both with regard to economy and to dispatch, by making use of the points ascertained trigonometrically by the officers of the ordnance.

Your committee are of opinion, that the new survey should supersede all local topographical proceedings, whether under the authority of grand juries, or otherwise. It is evident that the ordnance survey will supply all that can be required for county purposes. And however creditable to the artists who have executed them, are the maps of Roscommon, Longford, Mayo, Kilkenny and Dublin, yet most of the other county maps being laid down upon a variety of scales with very imperfect instruments, and without pretension to scientific accuracy, it would be unwise to continue operations so liable to objection, as well as so expensive in their execution.

With a view to the diminution of expense, your committee are inclined to think that the Bavarian system is not an ineligible one, by which individual proprietors of estates are allowed to subscribe for copies of those parts of the map in which they feel interested. A survey, on the scale of six inches to the mile, might be applied to various purposes of private utility, more especially when combined with a valuation, and with the statistical information included in the population returns. The latter documents contain the number of families, houses, the size and description of farms; and, when accompanied by an accurate map and valuation, your committee are inclined to hope they may furnish individual proprietors, at a moderate price, whether inhabitants or absentees, with valuable information respecting the condition of their estates, and the best means of improving them.

2. With respect to the valuation, your committee are not as yet in possession of sufficient evidence to enable them to form a detailed plan, or to do more than to suggest some leading general principles: they, however, regret this the less, because the survey must necessarily take precedence, the basis of the valuation being obviously the proposed maps of counties, baronies and parishes, divided into their respective townlands. Tracings of these skeleton maps may be furnished, as the filling up of the triangulation proceeds. In effecting the valuation, your committee conceive that three principles must be adhered to and combined. 1. A fixed and uniform principle of valuation applicable throughout the whole work, and enabling the valuation not only of townlands, but that of counties, to be compared by one common measure. 2. A central authority, under the appointment of government, for direction and

superintendence, and for the generalization of the returns made in detail. 3. Local assistance, regularly organized, furnishing information on the spot, and forming a check for the protection of private rights. In a future session it will be the subject of consideration, how far these principles are accurate, and in what manner it will be the pleasure of parliament to carry them into effect.

Your committee are fully aware of the difficulty of the proposed valuation, and how much consideration it will require in all its details. During the recess, they trust that the attention of the Irish government, of the magistracy, of grand juries, and of the proprietors of land, may be given to the question, and that early in the next session a bill may be introduced, likely to meet the assent of the legislature.

In concluding this report, your committee must again repeat their recommendation, that the work may be proceeded upon with as much dispatch as is consistent with accuracy of execution. It is not unworthy of remark, that all former surveys of Ireland originated in forfeitures, and violent transfers of property; the present has for its object the relief which can be afforded to the proprietors and occupiers of land from unequal taxation. The general tranquillity of Europe, enables the state to devote the abilities and exertions of a most valuable corps of officers to an undertaking, which, though not unimportant in a military point of view, recommends itself more directly as a civil measure. Your committee trust that the survey will be carried on with energy, as well as with skill, and that it will, when completed, be creditable to the nation, and to the scientific acquirements of the present age. In that portion of the empire to which it more particularly applies, it cannot but be received as a proof of the disposition of the legislature to adopt all measures calculated to advance the interests of Ireland.

21 June 1824.

APPENDIX D

A letter from William Edgeworth, Esq. civil engineer, to Alexander Nimmo, Esq. civil engineer, M.R.I.A.[1]

Dublin, January 1, 1823.

Dear Sir,

At your request I send you an account of a few of the principal triangles upon which the map of the county of Roscommon was constructed.

I have calculated the sides from a base measured on the road from Longford to Edgeworthstown, an account of which was published in my father's [Richard Lovell Edgeworth] report on the Bog District, No. 7, and, with a diagram of some triangles, is to be found in the Second Report of the Commissioners for improving Bogs in Ireland.

On my map of the county of Longford I have published the principal triangles upon which it was founded; and the latitude was determined from observations of the pole star, with an instrument of sixteen inches diameter, that Major Taylor most kindly lent to me.

The longitude of Edgeworthstown was determined from the Observatory of Dublin, by the valuable assistance of Dr [John] Brinkley [d. c.1763, d. 1835], who was so good as to make corresponding observations of white lights and explosions of gunpowder; four in one night agreed with the mean, within a second of time.

So that the longitude of the stations in the county of Longford may be considered as certain within a furlong. I have connected the triangulation through Roscommon with some of the stations made use of by Mr [William] Bald in his excellent map of Mayo.

Even with the slight data, that I can now give, the difference of latitude and longitude of the east and west coast of this island is known within a few seconds of time. The principal angles in Roscommon I took in the year 1814, with a six-inch theodolite made by Troughton.[2]

1 *The Transactions of the Royal Irish Academy*, vol. xiv (1825), pp 63–7.　2 Troughton's were based at 136 Fleet Street, London, at the 'Sign of Orrery'.

But I am now in possession of a repeating circle of eighteen inches diameter of his make; and a repeating theodolite of Reichenback [sic], which, from the trials that Major [Thomas] Colby and Captain [Henry] Kater kindly encouraged me to make of this instrument, at some of the trigonometrical stations in England, in comparison with the celebrated theodolite of [Jesse] Ramsden, I think I could be as certain of an angle to two seconds, as formerly I was to twenty seconds.

So that it would be well worth while to employ this repeating theodolite to correct, by a few well-chosen triangles, Galway and Sligo with Dublin, and to determine exactly the distance on the meridian between Dublin and Armagh Observatories. A few more triangles would connect Armagh with the stations on the coast of Ireland, which have been intersected by Major Colby.

If I were to give a diagram of all the triangles that I determined in Roscommon, you would find a station nearly in every square mile, as my object was to secure the accuracy of the map.

The manner in which I laid down the triangles on paper may be found useful to those few who are employed in similar labours. After having carefully drawn, mile squares of four inches asunder, and laid down a long base, I made use of a nine-inch protractor of Troughton's, with extending conical points. Over one of these points I placed a little pinhole in thin brass, so that I could see the opposite point through it; and, instead of marking the paper with the points, I intersected a little square cube with a fine perpendicular tine marked on it, where the station to be determined was likely to come. I moved it back and forwards, till the protractor, when set to the division, showed where the line should be drawn, which I did without taking up the protractor. In this way I marked every station round, at once, from the angles in the field book.

This may be called surveying on paper, as I made use of the protractor in laying down the angles, as I had done the theodolite in the field.

And when the paper was kept of equal dryness in the large triangles, I could perceive an error of a minute. I here give you a table of the angles to twenty seconds, and the sides calculated in feet, with the latitudes and longitudes of a few of the stations.

I am, dear Sir,
Yours sincerely,
William Edgeworth

APPENDIX E

Thomas Colby, Preface to the *Memoir of the city and north-western liberties of Londonderry: parish of Templemore* (London, 1837).

To carry on a minute survey of all Ireland so as to meet the various objects proposed by the Committee of the House of Commons (for the Survey and Valuation of Ireland) [Spring Rice Committee], on whose recommendation the townland survey was ordered; no collection of ready instructed surveyors would have sufficed. It, therefore, became indispensable to train and organize a completely new department for the purpose. Officers and men from the Corps of Royal Engineers formed the basis of this new organization, and very large numbers of other persons possessing various qualifications were gradually added to them to expedite the great work. The code of instructions which I framed and issued at the commencement of the survey, had reference principally to devising methods by which large numbers could be employed on it, at a moderate expense, with little risk of confusion or error; and provided for the collection of some subsidiary information, which might become useful in facilitating the construction of future roads and lines for communication. But the present volume comprises also a large mass of information, not contemplated in those instructions; and it is requisite to apprise the public of its origin.

Having set the general direction of the arrangements for the surveys of England and Ireland, it would have been highly prejudicial to have devoted my time to the local charge of the Survey Office in the Phoenix Park; I therefore, brought with me from the English Survey, Lieutenant Larcom of the Royal Engineers to perform that duty. In that situation, every document relating to the survey of Ireland passed through his hands. The elaborate search of books and records required to settle the orthography of names to be used on the maps, led him to compare the progressive states of the country. A geological examination having been ordered under Captain [Joseph] Portlock's [b. 1794, d. 1864] direction, and the organization framed for carrying on the survey, affording means for collecting and methodizing facts, which were never likely to recur, Lieutenant Larcom conceived the idea, that with such opportunities, a small additional cost would enable him, without retarding the execution of the maps, to draw together a work embracing every species of local information relating to Ireland. He submitted this idea to me, and I obtained the sanction of the Irish government for carrying it into effect. To him I have entrusted the execution, and the present volume is the first public result.

In a work so entirely new in its design, and so varied and elaborate in its details, the difficulty of obtaining complete materials can only be appreciated by those who have watched its progress; — and the persons engaged in it had many other duties to perform. A list of all those who have contributed more or less information would be little short of a list of the persons employed on the survey. But it is necessary I should specially mention the following gentlemen: Captain Portlock, who has charge of the Geological branch of the survey, and who, for this memoir, undertook also the Natural History and Productive Economy sections; having the assistance of Mr David Moore in the Botanical researches. The description of the National Features, Social Economy, and of the ancient and modern Buildings have been chiefly contributed by Captain [Robert] Dawson [b. c.1798, d. 1861], and his assistants, Mr Ligar, Mr Stokes, and Mr Williams. The History and Antiquities have been drawn up by Mr George Petrie [b. 1790, d. 1866], aided by Mr John O'Donovan [b. 1806, d. 1861]. As the other contributors have been less confined to particular sections, and the intimate connection between the several sections, renders it impracticable to assign their individual contributions, I only add, that I have been requested by Lieutenant Larcom, who has charge of the execution of work, to acknowledge the assistance he has received from Mr George Downes [b. 1790, d. 1846], who has contributed a variety of matter, and arranged the section 'People' in the city; and also from Mr Edward Singleton, to whom he has peculiarly committed the correction of tabular matter and numerical calculations.

Thomas Colby,
Colonel Royal Engineers.

Bibliography

COLLECTIONS

Cecil papers (Hatfield House).
Chief Secretary's Office registered papers (Ireland) (1824–2).
Edgeworth papers (NLI).
Hansard HC Deb. (1819–37).

LEGISLATION

11 James c. 7 [Ire.] (1614).
9 Anne c. 9, [Ire.] (1713).
46 Geo. III, c. 134 [G. Br.] (1806).
5 Geo. IV, c. 112 [G. Br.] (1825).
The Tithe Composition (Ireland) Act (1823).
6 & 7 Will. IV, c. 71 [G. Br.] (1836).

PRINTED MAPS

Arrowsmith, Aaron, *Ireland* (London, 1811).
Taylor, Alexander, *A new map of Ireland* (London, 1793).

NEWSPAPERS

Belfast Newsletter (1824)
Dublin Evening Post (1838)
Dublin Journal (1824)
The Economist (2023)
Freeman's Journal (1824–5)

The Gazette (1825)
The Gentleman's Magazine (1840)
The Irish Times (1996–2016)
The London Times (1866)
Morning Chronicle (1848)

PARLIAMENTARY REPORTS

First report from the select committee on Grand Jury presentments, HC (1822).
Lords Committee, State of Ireland (London, 1825).
Report from the select committee on Grand Jury presentments of Ireland, HC (1815).
Report from the select committee on Grand Jury presentments of Ireland, HC (1819).

Report from the select committee on Ordnance Survey (Ireland), HC (1846).
Report from the select committee on Ordnance Survey (Scotland), HC (1851).
Report from the select committee on the survey & valuation of Ireland, HC (1824).
Two reports from the select committee on Grand Jury presentments of Ireland, HC (1816)

PRIMARY SOURCES

Bald, William, 'An account of a trigonometrical survey of Mayo, read 30 Apr. 1821', *The Transactions of the Royal Irish Academy*, vol. xiv (Dublin, 1825).

Burgh, Thomas, *A method to determine the areas of right-lined figures* (Dublin, 1724).

Callan, Peter, *A dissertation on the practice of surveying* (Drogheda, 1758).

Gibson, Robert, *Practical surveying* (Dublin, 1752).

Mackenzie, Murdoc, *A treatise of maritime surveying* (London, 1774).

Monck Mason, William, *Suggestions to the project of a survey and valuation of Ireland* (Dublin, 1825).

Nimmo, Alexander, 'A letter from William Edgeworth to Alexander Nimmo, 1823', *The Transactions of the Royal Irish Academy*, vol. xiv (Dublin, 1825), 63.

Ordnance Survey of Ireland, *Memoir of the city and northwestern liberties of Londonderry: parish of Templemore* (London, 1837).

Owen, Tim, and Elaine Pilbeam, *Ordnance survey: map makers to Britain since 1791* (Ordnance Survey, 1992).

Portlock, Joseph, *Memoir of the life of Major-General Colby* (London, 1869).

Report on the Ordnance Survey of the United Kingdom for 1855–56 (South Hampton, 1856).

Statement of progress in Ordnance Survey of Ireland (London, 1837).

Stooks Smith, Henry, *The register of parliamentary contested elections*, 2nd ed. (London, 1842).

The dispatches of Field Marshal the duke of Wellington (London, 1844).

The Transactions of the Royal Irish Academy, vol. xiv (Dublin, 1825).

White, Thomas, *The Ordnance Survey of the United Kingdom* (London, 1886).

Wyld, Samuel, *The practical surveyor* (London, 1725).

SECONDARY SOURCES

Andrews, John, *A paper landscape: the Ordnance Survey in nineteenth-century Ireland* (Dublin, 1975).

Andrews, John, *History in the Ordnance map* (Newtown, 1993).

Andrews, John, *Maps in those days: cartographic methods before 1850* (Dublin, 2009).

Andrews, John, *Plantation acres: an historical study of the Irish land surveyors* (Omagh, 1985).

Baigent, Elizabeth, 'Topographic mapping and the state' in Woodward (ed.), *The history of cartography*, iv (Chicago, 1989).

Barber, Peter, 'Mapmaking in England, ca. 1470–1650' in Woodward (ed.), *The history of cartography*, iii (Chicago, 1989).

Boyce, George, *Nineteenth-century Ireland* (Dublin, 2005).

Close, Charles, *The early years of the Ordnance Survey* (London, 1969).

Connolly, Thomas, *The history of the corps of royal sappers and miners* (London, 1855).

Crosbie, Barry, *Irish imperial networks: migration, social communication and exchange in nineteenth-century India* (Cambridge, 2011).

Dictionary of Irish biography. www.dib.ie.

Doherty, Gillian, *The Irish Ordnance Survey: history, culture and memory* (Dublin, 2004).

Dolan, Terence, *A dictionary of Hiberno-English: the Irish use of English* (Dublin, 2006).

Dooley, Terrence, *Sources for the history of landed estates in Ireland* (Maynooth, 2000).

Edgeworth, Maria, *The life and letters of Maria Edgeworth* (New York, 1895).

Hayes, Nick, *The book of trespass: crossing the lines that divide us* (London, 2021).

Hewitt, Rachel, *Map of a nation* (London, 2011).

Knight, Charles (ed.), *Biography, or third division of 'the English encyclopaedia'*, ii (London, 1867).

Lennon, Colm, and John Montague, *John Rocque's Dublin: a guide to the Georgian city* (Dublin, 2010).

O'Cionnaith, Finnian, *Mapping, measurement and metropolis: how land surveyors shaped eighteenth-century Dublin* (Dublin, 2012).

O'Cionnaith, Finnian, *Land surveying in Ireland, 1690–1830* (Dublin, 2022).

O Donoghue, Brendan, *The Irish county surveyors, 1834–1944* (Dublin, 2007).

Ordnance Survey in Ireland: an illustrated record (Dublin, 1991).

Parsons, Cóilín, *The Ordnance Survey and modern Irish literature* (Oxford, 2016).

Wilkins, Noel, *Alexander Nimmo: master engineer, 1783–1832* (Dublin, 2016).

Wolf, Nicholas, *State, religion, community, and the linguistic landscape in Ireland, 1770–1870* (Wisconsin, 2014).

Woodward, David (ed.), *The history of cartography*, iii (Chicago, 1989).

PAPERS

Andrews, John, '"More suitable to the English tongue": the cartography of Celtic placenames', *Ulster Local Studies*, 14:2 (1992), 7–21.

Andrews, John, 'Charles Vallancey and the map of Ireland', *The Geographical Journal*, 132:1 (1966), 48–61.

Andrews, John, 'The French school of Dublin land surveyors', *Irish Geography*, 5 (1965), 275–92.

Andrews, John, et al., '*Translations* and *A paper landscape*: between fiction and history', *The Crane Bag*, 7:2 (1983), 118–124.

Clout, Hugh, 'The "cadastre" as a source for French rural studies', *Agricultural History*, 43:2 (1969), 210–24.

Crosbie, Barry, 'Ireland, colonial science and the geographical construction of British rule in India, c.1820–1870', *The Historical Journal*, 52:4 (2009), 963–87.

Harely, J.B., 'The re-mapping of England, 1750–1800', *Imago Mundi*, 19 (1965), 56–67.

Horner, Arnold, 'Retrieving the landscapes of eighteenth-century County Kildare: the 1755–60 estate maps of John Rocque', *Archaeology Ireland*, 31:2 (2019), 19–23.

McCormac, Stephen, 'The tithe war; reports by Church of Ireland clergymen to Dublin Castle', *History Ireland*, 4:13 (2005).

Nash, Catherine, 'Irish placenames: post-colonial locations', *Transactions of the Institute of British Geographers*, 24:4 (1999), 457–80.

O'Cionnaith, Finnian, 'Piracy, property and politics: Charles Vallancey and the Down Survey of Ireland', *Irish Architectural and Decorative Studies*, 14 (2011), 96–109.

Ó Drisceoil, Proinsias, 'Civilizing Ireland, Ordnance Survey 1824–42, ethnography, cartography, translation', *History Ireland*, review, 15 (2007).

Smith, Gillian, 'An eye on the survey: perceptions of the Ordnance Survey in Ireland, 1824–1842', *History Ireland*, 9:2 (2001).

Varley, John, 'John Rocque: engraver, surveyor, cartographer and map seller', *Imago Mundi*, 5 (1948), 83–91.

THESIS

Smyth, William, 'Sir Richard Griffith's three surveys of Ireland, 1826–1864' (PhD, NUI Maynooth, 2009).

Index